THE NEW LEVIATHAN

THE NEW LEVIATHAN

THE STATE VERSUS THE INDIVIDUAL IN THE 21ST CENTURY

FOREWORD BY
GEORGE F. WILL

EDITED, WITH AN
INTRODUCTION BY
ROGER KIMBALL

ENCOUNTER BOOKS
NEW YORK · LONDON

First American edition published in 2012 by Encounter Books,
an activity of Encounter for Culture and Education, Inc.,
a nonprofit, tax exempt corporation.
Encounter Books website address: www.encounterbooks.com

Manufactured in the United States and printed on acid-free paper.
The paper used in this publication meets the minimum
requirements of ANSI/NISO Z39.48–1992
(R 1997) (*Permanence of Paper*).

FIRST AMERICAN EDITION

LIBRARY OF CONGRESS CATALOGING-IN-PUBLICATION DATA

The new Leviathan : the state versus the individual in the 21st century / edited by Roger Kimball ; foreword by George Will.
p. cm.
ISBN 978-1-59403-632-3 (hardcover : alk. paper)
ISBN 978-1-59403-645-3 (ebook)
1. Liberty—History—21st century. I. Kimball, Roger, 1953–
JC585.N475 2012
320.01′1–dc23
2012016892

CONTENTS

FOREWORD

THIS BOOK is a double-barreled blast – using *blast* in two senses. One meaning of that word is a forceful, indeed explosive, discharge. The second meaning, a colloquialism, is a party tending to happy raucousness. What you hold in your hand is a compendium of constructive explosions from men and women intelligently exasperated by current tendencies in American politics and culture – but also exuberantly combative against those tendencies.

Early in the Obama administration, the clearheaded people at Encounter Books had a splendid idea. They would invite accomplished writers with expertise in particular fields to distill their discontents into 5,000 or so words. These distillations would be called Broadsides. The results, as you will see, are both efficient and exhilarating.

In the *Oxford English Dictionary*, one definition of the word *broadside* is "a strongly worded critical attack: *broadsides against political correctness*." Each of the chapters in this volume is such a broadside. Another definition, however, is "a nearly simultaneous firing of all the guns from one side of a warship." The book itself is a broadside in this sense. In these pages, the right side – in two senses – of the ship of American politics is heard from, resoundingly.

Blaise Pascal once wrote to a correspondent, "I have made this [letter] longer than usual, only because I have not had the time to make it shorter." A columnist who must compact his thoughts on any subject into 750 words knows exactly what Pascal meant: Brevity is a challenge. But not an insuperable one, as every chapter in this book demonstrates. Each of these essays is a bright, gemlike bead. All of these beads are threaded on the sturdy string of a shared understanding of the importance – and danger – of this moment in American history.

The temperature of American politics just now is unusually high – unusually but not excessively. The temperature of contemporary argument is proportional to the stakes. We are, after all, arguing about fundamentals: the proper relationship of the citizen to the state, the actual competence of government, and the continuing vitality of the Madisonian project of maintaining a government of limited, because enumerated, powers.

The essays in this volume constitute a collective rejoinder to the insufferably high-minded scolds who are forever deploring "partisanship." What they really deplore is determined, principled resistance to the progressive agenda. That agenda depends on erasing from the American consciousness the first two paragraphs of the Declaration of Independence. Woodrow Wilson, the first person to carry pure progressivism into the presidency, urged Americans to disregard those paragraphs. He understood that they constitute an impediment to the progressive goal of limitless growth of the regulatory, administrative state. If government really does exist, as the Declaration says, to "secure" our rights – rights that pre-exist government – and if government therefore is not a fountain of whatever rights it is pleased to confer upon the governed, then the progressive project must be stymied.

At the strong beating heart of this volume is the belief that progressivism is in radical conflict not only with the Declaration but also with realism. These essays are a summons to realism about the fecundity of freedom. They are a call for government to respect the spontaneous creativity of American society – which needs less, not more, supervision from the state. And they call for an unsentimental assessment of the world, which remains a dangerous place.

Those who have enlisted in the swelling resistance to progressivism have one great advantage. It is, as Wilson recognized, that progressivism is discordant with the American creed to which most Americans remain committed. The resistance to progressivism has, however, one great problem: It is difficult to get the attention of Americans. We live in a society filled with distractions. George Eliot wrote in *Middlemarch*, "If we had a keen vision and feeling of all ordinary human life, it would be like hearing the grass grow and the squirrel's heartbeat, and we should die of that roar which lies on the other side of silence." Living in contemporary media-drenched America, one wonders where silence can be found. Today, Americans live on the receiving end of an incessant communications blitzkrieg. Day in and day out, they are bombarded with commercial, journalistic, political, and cultural messages. Fortunately, they have developed mental filters to protect them from the cacophony. By now they are, in effect, wired to reduce almost all the noise to barely noticed static. Otherwise they would go mad from the roar.

Hence this volume of crisp, efficient arguments. Readers will find these essays not only informative but also entertaining and exhilarating. Political combat should not be a joyless chore; there should be pleasure in its rough-and-tumble. So enjoy this volume. It is a banquet of intelligent pugnacity and a handbook for the fun of rescuing progress from progressivism.

George F. Will

INTRODUCTION

PUBLISHING BOOKS is at the center of what we do at Encounter. But a book is by nature a long-gestating creature. Even after being written, a book typically takes six to nine months to make its way to the market.

Books offer essential, thoughtful perspectives on the issues that confront us. But in the age of the 24-hour news cycle, the crucial work performed by books needs to be supplemented by a form of commentary that is efficient enough to be timely yet extensive enough to elaborate a case thoughtfully. The rise of the Internet, the blogosphere, and outlets like Twitter have provided a deluge of nearly instantaneous commentary on every conceivable subject. Valuable as that new media has been, however, it has tended to be ephemeral in its effects and abbreviated in its analysis. A tweet of 140 characters can tell you that a fire has broken out. But it cannot elaborate on the causes, the culprits, or the right remedial action.

What is needed is a new – or rather, a revival of an old – genre that is supple enough to respond quickly to unfolding events and yet authoritative and detailed enough to have an important effect on the debate over policy – over, that is, the direction of our country, our government, and the way we live our lives.

Enter Encounter Broadsides. In an age in which debate about critical matters is often compressed into the literary equivalent of a geometric point, we saw that there was a new opportunity for commentary that is brief but thoughtful, authoritative yet timely. With Encounter Broadsides, we aimed to capitalize on that opportunity, providing new ammunition for serious debate. At 5,000 to 7,000 words, Encounter Broadsides are short enough to be read in a sitting but long enough to bolster assertion with argument. Throughout the series, we've aimed to combine an 18th century sense of political urgency and rhetorical wit with 21st century technology and channels of distribution.

We started thinking about this new publishing venture in the spring of 2009 and published our first Broadside that autumn. To date, we've published more than 30 Broadsides on a wide variety of subjects, from the battle over health care and the economic crisis to immigration, the attack on national sovereignty, the higher education bubble, and the war on terrorism.

It is no secret that this is a critical moment in the history of the West and of America in particular. The economic crisis has precipitated a loss of confidence in the value of free markets unlike anything we have seen in decades. Socialism, and the soft totalitarianism that follows in its wake, is making a comeback everywhere. At the same time, radical Islam confronts democratic society with a categorical and intransigent threat to its existence even as newly rampant authoritarian regimes from Russia and Iran to China and Venezuela are flexing their muscles. Truly, as the old Chinese curse would have it, these are interesting times.

We hope Encounter Broadsides will be to this troubled period of American history what broadsides like *The Federalist Papers* and Tom Paine's *Common Sense* were to an earlier revolutionary period. A wake-up call. An alarm bell. A blueprint, if I may employ a once popular phrase, for hope and change. Accordingly, we have aimed not merely to comment on but also to intervene in the debate, bringing fresh perspectives to controversies that too often have been interred in the shallow grave of politically correct orthodoxy. The goal of Encounter Broadsides is to change minds, not merely to add to the pile of commentary. Ultimately, we have sought to help shape policy and rescue the American dream from the nightmare of the new collectivism that is threatening our liberty, our prosperity, and our national security.

In *The New Leviathan: The State Versus the Individual in the 21st Century*, we've gathered a revised and updated baker's dozen of Encounter Broadsides that bear on the pressing issue adumbrated in the subtitle of the book: the relationship between the state and the individual in this increasingly regulated and bureaucratized world.

Back in March 2012, the pollster Scott Rasmussen published a brief essay called "The Real 'Entitlement Mentality' That Is Bankrupting America" on his website RasmussenReports.com. Republicans, Rasmussen noted, often grumble about the "entitlement mentality." Usually, they dilate on the growing habit of dependency and appetite for "goodies provided by the government and financed by taxpayers."

It would be hard to overestimate that aspect of the problem. It is a corollary of that "psychological change" in a people that Friedrich von Hayek diagnosed in *The Road to Serfdom*: a transformation from the practice of autonomy and self-reliance to the habit of dependency. It was, Hayek wrote, both a regular result and precondition of "extensive government control." Cause and effect fed upon and abetted each other. It was (as Hayek also noted) a textbook case of what Tocqueville described in his famous paragraphs on "democratic despotism" in *Democracy in America*. How would despotism come to a modern democracy?, Tocqueville asked. Not through the imposition of old-fashioned tyranny. No, that instrument is too blunt, too crude for modern democratic regimes. Much more effective is the disguised tyranny of infantilization. Turn government into the sole provider of all those "goodies," and you enslave the population far more effectively than old-style tyranny ever managed.

All this is true, and it deserves our constant attention. But Rasmussen shifted his focus to the other side of the equation. In order to work, the dependency agenda needs not only to cultivate the sheep, a population of dependents. It also needs to foster a population of controlling bureaucrats, the shepherds or warders of the system. And this brings us to what Rasmussen calls "the real entitlement mentality that threatens to bankrupt the nation: A political class that feels entitled to rule over the rest of us."

Let's pause over that observation: The "real entitlement mentality" revolves around "a political class that feels entitled to rule over the rest of us." As Rasmussen noted, this mentality is not solely a Democratic or a Republican trait. It affects – or infects – "the nation's political leaders of both parties." Hence the intractability of the problem. It's not just our habits of dependency that need to be broken. The habits of control and the penchant for feeding dependency on the part of our political leaders also need to be curbed. Rasmussen is right: "While most voters view excessive government spending as the problem, those who feel entitled to rule over the rest of us see the voters as the problem. And that's the real entitlement crisis facing the nation today. The political class wants to govern like it's 1775, a time when kings were kings and consent of the governed didn't matter."

Back in the 1770s, some exasperated and enterprising American colonists demonstrated that the consent of the governed did matter by littering Boston Harbor with English tea. It is part of our ambition in *The New Leviathan* to recall that exemplary demonstration, reminding the world that the soft tyranny of 1775 gave way to the ferment of 1776. Those presuming to be our political masters believe we are inured to dependency and Big Government. Not everyone, however, likes being a ward of the state. More and more people, it seems, wonder how the warders got their keys and authority to force the rest of us to accept their bidding. This, at bottom, is what *The New Leviathan*, endeavors to ask: Will we be wards or free citizens?

ROGER KIMBALL

JOHN R. BOLTON

HOW BARACK OBAMA IS ENDANGERING OUR NATIONAL SOVEREIGNTY

For several decades, Americans have slept while their national sovereignty has been threatened, chipped away, and eroded by a series of innocuous-sounding and nearly imperceptible decisions. Building on years of writing, conference going, resolution passing, and networking, opponents of unfettered U.S. sovereignty have been fashioning constraints on the exercise of our fundamental democratic rights, national power, and legitimacy. We have been locked in a struggle between sovereignty and "global governance" that most Americans didn't even know was happening. Not surprisingly, therefore, the "Americanists" have been losing to the "globalists," and the general public does not yet appreciate the chasm between these two worldviews. In fact, there hasn't been much of a battle elsewhere in the world either; we can have a truly robust debate only in America because of the basic faith we have in our own institutions and freedoms.

The important point is to get the discussion started. It is time for a fire bell in the night, a little contemporary common sense about what has been going on all around us. This is not a confrontation over that favorite buzzword, "globalization," and its implications for commerce, culture, and travel, but a debate about power and government – *our* power and *our* government.

Key Issues in the Sovereignty Debate During the Obama Era

What Is "Sovereignty," and Why Is It Especially Important for the United States?

Sovereignty may seem like an enormous abstraction, gauzy and hard to understand. Indeed, it has a huge range of definitions, complicated and often contradictory, thus ironically making it easier for some people to believe that sovereignty is less important than it actually is. Coined originally in Europe to describe the authority of kings and queens – the "sovereigns" – the concept evolved rapidly after the 1648 Peace of Westphalia to refer to nation-states. National sovereignty now generally encompasses the fullest range of state power: dealing with other international actors (foreign and defense policy); control over borders (immigration and customs); and exercising authority domestically (economic and social policy). Whatever the intricacies and complexities of measuring and exercising legitimate governmental authority, these powers are basic.

Despite the raging academic debates over the precise definition and measurement of sovereignty, for Americans, the idea is actually quite straightforward. The Founding Fathers understood it implicitly, and they took care in the Declaration of Independence to explain why they were ready "to assume among the powers of the earth, the separate and equal station to which the laws of nature and of nature's God entitle them." On July 4, 1776, our sovereignty moved from George III to us, "We the People of the United States," as the Constitution later described it.

This is fundamental. For Americans, sovereignty is not simply an academic abstraction. For us, sovereignty is our control over our own government. Thus, advocates of "sharing" or "pooling" U.S. sovereignty with international organizations to address "global" problems are really saying that we should cede some of our sovereignty to institutions that other nations will also influence or even control. That is unquestionably a formula for reducing U.S. autonomy and reducing our control over government. Since most Americans believe they do not have adequate control over the federal government *now*, it is no wonder they are reluctant to cede even more of that control to distant bodies where our influence is reduced or uncertain. Indeed, wasn't that what our Revolution was about in the first place?

What Is "Global Governance," and Why Is It a Threat to U.S. Sovereignty?

Opponents of U.S. sovereignty used to applaud "world government," thus providing an easy target, since there has never been more than a shred of sympathy here for such an idea. Over time, academics and activists alike have therefore adopted the phrase "global governance" to describe a more piecemeal, less rhetorically threatening approach, reflecting also that not all global governance advocates themselves feel comfortable that their final objective is world government. The soothingly titled 1995 blueprint *Our Global Neighborhood* argues that global governance "is part of the evolution of human efforts to organize life on the planet, and the process will always be going on."

This underlines the debates between Americanists – who want to preserve our sovereignty – and globalists, who want to see it, in whole or part, constrained by or transferred to international organizations.

Most Americans, busy with their daily lives, have paid scant attention to the global governance debate in places like the United Nations, the European Union, and the universities. Nonetheless, academics and the international left, despite their differences, can be heard repeating endlessly, like a Greek chorus, that national sovereignty is diminishing inexorably because of the press of global problems. They emphasize the EU example, where the drift of national authority toward EU headquarters in Brussels and away from London, Berlin, and other capitals has indeed seemed inevitable and irreversible. Global governance advocates frequently minimize the importance of reduced sovereignty, citing, for example, the treaty-making authority. Although normally understood as an elemental example of exercising national sovereignty, treaties, say the globalists, actually limit sovereignty by reducing the scope for unilateral action. Since treaties have been around from time immemorial, what is the problem today with more ambitious treaties that diminish sovereignty somewhat more visibly? Isn't the whole argument just one of degree rather than basic philosophy? Why be so uncomfortable?

This verbal and conceptual bait and switch has, for its proponents, the further advantage of obscuring what is happening at any particular point in the seemingly endless process of negotiation that facilitates diminutions in U.S. sovereignty. Unquestionably, most threats to sovereignty grow like a coral reef rather than manifesting themselves in a particular crisis or a made-for-TV decisive moment. Moreover, the debate over sovereignty and global governance is diffuse and opaque because the battlefront stretches over a vast territory and the scope of activity along that front varies dramatically.

The field of combat is neither well understood nor well watched by politicians or the media. There is nothing mysterious or sinister about the process of international negotiations, including those with profound sovereignty implications. Indeed, it is precisely the ordinariness and depressingly unremarkable nature and pace of such negotiations that guarantee they do not cause red flags to pop up until each negotiation is essentially complete and the final agreement available for public and legislative review. Even then, the final texts are likely to be obscure, technical, and jargon-filled.

The key lies in seeing the big picture. In fact, global governance advocates have crossed a clear line of demarcation. The millennia-old notion of treaties – whether political, military, or economic – expanded after World War II into a completely different realm, a conceptual breakout distinguishing what has been afoot for the past half-century from the historical treaty process. The EU led the way with its regional experiment, and EU diplomats and their worldwide allies sympathetic to their transnational aspirations have been spreading the gospel.

So common and well accepted is this approach in Europe that its leaders now disdain to hide their objectives, in effect aspiring to do worldwide to national sovereignty what they have so successfully done in Europe. Fittingly and revealingly, the EU's first president, former Belgian Prime Minister Herman Van Rompuy, upon taking office on November 19, 2009, called 2009 "the first year of global governance, with the establishment of the

G-20 in the middle of the financial crisis. The climate conference in Copenhagen is another step toward the global management of our planet." Advocates of global governance in the United States are not yet so outspoken in general public discourse, but they believe exactly the same things and say so in their obscure academic journals and debates. They have long been hard at work on this issue, and they almost uniformly supported Barack Obama for president in 2008.

What Is President Obama's View on U.S. Sovereignty?

Barack Obama is our first post-American president – someone who sees his role in foreign policy less as an advocate for America's "parochial" interests and more as a "citizen of the world," in his own phrase. He broadly embodies many European social democratic values, including those regarding sovereignty, so it was not surprising that an ecstatic student said after hearing him on one of his first overseas trips, "He sounds like a European." Indeed he does.

Understanding Obama's view of America's proper role in the world and how it relates to other nations is critical. Strikingly, he neither cares very much about national security issues nor has had much relevant professional experience. During the 2008 campaign, he repeatedly contended that the world was not very threatening to U.S. interests, and in his first year in office, other than the usual processionals abroad, he has spent as little time as possible on international issues. His preoccupation with radically restructuring our domestic economy is obvious.

Obama's worldview is almost exclusively Wilsonian, as his public statements reveal. In his September 2009 address to the U.N. General Assembly, for example, Obama said:

> *[I]t is my deeply held belief that in the year 2009 – more than at any point in human history – the interests of nations and peoples are shared. . . . In an era when our destiny is shared, power is no longer a zero-sum game. No one nation can or should try to dominate another nation. No world order that elevates one nation or group of people over another will succeed. No balance of power among nations will hold.*

In 1916, Woodrow Wilson said, "There must be, not a balance of power, but a community of power; not organized rivalries, but an organized common peace" resting on "the moral force of the public opinion of the world." Removing the dates in these remarks makes it nearly impossible to differentiate Wilson from Obama.

Thus, while Obama's naive multilateralism is not unprecedented in U.S. history, his disregard of the 90 years of global conflagration, carnage, and catastrophe since Wilson is both breathtaking and unnerving. It reflects, moreover, the obsession with process rather than substance that permeates Obama's broader international perspective; for example, his belief that negotiation is actually a policy rather than merely a technique.

Critically, however, Obama's worldview extends well beyond Wilsonian multilateralism. Asked by a reporter about American exceptionalism, Obama replied, "I believe in American exceptionalism, just as I suspect that the Brits believe in British exceptionalism and the Greeks believe in Greek exceptionalism." There are 193 members of the U.N., and Obama could have gone on to mention "Peruvian exceptionalism," "Nigerian exceptionalism," and "Papua New Guinean exceptionalism." Obviously, if everyone is exceptional, no one is.

U.S. exceptionalism comes in many varieties, but they share the core notion that our founding and history give

America a special place in the world. John Winthrop, governor of the Massachusetts Bay Colony, paraphrased scripture and said, "We must consider that we shall be as a city upon a hill," which Ronald Reagan edited slightly to describe us as "a shining city on a hill." Others call us "the New Jerusalem," but it was the perceptive Frenchman Alexis de Tocqueville who first wrote, in *Democracy in America*, that "[t]he position of the Americans is therefore quite exceptional, and it may be believed that no democratic people will ever be placed in a similar one."

Obama's remoteness from American exceptionalism has been revealingly noted by his enthusiasts as well as his critics. Following Obama's speech on D-Day's 65th anniversary, for example, Evan Thomas of *Newsweek* hailed Obama as a marked contrast to Ronald Reagan, who spoke at the 40th anniversary.

> *Well, we were the good guys in 1984, it felt that way. It hasn't felt that way in recent years. So Obama's had, really, a different task.... [R]eagan was all about America.... Obama is "we are above that now." We are not just parochial, we're not just chauvinistic, we're not just provincial. We stand for something. I mean in a way Obama's standing above the country, above – above the world, he's sort of God. He's going to bring all different sides together.*

One can imagine Obama saying nearly the same thing about himself.

Obama is the first person holding such views to be elected president, but he merely reflects what has long been the dominant opinion within the Democratic Party's top leadership. John Kerry in the 2004 campaign argued that U.S. foreign policy has to pass a "global test" of legitimacy, essentially meaning approval by the U.N. Security Council. In his

1988 acceptance speech at the Republican convention, then Vice President George H. W. Bush captured the contrast between himself and his opponent, Massachusetts Gov. Michael Dukakis, tellingly: "He sees America as another pleasant country on the U.N. roll call, somewhere between Albania and Zimbabwe. And I see America as the leader – a unique nation with a special role in the world."

Bush's 1988 description of Dukakis easily fits Obama today, as his repeated implicit denigration of a special role for America shows. ("No world order that elevates one nation or group of people over another will succeed.") With Obama's predilections in mind, let us turn to the pending issues where Obama's decisions and policies can decisively affect U.S. sovereignty.

Imminent Threats to U.S. Sovereignty and Continuing Erosions

Threats to U.S. sovereignty are both imminent and long-term. They do not all share common characteristics, nor are they necessarily immediately obvious as threats. One element that runs through many of them, however, is the concept of international "norming" – the idea that America should base its policies on the international consensus, rather than making its own decisions as a constitutional democracy. Using norming, the international left seeks to constrain U.S. sovereignty by moving our domestic political debate to align with broader international opinion as they define it. Because of the centrality of individual freedom in the United States, norming advocates are invariably on the left of the political spectrum; there are simply no other nations out there are as liberty-oriented as we are.

One way to drive norming is through votes in multilateral organizations like the 192-member United Nations.

Operating under the "one nation, one vote" principle, the General Assembly routinely passes resolutions where the United States finds itself not only in opposition but often with only a handful of others voting with it. "One nation, one vote" has a surface democratic ring to it, but it is in fact profoundly antidemocratic and certainly affords no legitimacy to what happens on the General Assembly floor. While being "isolated" in international bodies may be uncomfortable, a point the international left stresses to embarrass us, it often may be the only way to protect our sovereignty and our interests. After all, if American exceptionalism means only that it took us longer and a different route to get to European social democracy, the whole enterprise would hardly have been worth it.

Let us turn now to several critical areas where U.S. sovereignty is under siege.

American National Security

Strong defenses are critical to national survival, so it is hardly surprising that opponents of unfettered U.S. sovereignty strive endlessly to constrain our ability to act in self-defense. Limiting or transferring decisional authority on security issues to international bodies is thus a core divide between Americanists and globalists.

Nowhere is this issue more graphically framed than in debates over the legitimacy of the use of force. In 1999, during NATO's air campaign against Yugoslavia – which the U.N. Security Council had not authorized because of a threatened Russian veto – Secretary-General Kofi Annan complained that "[u]nless the Security Council is restored to its preeminent position as the sole source of legitimacy on the use of force, we are on a dangerous path to anarchy." Shortly thereafter, Annan said that military action taken without council approval constituted a threat to the "very core of the international security system.... Only the [U.N.] Charter provides a universally accepted legal basis for the use of force."

This, of course, is conceptually identical to Kerry's argument for a "global test" for U.S. foreign policy, namely, that someone else must approve it before it can be considered legitimate. Interestingly, shortly after Annan's comments, then Delaware Sen. Joe Biden said, "Nobody in the Senate agrees with that. Nobody in the Senate agrees with that. There is nothing to debate. He is dead, flat, unequivocally wrong.... It is a statement that an overexuberant politician like I am might make on another matter, but I hope he did not mean it, if he did. I love him, but he is flat-out wrong." We will now see, of course, whether Vice President Biden's opinion remains the same under President Obama.

A dramatic contrast to the global-test approach to foreign policy, which still involves effective multilateral activity, is the U.S.-led Proliferation Security Initiative (PSI). PSI now has more than 100 participating countries working to stop the international trafficking of weapons and materials of mass destruction. PSI has no secretary-general, no bureaucracy, no headquarters, no endless diplomatic meetings. It simply focuses, often clandestinely, on working to prevent or interdict shipments of contraband material. As one British diplomat put it, "PSI is an activity, not an organization." In fact, PSI is precisely the kind of multilateral activity that protects our national security while respecting our sovereignty, and thus disproves the charges of those who complain that U.S. sovereignty advocates favor only unilateral action and therefore lack "legitimacy."

These contrasting approaches highlight the options facing President Obama. Moreover, many national security issues, particularly those involving the use of force, merge quickly into the appropriate role of "international law." While respected scholars disagree strongly on the force and scope of international law, those urging its expansion most emphatically are also those most at odds with the continuing vitality of American sovereignty. Thus, while many in the mainstream of American politics debate the utility, wisdom, and implications of international law policies, we can focus on the sharp edges, where international law advocates are trying to tie Gulliver down in ways most Americans find utterly unacceptable.

Law, "International Law," and American Sovereignty

To President Obama, the concept of international law is palpable, as his September 2009 speech to the U.N. Security Council emphasized: "[W]e must demonstrate that international law is not an empty promise and that treaties will be enforced." Many in his administration are doing their utmost to subvert America's well-deserved reputation as an adherent of the rule of law by subordinating it to the dangerous concept that international law, as defined by its high priests, overrides our domestic law, including in the judiciary. Actually, what is or is not legally binding about international law, particularly customary international law, is wide open to dispute. Customary international law used to refer to "state practice" in international affairs, a generally sensible way of deciding such questions as navigation protocols, reflecting what seafaring states have done over the centuries. In recent decades, however, the academic left has seized on customary law as a fertile field for imposing its own ideological standards internationally and binding countries to "laws" they never explicitly approved.

Because democratic debates in constitutional systems

like ours are so unsatisfying and often so unproductive for America's statists, they have, in essence, launched an international power play to move outside our legal systems. They find much greater prospects for success in international forums like the United Nations than in the U.S. Congress. Hence, the role and limits of international law, determining what is legally binding for our international conduct and domestic policy, will be a critical area of debate in the coming years.

The most visible, immediate impact of President Obama's fascination with international law appears in the global war against terrorism, a term he tries to avoid. Instead, he adopted the view widely held in Europe and among legal theorists that terrorist threats and attacks should be treated under the criminal law-enforcement paradigm, rather than as attacks on America subject to the law of war. The question is whether we treat terrorists simply as bank robbers on steroids or as national security threats to which we should respond in legitimate self-defense. The Obama administration strongly supports the criminal law paradigm, which most Americans emphatically reject.

Thus, reflecting the law-enforcement approach, Obama rapidly ordered the closure of the Guantanamo Bay terrorist detention facility and either the release of those still detained or their transfer to the United States. He also pushed to abandon "enhanced interrogation" techniques and insisted upon trying as many terrorists as possible in civilian courts, under ordinary criminal law procedures rather than in military tribunals. This mindset's strong ideological roots reflect the administration's fundamental acceptance of leftist conventional wisdom on international law. Under this view, for Obama, closing Gitmo is not just good policy but, more importantly, "norms" America with international opinion on handling terrorists.

Why we should defer to international norms on terrorism is, to say the least, unclear. The U.N. has repeatedly tried and failed to reach a comprehensive definition of terrorism. Its continuing inability to agree on something so fundamental helps explain why the U.N., particularly the Security Council, has been AWOL in the war on terrorism and why international norms should not dissuade us even slightly from legitimate self-defense efforts.

Unfortunately, mishandling the war against terrorism doesn't end with distorting the correct legal and political paradigms to combat it. The Obama administration has broader ambitions as well, including an ill-concealed desire to join the International Criminal Court (ICC). Although billed as a successor to the Nuremberg tribunals, the ICC, in fact, amounts to a giant opportunity to second-guess the United States and the actions we take in self-defense. The ICC's enormous potential prosecutorial power awaits only the opportunity to expand almost without limit. The Clinton administration initially signed the ICC's founding document, the Rome Statute, in June 1998, but there was no prospect that the Senate would ratify it. The Bush administration unsigned the treaty and entered into more than 100 bilateral agreements with countries to prevent our citizens from being delivered into the ICC's custody. To date, the ICC has proceeded slowly, partly in the hope of enticing the United States to cooperate with it, and the Bush administration succumbed to it in its final years. The ICC's friends under President Obama want to go even further. Secretary of State Hillary Clinton said in 2009, for example, that it was "a great regret but it is a fact we are not yet a signatory" to the Rome Statute, signaling unmistakably what she hopes to do.

The Obama administration's willingness to submit U.S. conduct to international judicial review also extends to the concept of "universal jurisdiction," which permits even countries utterly unrelated to an event to initiate criminal prosecutions regarding it. The administration has yet to say, for example, that it will oppose potential European efforts to prosecute those responsible for enhanced interrogation techniques. This devotion to international norms is designed to intimidate U.S. decision makers, military forces, and intelligence agents, and violates basic democratic precepts that we are responsible for and fully capable of holding our government to its responsibilities under our Constitution.

In fact, limiting America's military options and capabilities through international agreements and organizations is a high priority for the Obama administration. It worked hard to negotiate with Russia significant reductions in America's nuclear weapons and delivery systems, now embodied in the "New START" treaty. The administration appears open to imposing new constraints on our missile-defense programs. These were previously eliminated in 2001 by the Bush administration's withdrawal from the 1972 Anti-Ballistic Missile Treaty, which barred us from building national missile defenses. President Obama has already abandoned missile-defense sites in Poland and the Czech Republic that were intended to protect the continental United States. Any missile defense budget cuts will cause enormous damage, no matter what is ultimately agreed with Moscow.

Moreover, the president's aspiration, articulated in his 2009 Prague speech, to achieve a world without nuclear weapons is well on track, whether or not other nuclear nations (and proliferators) follow suit. Obama has committed to a multitude of multilateral arms-control treaties and negotiations, such as again pressing for Senate ratification of the Comprehensive Nuclear Test Ban Treaty (previously defeated by a Senate vote of 51–48 on October 13, 1999). Undoubtedly, the Landmines Convention, another Clinton administration legacy (adopted in Ottawa in December 1997) will also reappear on the administration's agenda. In addition, the president wants to negotiate treaties to stop new production of fissile material, to prevent an outer space "arms race," and to regulate trade in conventional weapons that will have potentially enormous implications for our domestic debate over the Second Amendment and firearms control.

In addition, many senior administration officials have demonstrated their sympathy for using international "human rights" norms on the conduct of war to constrain the United States. Of course, no one advocates uncivilized or inhumane behavior, but the critical point is who defines such behavior and who holds those who violate the accepted standards accountable. Under our Constitution, we are fully capable of deciding how and when to use military force, how our warriors should conduct themselves, and how to deal with those who violate our standards. We do not need international human-rights experts, prosecutors, or courts to satisfy our own high standards for American behavior.

This is not the view, however, of those who want to constrain our sovereignty. After all, if we decided what is right and wrong, they couldn't second-guess us and bend us to their views. Having failed to win this point within our political system, however, they simply retreat into international organizations, hoping they and their international leftist allies can win there what they failed to win at home.

Israel is often a preferred target because it is small and even less popular in the elite circles of international law and norming than the United States. Thus, the U.N.'s

Goldstone report on Israel's 2008–09 Operation Cast Lead against Hamas in the Gaza Strip criticized Israel for violations of the law of war, such as the "disproportionate use of force," in ways that severely undermine Israel's inherent right of self-defense. If such conclusions become widely accepted, they will obviously have direct and substantial effects on our ability to undertake our own self-defense, which is, of course, exactly what the globalists have in mind. The U.N. Human Rights Council, established in 2006, has proved to be even worse than its completely discredited predecessor, spending most of its time examining Israel's defects rather than the world's worst human-rights violators. Nonetheless, based on its post-American ideology, the Obama administration rejoined the council. Unsurprisingly, U.S. membership has had no effect on council decisions, but our return has given it a legitimacy utterly lacking in our absence.

President Obama has used military force to protect America, but almost apologetically and with undisguised longing to do exactly the opposite. Thus, even when announcing a substantial increase in U.S. forces in Afghanistan to combat the Taliban, he avowed simultaneously his hope to begin withdrawing those forces in mid-2011. Such a clear signal of weakness only encourages the Taliban and al Qaeda to hold on until that point, when Obama could begin bringing troops home, perhaps even proclaiming, "Mission accomplished." Ironically, of course, the campaigns in Afghanistan and Pakistan employ armed drone aircraft to target and kill terrorist leaders and supporters, although, needless to say, the targets don't get *Miranda* rights read to them. The administration seems unwilling to reconcile these strikes with how it handles terrorists captured in the United States. Already, there are international complaints that the drone attacks are precisely the kinds of "targeted" or "extra-judicial" killings complained about for years when undertaken by Israel. But what conclusion will terrorists draw if they realize that, as with the Christmas Day 2009 bomber, you are likely to be safer if you attack the United States in its homeland rather than in the "Af-Pak" mountains? President Obama should adjust his antiterrorism policy in America to reflect the war paradigm in central Asia.

Economic and Environmental Policy Threats to Sovereignty

One popular global initiative arising in a variety of contexts and formats is to give global organizations taxing power that is independent of national governments. First proposed by Yale's James Tobin to tax currency transactions to reduce speculation, the idea of international taxes has expanded to such diverse sources of revenue as bank transfers, international airplane tickets, and royalties from subsea mining. Proceeds from the taxes could be used to finance U.N. agencies, for global warming programs, or for anything else creative minds can conjure.

Central to these proposals is funding international activities without any need for action by national governments, and this stems from frustrations with the United States. Congress has, over the years, frequently withheld "assessed" contributions from the U.N., and critics claimed we were thereby violating our obligations under the U.N. Charter. That claim itself is highly debatable, but there is no question that withholding funds shocked and awed the international bureaucracies. Accordingly, the search was on for ways to end-run Congress and obtain revenue sources that the people's representatives could not turn on and off at will.

The issue of international taxing authority will be

increasingly prominent and is an issue even in long-pending treaties that President Obama is pressing to ratify, such as the Law of the Sea Treaty (LOST). "Royalties" from undersea mining activities to fund the international authority created under LOST should be understood as one of the treaty's key defects and a dangerous precedent for future "self-funding" international regulatory schemes.

Unquestionably, the mother of all such plans is in the environmental area: the Kyoto/Copenhagen global warming enterprise. Buried in the failed Copenhagen negotiations were critical provisions to generate funding for "climate change" activities completely free of congressional action. There are many grounds to oppose Copenhagen's statist agenda, but the issue of taxation should be one of the most important. Whatever the reality of the earth's changing temperature and humanity's role in it, the fundamental debate should be over the proposed solutions. If increased taxation, regulation, and control at the national or international levels are the answers, we are clearly asking the wrong questions.

Mirroring the threat of the ICC and "universal jurisdiction" in national security, many proposed international economic regulatory schemes also contain tribunals with unchecked judicial or prosecutorial powers. This increased delegation of national authority into essentially unaccountable international tribunals translates as transferring more and more of our own governance beyond our effective constitutional control – and more erosion of U.S. sovereignty.

Sovereignty and Social Issues

The globalists have been extremely active in what we normally consider domestic social issues. Their tactical rationale is clear. Frustrated by not achieving their objectives in domestic U.S. politics, they take their issues international. There, in multilateral negotiations, they typically find far more sympathy for their objectives and policies than in Washington. Encouraged by this welcoming environment, the globalists, often working through nongovernmental organizations (NGOs), negotiate agreements embodying their own policy preferences. They then bring them back to America, often embedded in larger treaty documents that contain unrelated or at least innocuous provisions. By using this back door, the globalists hope to achieve indirectly what they cannot obtain more openly. Moreover, NGOs often participate in international negotiations almost as nation-states, giving the "civil society" activists a second bite at the apple to reach their policy objectives. Most Americans think the debate is over once an issue is resolved in our domestic politics. The globalist NGOs know better.

It is certainly true, and vitally important for protecting our sovereignty, that treaties require a two-thirds Senate vote for ratification, thus leading some to conclude that the backdoor approach is actually more difficult than conventional legislation, which requires only a majority in the House and Senate. Of course, through the increasingly popular vehicle of "legislative-executive agreements," large numbers of measures have been enacted into law by the House and Senate, including trade and tariff agreements and U.S. membership in the World Bank and the International Monetary Fund. The broader point is not process but legislative scrutiny. International agreements are essentially "take it or leave it" propositions, rarely amended during congressional debate. In addition, the domestic effects of many treaty provisions are far from obvious, often intentionally so, and therefore they do not receive adequate scrutiny. Moreover, many international conventions are adopted routinely and without much thought by other countries, leaving the United States, often one of the few nations not to immediately ratify, exposed to the complaint that we are isolated in the world, usually in the company of undesirables like Sudan and Burma. "What is wrong with the United States?" the treaty advocates lament. The efficacy of this form of political pressure cannot be discounted, although most often what is wrong with the United States is that we actually take treaties seriously, unlike many other countries that ratify them indiscriminately with little or no intention of abiding by them or even paying them much attention.

Take, for example, the issue of gun control, where many proponents are frustrated with their lack of popular domestic support. Beginning in the Clinton administration, pro-gun-control NGOs decided to go international under the guise of curbing international trafficking in "small arms and light weapons." While there is much to be said for responsible protections in arms exports, which United States law has long included, more strictly, in fact, than any other country, the NGOs' real objective was the international limitation on private ownership of firearms.

In 2002, the Bush administration essentially put a stop to those efforts in the U.N. system, a bar that lasted until Obama's inauguration. Now, Secretary of State Clinton is pushing hard for an Arms Trade Treaty that could do what the gun-control advocates have long been seeking. Ellen Tauscher, under-secretary of state for arms control and international security, said in February 2009 that the ongoing negotiations "have broadened so that we now have an A-to-Z list of meetings and forums on how to limit or eliminate small arms, anti-personnel land mines and other indiscriminate weapons." Note how, in her view, guns and rifles for hunting or self-protection are now "indiscriminate weapons" like land mines. Her formulation is a classic example of how advocates can obfuscate their real objectives and how they operate under the radar screen in domestic American politics until the international treaty is negotiated and brought back to Washington. Then, we are told, we must ratify it or be "isolated" in the world.

This approach has been used over the years against the death penalty. In the United States, at the national and state levels, we have a vigorous democratic debate over the death penalty, sometimes expanding it and sometimes contracting it. In every case, though, we do it after free and open debate. That, however, is not good enough for death-penalty opponents, who can't get what they want in the United States. They too have gone international, using the U.N.'s "human rights" bodies to repeatedly condemn the death penalty. In effect, death-penalty opponents are trying to mobilize international public opinion against the prevailing majority view within the United States, as well as trying in U.S. courts to use unrelated treaties to prevent the penalty from being applied. This often surprises people from democracies. During his first months in office in 2007, for example, U.N. Secretary-General Ban Ki-moon remarked that the issue of the death penalty was each nation's to decide on its own, reflecting his understanding as a citizen of South Korea, which still has the death penalty. Ban was all but tarred and feathered in U.N. circles for not recognizing the long string of U.N. resolutions opposing the death penalty. In America, citizens might well have asked, "What business is it of the U.N. even to have votes on the legitimacy of the death penalty?"

The same internationalization of domestic issues appears in a host of other social issues: abortion; family law and the relationships between parent and child (the Convention on the Rights of the Child); and discrimination based on gender (the Convention on the Elimination of All Forms of Discrimination Against Women), race (the U.N. Committee on the Elimination of Racial Discrimination), or disability (Convention on the Rights of Persons with Disabilities). The issue here is not, for example, appropriate protections against discrimination, but who should decide such questions. Should it be American citizens operating under our Constitution or international agreements with nations that care little about fundamental freedoms or the importance of democratic debate? This is where the rubber truly meets the road on sovereignty.

Protecting American Sovereignty in the Age of Obama

We must take threats to American sovereignty and efforts to expand the scope of global governance seriously. Failure to do so, and its inevitable consequences, will only be our fault. As James Madison said in 1788 during the debate over ratifying the Constitution: "[T]here are more instances of the abridgment of the freedom of the people by gradual and silent encroachments of those in power than by violent and sudden usurpations. . . ."

So what must we do during the remainder of the Obama presidency, given the enormous authority for international affairs vested in the executive branch and his current considerable majorities in both houses of Congress? While the answer is discouraging, it should remind us yet again why elections matter.

First, and most important, we must understand better how and where sovereignty issues arise. Too often, even in areas directly affecting national security, we do not appreciate the issues at stake. Important threats to sovereignty may arise more often on what we consider domestic policies. All of us, therefore, need to be alert to the implications of policy issues for U.S. sovereignty. You can be sure the globalists are. Moreover, defenders of American sovereignty, working through their own organizations, must develop international capabilities like the left's NGOs if they do not already have them. That will ensure both awareness of what the globalists are up to and provide mechanisms to counter them in the often obscure corridors of international organizations, conferences, and negotiations.

Second, we must make foreign policy, national security, and sovereignty issues top priority in evaluating candidates at the federal level, starting with the president. Even at a time of grave economic challenge, we must remember that our international adversaries are not waiting for us to get our domestic house in order. Neither are those seeking to diminish our sovereignty. Indeed, they very well understand the admonition, "Never let a good crisis go to waste." In congressional and presidential elections, we should insist that candidates explain their views on sovereignty and, if they are incumbents, what they have done to protect it during their terms in office.

Third, we must ensure that our senators and representatives are reminded regularly that sovereignty issues are important to us. Their attention at election time will be easier to get if they are constantly aware while in office that their constituents think these issues are important.

All of this implies that the importance of threats to American sovereignty needs more attention from our political leaders and our media. But most important of all, it needs more attention from us, the citizenry. After all, it's our sovereignty that's at stake. If we don't take it seriously, no one else will.

DANIEL DiSALVO

GOVERNMENT UNIONS AND THE BANKRUPTING OF AMERICA

THE GREAT RECESSION has exposed to public scrutiny the generous pay and benefits that many government employees receive. At a time when many states (to say nothing of that superstate, the federal government) are staggering under unprecedented debt, the Shangri-la of public-sector, government unions has aroused widespread criticism as well as the envy of average workers in the private sector. In February 2011, the newly elected Republican governor of Wisconsin, Scott Walker, gave voice to those resentments, saying, "We can no longer live in a society where the public employees are the haves and the taxpayers who foot the bill are the have-nots." Addressing the issue of fiscal continence as well as the issue of fairness, Walker sparked a national debate over the legitimacy and desirability of a unionized government workforce. His proposal called for the state's public employees to pay a bit more of their pension and health care costs (still less than the national average for government workers and far less than the private-sector average); it rolled back collective-bargaining rights for most government workers; and it took the state out of the business of collecting union dues.

Walker's proposals elicited a heated response from public employees and their Democratic allies. Some 60,000 protesters descended on the state Capitol in Madison, and teachers effectively went on strike for a couple of days by calling in sick in large numbers. Democratic state senators fled to Illinois to prevent a vote on the measure. Even President Obama accused Walker of launching an "assault on unions." Nevertheless, after three weeks of fruitless negotiations with absentee Democrats, Walker and his Republican colleagues in the Legislature forged ahead and enacted significant changes to Wisconsin's public labor laws.

The steps taken by Wisconsin's Republican leaders were quickly seconded in Ohio, where the state's governor, John Kasich, and the state Legislature passed similar measures only to see them overturned before taking effect by the state's unions and their allies in a referendum. The legislative battles playing out in the Midwest follow on the heels of actions taken by New Jersey's hard-charging governor, Chris Christie, who improbably became a national celebrity through his battles with his state's public-employee unions. Christie targeted for reform the burdens that public workers' health and pension benefits place on the Garden State's long-term finances. He dared to propose measures that just yesterday were considered "impossible" or "political suicide." The teachers unions reacted with fury, spending millions on attack ads in 2010 to block Christie's proposals. Yet in cooperation with a state Legislature controlled by Democrats, Christie has changed pension rules, instituted a 2 percent property-tax cap, and required teachers to make small contributions to their health-insurance plans. He is now seeking to reform the teacher tenure system.

Other states – such as Nevada, Michigan, New York, California, and Pennsylvania – are also revisiting the status and role of unionized government workers in their politics. The reason for this wave of concern is that in the past half-century, unions representing public servants have become political powerhouses. In recent campaigns and elections, they have provided large sums of money to candidates, almost all of it to Democrats, at all levels of government. They make huge independent expenditures on campaign ads, again almost always for Democratic candidates. In addition, they provide the foot soldiers for voter registration and get-out-the-vote drives. “We’re the big dog,” says Larry Scanlon, the political director of the American Federation of State, County, and Municipal Employees (AFSCME), the largest union of government workers in the country. AFSCME’s website brags that candidates “all across the country, at every level of government” have learned to “pay attention to AFSCME’s political muscle.” And the union has used that formidable muscle to elect allies and secure generous pay and substantial benefits for their members at significant cost to taxpayers.

The main reason for the unions’ success is that the political process affords public-sector unions much more influence over their members’ employers – that is, the government – than private-sector unions could ever dream of. Government unions help elect politicians who then act as “management” in negotiations over pay, benefits, and work rules. “We elect our bosses, so we’ve got to elect politicians who support us,” AFSCME’s website flatly states. The result is a cycle that is hard to break. Unions extract dues from their members and funnel them into politicians’ campaign war chests, then those same politicians agree to generous contracts for public workers – which in turn leads to more union dues, more campaign spending, and so on. It is a cycle that has dominated the politics of some of America’s states with dire consequences.

The principal function of unions is to represent their members' interests. Therefore, those in the public sector have interpreted the reform proposals of Christie, Walker, and Kasich as a serious threat. Defenders of public-employee unions, like former Secretary of Labor Robert Reich, charged that humble public workers were being targeted as "scapegoats" for the Great Recession. They argue that most government employees live modest lives and aren't paid better than workers in the private sector. Criticizing public servants, they say, only serves to divert attention from the corporate executives who perpetrated the economic crisis. The unions help sustain a professional public service and preserve a segment of the hard-pressed middle class that would otherwise be thrust into a cruel race to the bottom. The arguments of the unions and their defenders have some merit. But ultimately, they are unpersuasive.

Attention to government unions has revealed two pressing problems. First, the unions exercise considerable political clout in a partially acknowledged symbiosis with the Democratic Party, and second, the economic consequences of that alliance are fiscally unsustainable promises and inflexible government. These two interrelated problems were present before the financial crisis, but when it took the economic tide out, the strain on government finances and taxpayer wallets was readily apparent. In the wake of the Great Recession, it has become clear across the country that the road to genuine reform runs straight through these unions. How to deal with them and their Democratic allies presents state and local officials with a huge challenge that is likely to occupy them for years. But deal with them they must: Business as usual with public-sector unions has produced staggering government obligations. The stakes in these battles are high.

They involve the long-term fiscal health of the nation, the balance of power between the nation's two political parties, and the government's efficiency and effectiveness. Ultimately, insofar as the fiscal health of the country is at stake, we are confronted with a threat to the power and prestige of the United States on the world stage.

The Takeoff

The story of the American labor movement is a tale rich with the organizing struggles of miners, ladies' garment workers, and autoworkers. Today, however, the conventional wisdom is that organized labor in America has been enfeebled. The inability of President Barack Obama and large Democratic majorities in the 111th Congress to pass labor's highest legislative priority, the Employee Free Choice Act (often called "check card"), is supposedly indicative of unions' political impotence. In 1955, organized labor represented one-third of the nonagricultural workforce. Today, it represents only 11.6 percent – and only 6.9 percent of private-sector workers. While there is much to be said for the "union decline" thesis, most observers have greatly underestimated labor's political power because they have overlooked public-employee unions. In spite of declining private-sector union membership, the unique attributes of government unions have helped maintain labor's power in American politics. In 2009, a major barrier was breached. For the first time, more government employees (7.6 million) than private-sector employees (7.1 million) belonged to unions. And this was despite the fact that 83 percent of workers labor in the private economy, while 17 percent are in the public sector.

Before 1960, few government workers were union members. Party machines or civil-service rules determined who worked for the government and what they did. Many states even had laws on the books that forbade government workers from joining unions. Even in places where joining a union was legal, union rights were highly restricted. Over the course of the 1960s and early 1970s, however, there was a largely unnoticed "rights revolution." Public-employee unions won the right to organize and bargain collectively – a legally enforced process that determines binding contractual agreements for the terms and conditions of employment – with various units of government. Today, all but 12 states have collective bargaining for at least some public servants (usually those in the protective services, such as police and firefighters), and in only five states is public-sector collective bargaining completely proscribed. The growth of public-employee unions surged. By 1980, 36 percent of public employees belonged to unions – a figure that has remained roughly stable ever since. Yet disparities in state and local laws mean that the percentage varies widely from state to state. New York is at the top of the heap, with 69 percent of its state employees in unions, while many Southern states have membership rates below 10 percent.

That powerful government unions exist at all is a striking political development. The prevailing attitude among policymakers across the political spectrum was downright hostile well into the 1950s. President Franklin D. Roosevelt, one of labor's best friends, wrote in 1937 that "meticulous attention should be paid to the special relations and obligations of public servants to the public itself and to the Government.... The process of collective bargaining, as usually understood, cannot be transplanted into the public service." Other champions of organized labor thought the same way. Although he later revised his position, the first president of the AFL-CIO, George Meany, believed as late as the 1950s that it was "impossible to bargain collectively with the government." Meany and Roosevelt's reasoning was that the elected representatives of the people would be forced to share their governing authority with unelected union officials whom voters could not hold accountable. The integrity of democratic self-government would thus be compromised.

For government unions to emerge, two things had to happen. The first was the destruction of the party machines at the state and local levels. Machine control of government work increased turnover in public employment by hitching it to election results. Patronage appointees rarely developed a culture of professionalism. Reformers sought to take patronage away from party bosses and ward heelers and reduce the politicization of government work by enacting civil-service laws. By the end of the 1950s, reformers had largely succeeded. The most important consequence of civil-service reform was that public employees gained nearly lifetime job security, which enhanced their collective-action incentives. These laws also lifted the floor of worker protections on which union-negotiated contracts were built.

The second precondition was the solidification of the alliance between the Democratic Party and organized labor. Roosevelt's signing of the Wagner Act in 1935 married labor to the Democrats. Private-sector union membership surged. By midcentury, Democrats began to rely heavily on labor unions for both campaign financing and grassroots organizing. Therefore, both Democrats and labor had a strong incentive to increase the size of the labor movement. Government workers were the new recruits, especially as private-sector union membership declined.

To give government workers the incentive to join unions, a series of measures granting them collective-bargaining rights was passed. In 1958, New York City Mayor Robert Wagner Jr. issued Executive Order 49, known as "the little Wagner Act." In 1959, Wisconsin passed the first statewide collective-bargaining law for public employees. And in 1962, President John F. Kennedy issued Executive Order 10988, which reaffirmed the right of federal workers to organize and codified some workers' rights to bargain collectively. Over the next decade, other states and cities passed a host of laws providing public-employee unions with collective-bargaining rights. Consequently, as private-sector unions withered in the 1970s, government-union membership took off.

The growth of government workers inside the labor movement's ranks produced a noticeable change in the demographic profile of union members. In the 1950s, the typical union member was a high school-educated white male who lived in a major city. Today, white-collar workers are a majority of union members, and gender parity has almost been achieved. A quarter of union members have college degrees, most live in the suburbs, and unions have become multiracial. The sort of jobs union members do has also drastically changed. Union members today are more likely to be teachers, police officers, or firefighters than they are to be electricians, iron workers, or coal miners. In sum, unions today represent a very different segment of the workforce than they did when America was the world's leading manufacturer.

The shift in the makeup of the labor movement has had an impact on public perceptions of it. In the 1950s, many families had at least one member who was in a union. Today, few Americans know anyone who belongs to a private-sector union. In 2009, just 48 percent of Americans approved of labor unions – the lowest percentage Gallup has recorded since 1937. Gallup reported that while two-thirds of the public believed unions were good for their members, 51 percent believed they were bad for the economy in general. And 62 percent said they felt that unions "mostly hurt" workers who were not members. These perceptions pose significant problems for the Democratic Party, which for much of the 20th century was the home of working-class voters and which today is deeply dependent on union campaign support. Consequently, while it is clearly not in the short-term interests of many Democratic incumbents, it might actually be in the party's long-term interests to distance itself from the public unions. They could then more easily claim to represent the interests of most workers, not just government ones.

The Government-Union Advantage

Once up and running, government unions became some of the most powerful interest groups in America, and their importance in political campaigns has grown by leaps and bounds. Government-workers unions now far exceed private-sector unions in political contributions. The money unions spend on politicking originates from citizens who pay taxes, which in turn pay public employees' salaries, a portion of which is deducted from their paychecks by the government in the form of union dues. The unions then use that revenue to fund, almost exclusively, the Democratic Party. Under the current arrangements, taxpayers thus partially subsidize a demand for bigger government and higher taxes. For example, from 1989 to 2012, according to the Center for Responsive Politics, six of the top 15 biggest spenders in America on direct donations to candidates (almost all of it to Democrats) were public-employee unions led by AFSCME. Interestingly, this was spending on federal elections by a union federation that represents mostly state and local workers. What explains this behavior is the huge number of federal dollars that go into state budgets. The AFSCME's aim is to shape federal spending in ways that are favorable to public workers.

For federal races in the 2010 elections, public-employee unions paid out more than $200 million in "independent expenditures," almost all of it to defeat Republican candidates. The AFSCME alone spent more than $90 million, and it was the biggest donor to the Democrats' efforts to win (or hold) gubernatorial and state Legislature seats. The union's president, Gerald McEntee, proudly said, "We're spending big. And we're damn happy it's big." Indeed, the AFSCME was the biggest campaign spender in 2010. Other spenders in the top 10 were the teachers unions (American Federation of Teachers and the National Education Association) and the Service Employees International Union (SEIU), at least half of whose members are government workers. Unlike business groups that contribute to Democrats and Republicans alike, the unions provide Democrats with a unique source of support.

Even when campaign cash is not the coin of the realm, government unions can exert a powerful influence on election outcomes. The hold the unions exerted on former New Jersey Gov. Jon Corzine was suddenly dramatized when he addressed a Trenton rally of roughly 10,000 public workers in 2006 and blurted out, "We will fight for a fair contract!" Why was a multimillionaire self-financing candidate kowtowing to the unions? Because he was locked in a tight contest with insurgent Republican Chris Christie and needed their get-out-the-vote operation. Corzine knew that every vote would count. If the unions sat on their hands, he was done for. The point is that the political influence of the unions is compounded by their ability to mobilize voters for a specific candidate.

Government unions exercise their greatest influence, however, in low-turnout elections with limited media scrutiny – elections for school boards, for instance, and many elections for state and local offices. In addition, the millions spent by public-employee unions on ballot initiatives and referenda almost always support policy changes leading to higher taxes and bigger government. The California Teachers Association, for example, spent $57 million in 2005 to defeat referenda that would have reduced union power and limited government growth. In 2010, the Oregon Education Association and the SEIU contributed nearly three-quarters of the funds to the campaign in favor of ballot measures that raised taxes on businesses and individuals in Oregon. In San Francisco in fall 2010, there was also a ballot measure that, had it passed, would have required city workers to increase their contributions to their pension and health care plans. City-workers unions spent a million dollars in opposition, the Democratic County Central Committee told voters to not to support it, and Mayor Gavin Newsom said publicly that if it passed, he wouldn't implement it. The measure was defeated. (San Francisco currently spends more on pensions than on parks or its fire department.)

The power of government unions to decide election outcomes is magnified by the fact that in many jurisdictions, their members constitute a disproportionate slice of the electorate. Stanford University political scientist Terry Moe has documented this phenomenon in school-board elections across the country. School boards often form autonomous government units, and elections to them tend to be low profile. Average voters – especially those who are not parents with school-age children – are often poorly informed about the candidates and the issues in these races. Teachers unions, on the other hand, have a powerful interest in who wins these races. And since teachers themselves often make up a large share of the electorate, they are able to elect members of the school board who are beholden to them.

In between elections, government unions have significant advantages over private-sector unions and other interest groups in lobbying for their interests. A profound difference between public- and private-sector collective bargaining is that private-sector unions have a natural adversary in the owners of the companies with whom they negotiate. When private-sector unions negotiate with owners, the owners always have the enticement of keeping profits for themselves. But government unions face no such opposition. In the public sector, there are no profits for managers to keep. There are only the deep pockets that belong to someone else: the taxpayers.

Market forces also provide a powerful check on unions in the private sector. If private-sector unions demand too much compensation, they risk making their employer uncompetitive vis-à-vis its rivals. Union members' jobs are thus on the line if the company loses market share. On the other hand, because the government is the monopoly provider of many services, the pressure to be efficient is greatly relaxed. Finally, amid the "creative destruction" of the market, companies regularly go out of business, which means that private-sector unions must constantly redouble their organizing efforts. The government, on the other hand, never goes out of business. Therefore, once a group of public employees has formed a union, the union persists. Not having to spend more on organizing frees up more scarce resources for political activity.

Government unions also have a number of advantages over regular interest groups. First, they have access to politicians through the collective-bargaining process.

Other interest groups must fight for such access. Second, government unions have a constituent base that can easily be mobilized for electoral participation, while most other interest groups do not. Third, most interest groups dedicate a major portion of their administrative overhead to fundraising. Government unions, by contrast, enjoy a steady revenue stream from union dues. In fact, the government often collects the dues, which drastically reduces the unions' administrative costs. And such savings on overhead can be redirected into electioneering and lobbying.

In American government, political power is often obscurely apportioned. Therefore, beyond direct lobbying of elected officials, government unions have sought to form alliances with actuaries, pension-fund board members, and other little-known officials with power over issues of concern to them. It is through such channels that seemingly small changes in the fine print of pension and health care plans can end up having big consequences.

And if working quietly behind the scenes doesn't cut it, unions often go public to pressure legislators. The tactics include rallies at the state Capitol along with ads on television, radio, and the Internet. The governor of New York, Andrew Cuomo, described how government unions operated in the Empire State: "We've seen the same play run for 10 years. The governor announces the budget, unions come together, put $10 million in a bank account, run television ads against the governor. The governor's popularity drops; the governor's knees weaken; the governor falls to one knee, collapses, makes a deal."

Defenders of government-workers unions often point out that their political power is limited because strikes are illegal in all but two states. (Of course, that doesn't mean strikes haven't been called.) Yet despite being a potent weapon in industrial labor relations, the strike is not a weapon that government unions need to exercise influence. This is because government unions replaced the strike with a process called binding arbitration. When the government and its unionized workers cannot come to an agreement, many states and cities require the dispute to be settled by a third party. The structure of the situation privileges the unions' position by giving them the incentive to keep their final offer high enough to ensure stalemate, with the understanding that an arbitrator will split the difference between the two sides and thus award the union more than the government's last bid. In 1981, Coleman Young, then mayor of Detroit, remarked, "We know that compulsory arbitration destroys sensible fiscal management... [and has] caused more damage to the public service in Detroit than the strikes [it was] designed to prevent."

All of these advantages make government unions a threat to the Madisonian system in which the clash of competing private interests normally conduces to the public interest. When one group has so many advantages over the others and is deeply embedded in one of the two major political parties, it threatens to overwhelm the public interest.

The Taxpayer's Burden

Government unions' political power increases the cost of government – most obviously in the form of greater compensation for government workers. Scholars disagree about how best to measure the differences in compensation between public- and private-sector workers. Depending largely on actuarial assumptions related to the price of future benefits, some find government workers make more in total compensation; others find they make slightly less than private-sector employees. But there are a few points that elicit broad agreement. Generally speaking, the public sector provides a pay premium for jobs at the low end of the labor market, while the private sector pays more, sometimes fantastically so, at the high end. In addition, government workers tend to work fewer hours and have more vacation days per year. The private sector usually requires workers to be much more flexible and to work longer hours. Considering all jobs, government workers today earn more per hour, on average, in total compensation (wages and benefits) than workers in the private sector. It is not worth emphasizing the aggregate pay differential, however, since much of it is easily explained by demographic differences. There are more white-collar jobs in government, which means that public employees tend to be better educated. In addition, most public employees live in urban areas where the cost-of-living and salary scales are higher.

Not as easily captured in many comparable-worth studies are those government workers who lack counterparts in the private sector, such as policemen, firefighters, and corrections officers. And these are the workers who have used their unique status to leverage some of the best compensation packages. In Massachusetts, for instance, a number of state troopers make more in salary than the governor. And a few corrections officers in California can make more than $300,000 a year with overtime. While jobs that require the risk of life and limb merit greater compensation, collective-bargaining contracts have provided a sizable bonus.

Another factor that drives up public-sector pay is the long tenure of many government workers. Staying in a job and accepting incremental raises drives the pay scale up. Turnover in the public workforce is very small compared with the private sector, which indicates that people feel comfortable in their jobs. This is measured by what economists call the "quit rate," which is when workers voluntarily leave their jobs. In 2009, the quit rate in the public sector was one-third that of the private sector. Put differently, many more people quit in the private sector than in the public sector. If public employment has such a good retention rate, it hardly seems that such workers are being exploited.

Ultimately, union wages and salaries are not out of line with pay in the private sector. That is partly because pay increases must be factored into the government's budgets each fiscal year. Therefore, when the road to bigger paychecks has been blocked, the unions have turned their attention to benefits. Because benefits are future compensation, they don't pose the same political costs for lawmakers. Indeed, the coming years are going to be especially challenging for state and local lawmakers throughout the country. The unions' most cherished benefit is the pension. In California, for example, state workers often retire at 55 with lifetime pensions that equal or exceed what they made on the job. In 2011, the Golden State is confronted with a $25.4 billion budget gap but will pay pensions of $100,000 or more annually to some 12,000 retirees.

Part of the explanation for the "pension tsunami" is that about 80 percent of public workers have "defined benefit" retirement plans. Under these plans, when an employee retires, he or she receives a pension on the basis of a formula. In many states and localities, that formula is 2.5 to 3 percent of a worker's average salary during their three highest-earning years times the number of years worked. For example, in New York State, if a state worker whose top salary was $80,000 wanted to retire at 55 after working for 30 years, his pension benefit would be $4,000 a month, or $48,000 annually. If the worker was not a government employee, he or she would need nearly $1 million in savings to have the same monthly retirement income. Such defined benefit plans are now rare in the private sector (only 18 percent of workers have them). Most workers in the private sector instead rely on "defined contribution" plans, which are similar to a 401(k).

How, a reasonable citizen might ask, were lawmakers ever induced to make such promises? Easy. Lawmakers discovered that pension "sweeteners" could be very good politics – that is, "good" for their re-election. Unable to raise pay any higher, calculating politicians placated the unions with future pension commitments. The money is then allocated, but it doesn't have to be paid immediately. The bill comes due when they are long out of office. Politicians could also appear generous by providing public services to citizens without raising taxes to pay for them. And sleight-of-hand budgeting and rosy actuarial assumptions obscured the truth about the fiscal health of state pension funds. Consequently, legislators who got into bed with the unions also deserve a great deal of the blame for governments' fiscal straits.

The long-term problem is that government has become too big, too cumbersome, and too expensive. Northwestern University economist Joshua Rauh estimates the states' current pension liabilities at $3 *trillion.* Some states are worse off than others. Those with strong government-workers unions tend to have greater unfunded liabilities. The Pew Research Center offers a less drastic but still worrisome calculation (made before the recession) that the states are on the hook for $1 trillion in retiree pension and health care costs. However liabilities are calculated, many states cannot renege on many of the promises they've made, because pensions are guaranteed by their constitutions.

Unions and their supporters respond to such arguments

by waving them away. They point out that pension payments only account for about 4 percent of the states' average spending. What's a measly 4 percent? But this figure by itself is misleading. Some states spend as much as 10 percent of their annual budgets on pensions. And because even that figure might seem low, it must be put in context. Major portions of the states' budgets are fixed by federal mandates and bond payments. The percentage of the budget in which lawmakers can actually exercise discretion is much smaller than it first appears. This makes that small percentage devoted to pensions loom much larger, especially when it is increasing. Combine that with health care commitments to retirees, and the percentage of revenue goes up even further.

For all the talk about how public employees' pension costs can "crowd out" other government priorities, it should not be forgotten that retiree health care costs do the same thing. The Pew Center on the States estimates that the states currently have a $550 billion unfunded liability for promised retired-employee health coverage besides Medicare. Consequently, in Massachusetts, hundreds of millions of dollars in school funding never reached a classroom because they have been used to pay for the health care of education workers. This sort of outcome helps explain why the major increases in spending on education in the past 30 years have had so little effect on student performance.

The result is that taxpayers don't receive more government services for the greater costs they are paying. One group of economists reports that "since 1950, state and local spending has grown … fast enough to double the size of state and local government every 8 or 9 years." Such growth would be logical if it were improving infrastructure, because better roads, bridges, and mass-transit systems increase economic efficiency. But that hasn't happened. Spending on infrastructure has been flat as a percentage of GDP since 1950. The implication is that employee compensation has gobbled up most of the growth in state and local spending.

While the economic downturn of 2008–11 has caused a fiscal calamity for states and cities, their budgets were fraught with problems long before the recession hit. As John Hood has pointed out in *National Affairs*, these were due to unsustainable public-employee pension obligations, excessive borrowing, and overly optimistic budgeting in years of relative prosperity. The basic consequence is that taxpayers are now stuck spending more – a lot more – for less. If a government must spend more on pensions and health care for its workers, it cannot spend more on schools, roads, and poor relief. As former California Gov. Arnold Schwarzenegger's economic adviser David Crane has pointed out, pension and health care obligations to his state's employees threaten to "crowd out funding for many programs vital to the overwhelming majority of Californians," including "higher education, transit, and parks." In other words, the core functions people expect their governments to perform get shortchanged. State and local governments are now confronted with the difficult choice of either raising taxes or making deep cuts to critical programs.

Reducing Government Performance

The rise of government unionism helps explain the distinct private and public "worlds of work," as Harvard policy scholar John Donahue has put it. The former is ultra-competitive and the rewards highly unequal, while the latter still provides multiple protections and greater equality in the pay scale. Government unions have shaped the conditions of their members' employment in ways that shield them from the fierce struggle that rages in the private sector. In the private sector, intense competition, constant evaluation, long hours, and pay-for-performance standards are the norm. Comparatively speaking, the public sector is an oasis of stability.

The differences between public- and private-sector work stem in part from allowing public-employee unions to have a large say in setting the conditions under which they work. Negotiating work rules means that they have the power to shape the daily routines of public servants. Because government workers are, in effect, the face of government that most people see, what they do shapes how well the government performs. Unfortunately, they tend to make government less effective and more expensive. American government does not, therefore, spend taxpayers' dollars very efficiently. The World Economic Forum ranks America 68th in the world on this score.

Unions also negotiate salary scales, promotion schedules, and other aspects of the workplace. This makes government work more attractive for some people than for others. Given the pay premium at the low end of the labor market for government work, those with limited skills increasingly seek it out. At the high end of the labor market, which requires much schooling and long years of experience, the fact that government work is less well compensated than the private sector can make it less appealing. Some scholars argue that a "brain drain" occurs when talented people leave government work for the handsome salaries and plush offices they can secure in the private market. Some workers may also opt out of government work to avoid the slow promotion process that prevails in the public sector. And highly educated employees who decide to stay in government work can sometimes be less innovative and less willing to experiment than their private-sector brethren.

Because the task of unions is to represent all their members as equally as possible, negotiated work rules protect high-performing and underperforming workers alike. The problematic result is that it is difficult for agency managers to reassign workers and nearly impossible to fire bad public employees. The termination process is so drawn out and costly that many managers often forgo it. Speaking of his state's teacher-tenure provisions, Nevada Gov. Brian Sandoval remarked, "It's practically impossible to remove an underperforming teacher under the system we have now." In the first decade of the 21st century, the Los Angeles school district spent $3.5 million to sack seven teachers (out of 33,000).

While many factors contribute to the performance of state and local government, government unions tend to reduce efficiency and introduce greater rigidity. The Pew Center on the States grades state government performance, and those that came out on top, such as Virginia and Texas, prohibit collective bargaining in the public sector. States with powerful government unions, such as California, New Jersey, and Rhode Island, received some of the worst grades. The implication is that offering the leaders of public bureaucracies greater flexibility can produce positive results.

The Way Out

The struggles of the 1960s invigorated government unionism; the Great Recession may end up gutting it. Indeed, the next year is going to be an especially challenging one for state and local lawmakers throughout the country.

Many are confronted with painful choices in order to close yawning budget gaps. There are two basic alternatives (which can be combined). One is to try to diminish government-union power through structural reforms – such as limiting or ending collective bargaining and stopping governments from collecting union dues – that would sever the problematic links between unions and elected officials. The other is to work within existing arrangements and seek concessions from the unions on pay, pensions, health care, and work rules.

In light of the threat posed by government unions to fiscal sanity and democratic self-government, some governors, notably in Wisconsin, have adopted the first approach. They are rolling back the 1960s collective-bargaining-rights revolution by narrowing the subject of collective bargaining to wages only for most workers. Pension and health benefits will no longer be legally mandatory subjects of negotiation.

The hope is that this will give agency managers greater flexibility in determining benefits and how public servants do their jobs. The principal effect of these changes in collective-bargaining rights is likely to be lower pension and health care benefits for new employees, which can reduce long-term spending. And it will make it more difficult for unions to win back concessions made in hard economic times when growth returns.

Critics of Walker argue that "basic democratic rights" are being taken away. If they were so fundamental, however, all government workers would have them. But many don't. Texas, Virginia, North Carolina, South Carolina, and Georgia prohibit all collective bargaining with government-workers unions. Twelve other states only grant certain categories of public employees collective-bargaining rights. Even if most government workers were stripped of collective-bargaining rights, they would retain more protections than private-sector workers, since most worker protections – such as merit-based hiring or the need for just cause to discipline or fire an employee – stem from civil-service laws passed well before collective-bargaining rights were put on the books. Government workers could still band together and exercise their rights as citizens by trying to elect politicians of their choice and by petitioning the government. Furthermore, much informal negotiation between the government and workers' representatives could still take place even if collective bargaining were not legally mandated. This in fact occurred in many states and cities prior to the adoption of collective-bargaining laws.

To weaken unions' political power in future negotiations, reform-oriented governors have also sought to stop the government from collecting union dues. They aim to change the default option to one in which workers wouldn't pay union dues unless they voluntarily decided to become a union member, even if they are covered by a union contract. This arrangement is called an open shop and currently exists in nearly half the states. Wisconsin has eliminated "agency shops" in government, in which money is automatically deducted from paychecks. The likely effect of the new laws in Wisconsin will be to vastly reduce the amount of revenue the unions take in. In the long run, they would reduce membership, undermine a huge source of funds for Democrats, and reduce taxpayer support for a lobby that promotes larger government and more taxation. The Badger State is trying to provide a model for reform that would put it on a path toward the saner and more responsible way of conducting government affairs, which was endorsed long ago by Franklin D. Roosevelt and George Meany.

Short of such a direct "assault," in President Obama's

words, on the public unions, other governors have sought to work within existing arrangements toward similar ends. They have called for "shared sacrifice" to get public employees to contribute more toward their pension and health care plans, as they believe current commitments are untenable. "[Pension reform] is not a Democrat or Republican issue," says Los Angeles Mayor Antonio Villaraigosa. "The fact is our pensions aren't sustainable." Villaraigosa is a former teachers-union organizer and a Democrat. He supports lowering pension benefits for new police officers and firefighters and requiring other public employees to pay more of their retirement health benefits. Another common proposal in this area is to stop governments from offering defined benefit plans and switch to defined contribution pension plans. The idea is to pay newer employees slightly more in salary and less in deferred pension and health care compensation. Reducing deferred payments has the virtue of reducing the number of opportunities politicians have to keep liabilities off the balance sheet. In 2010, public-employee unions in Vermont, Iowa, Minnesota, and Wyoming conceded to modest reductions in pension benefits. But more will need to be done to bring the states' pension funds into balance.

The difficulty with this approach is that calling for such reforms without touching unions' financial and political power leaves the dysfunctional relationships between public-employee unions, politicians, and the government intact. The unions can be counted on to make strategic sacrifices in the here and now to ensure that they can claw back losses when more favorable economic conditions return in the future. Consequently, the trouble with government unions is likely to persist in America's biggest Democratic strongholds.

In sum, we are likely to see a patchwork of reforms

across the nation. Some states like Indiana and Wisconsin have enacted deep reforms that weaken the political power of government unions in their states. Other states, like California, Pennsylvania, and New York, have followed Chris Christie's model in New Jersey, demanding concessions from public-employee unions but leaving prevailing arrangements in place. The viability of either reform strategy will depend on the particular fiscal and political conditions in the states and cities.

The attack on reformers by the unions and their defenders is designed to make any of the changes to current practice seem excessive. But by defending the status quo – when it means undermining the fiscal health and thereby the global power of the United States – the unions risk appearing irresponsible and selfish. The American people are now learning the dangers of handing over so much governing authority to unelected union officials whose interests are not synonymous with theirs. They must take the next step and pressure their elected representatives to take it back.

RICHARD A. EPSTEIN

WHY PROGRESSIVE INSTITUTIONS ARE UNSUSTAINABLE

Classical Liberal vs. Modern Progressive

The modern economic malaise in the United States is captured by two numbers. The first is the decline in average family income, which has slid for the past three years and now stands at the same level, adjusted for inflation, that it was in 1996. The second is the persistent level of unemployment at 9.1 percent, which excludes those who are underemployed or have in frustration given up the search for jobs. Everyone across the political spectrum deplores the result and wishes to reverse the trend. But this unanimity of ends gives way to a fierce difference of opinion on means. Just what should be done?

The deep polarization of views clusters on a broad range of macro- and microeconomic issues. The former covers taxation, deficits, public expenditures. The latter is focused single-mindedly on jobs. The intimate connection between these two is evident from the constant political refrain of whether the priority for government action should lie with the elimination of unemployment or with getting the government's fiscal house in order. This entire set of problems is complicated further by the precarious position of the real estate markets, as the major decline in real estate values has led to a torrent of underwater residences subject to foreclosures whose frequency increases with the decline in employment levels. The overall landscape is still more clouded because the budgetary position of many states is precarious, to say the least. What should be done about these pressing matters? In dealing with this question, it is hardly productive to revisit the political sniping that takes place on both sides of the aisle. It is far more important to ask about the fundamental differences in approach to ending the admitted stagnation in the economic sphere.

For simplicity, I shall ignore the important issues at the state level and concentrate on the nationwide problems with public finance, unemployment, and housing. It is somewhat hysterical to call the current malaise a depression. The overall levels of material wealth are far higher than they were in 1935, and the toxic brew of high tariffs, major deflation, high marginal tax rates, and incessant cartelization of labor and agricultural markets is less potent today than it was at the height of the New Deal. But to say that today's economic climate is better than it was at the depths of the depression is not a ringing endorsement of the status quo – nor does it explain what should be done. Matters do not become, nor do they remain, this grim simply by chance. Consistent bad results can only be explained by consistent bad policies and not by some mysterious run of bad luck. Bad policies in turn rest on an unsound worldview. So this nation has reached a crossroads in its choice of first principles. The nation must choose between the oft-rejected classical liberalism of its founding period and the modern progressive stance that served as the foundation of Franklin Delano Roosevelt's New Deal.

I strongly embrace the former first vision and roundly

reject the latter. There is no middle ground on this topic. Nor is there any one way to explain why the progressive vision has led us so badly astray. But it is possible to see what went wrong by focusing on one part of the larger picture: namely, the relative durability of these alternative institutional arrangements. What is needed therefore is a rough measure of the useful half-life of social arrangements. Not even the most ideal set of institutions can just last forever. Every sound set of institutions must be defended, restored, and renewed to undo the damage that political factions of all ideological persuasions seek to turn social events and technological changes to partisan advantages. The problem of factions, both minority and majority, identified by James Madison in "Federalist No. 10," cannot be wished away by appeals to the virtues of deliberative democracy. What is needed is a choice of robust institutions that do not have to be re-engineered with each technological innovation or social change.

The terms *classical liberal* and *modern progressive* may seem quaint to some people, so let me explain why I use them. The former evokes references to 19th century theories of market liberalization, which were intended to reduce the dead hand of government over the operation of the economy. The second recalls the progressive movement of the first third of the 20th century, which championed the rise of the large administrative state to overcome the perceived weaknesses of the classical liberal synthesis. I use that term *progressive* here for two reasons. First, many Democrats and champions of large government use it as a form of self-identification. Second, their use of the term relocates the center of discussion away from such 1960s issues as criminal procedure, the death penalty, abortion, and affirmative action to the bread-and-butter economic issues dealing with the regulation of financial institutions, home mortgages, labor markets, and health care, all of which hearken back to the New Deal. In defending this modern roster of reforms, moreover, the modern progressives invoke a Keynesian renaissance that places discussions of stimulus packages, multiplier effects, and aggregate demand at the center of the discourse. The classical liberal has the opposite view. Governments are to supply public goods and maintain social stability, leaving innovation to the private sector.

The key components of the classical liberal theory are as follows. The first component is the call for limited government funded by tax revenues preferably generated under a flat tax (i.e., one that requires uniform rates for the taxable-income individuals, regardless of their aggregate income in any given tax period). In a sound system of public finance, the government's borrowing to meet the cost of capital improvements is acceptable, but borrowing to pay for short-term-consumption items is not. It is, in other words, proper to use borrowed funds to create long-term capital improvements but not to fund short-term government activity, like the payment of salaries for public employees. Accordingly, the purpose of taxation is to fund the creation of (nonexcludable) public goods that could not be created or maintained without some system of coerced public support. Public finance, however, is not to operate a disguised system of wealth transfer for individuals, which, if anything, it discourages as a road map to reduce taxation to a rarified form of "theft."

In putting these elements together, the theory departs in a conscious way from narrower forms of libertarian thought that see the sole proper use of government power to be the control of force and fraud. The hard-line libertarian thus has no reason to develop any theory of taxation or eminent domain in the first place, let alone a theory of optimal taxation on the one hand or sound public improvements on the other. I reject this extreme version of libertarianism not because it resonates at most only with a tiny minority of the population. I reject it for the best theoretical reasons. Taxation and eminent domain are both needed to solve a wide range of collective-action problems, whereby high transaction barriers prevent people from getting together voluntarily to work on projects that work to their joint advantage. Coercion is not the only threat to social order. Holdout problems by private individuals, each of whom wants a disproportionate share of social gain, must also be candidly addressed. The real question is how to shape their use so that they perform their assigned functions well. It is not to deprive any government of the tools that it needs to perform its essential functions to maintain and preserve public order.

The second component of the classical liberal system draws on traditional libertarian theory insofar as it relies on a system of strong property rights that allow individuals choice on how to use and dispose of their property as long as they do not encroach on the land of their neighbors or create nuisances – smells, filth, and waste – to their neighbors. But the opposite of the coin is every bit as important. Ordinary forms of economic competition may displace established businesses and thus be a source of private grievances. But the disappointed business should never be heard to say that ruinous competition should be treated as though it were a nuisance when its social consequences cut in the opposite direction. Nuisances shrink the overall size of the social pie that economic nuisance expands. Classical liberalism steers between the risks of anarchy and authoritarianism. Put simply, the theory is never that any individual can do what he will with what he owns. The theory is that the rules that preserve the like liberties of property owners should maximize their joint welfare by imposing parallel limitations against disrupting the quiet enjoyment that neighbors have of their own property.

The third component of the overall system requires a strong commitment to the principle of freedom of contract. Quite simply, the terms and conditions of individual employment contracts should be decided by employers and employees operating within the general confines of a competitive market. Such contracts should be left untouched by minimum-wage and antidiscrimination laws on the one hand and maintain a distinctive, privileged role for labor unions on the other. Unions are monopoly institutions whose combined activities are wholly exempt from the antitrust laws and who receive explicit backing from the government that strengthens their bargaining position against the government. That effort to undermine competitive markets is no better in the market for labor than it is for goods and services. During the heyday of classical liberalism, labor unions were in fact subject to the watchful eyes of an antitrust law and were afforded no special privileges of collective bargaining. Those principles of freedom of contract extended also to the operation of real estate markets and supported, among other things, the ability of a mortgage lender to quickly repossess property from debtors in the event of default, both to encourage lending in the first instance and to preserve the physical condition, and thus the value of property, after default took place.

In sum, the pillars of classical liberalism call for flat taxes, with revenues put to limited uses; strong property rights; and free markets. Each of these premises is systematically rejected in the progressive agenda as it evolved during the first third of the 20th century, culminating in

Roosevelt's New Deal. For these modern progressives, any notion of limited government at either the federal or state level is regarded as a misguided holdover from the simpler economic era that had long vanished from view with the industrialization of the post-Civil War period. At the public level, the progressives did not, of course, repudiate the use of taxation to fund the creation of public goods, which is so key to the classical liberal agenda. But they took strong exception to the classical liberal view that this objective, closely watched, marked the outer limits for the exertion of government power. In their view, the second permissible function of taxation was to take advantage of the pronounced, diminishing marginal utility of wealth and to arrange for a set of wealth transfers of indeterminate amounts from the rich to the poor through a wide variety of programs.

The theory behind this transfer program rests on the true but incomplete insight that the same dollar is worth more to a poor person than to a rich one. Using this theory, the government could improve welfare by social transfers, even if at the margin they might do some – progressives always thought small – damage to overall wealth creation. Of these, perhaps the most notable methods are as follows. The first is progressive taxation, in which the rate of taxation increases with income. The rate of progressivity could be modest, if the lowest rate is, say, 10 percent and the highest is 20 percent. Or it could be far steeper, with a differential from, say, 0 percent to 75 percent. One weakness of the theory is that it does not indicate *which* progressive rate structure is desired but only claims that *some* such rate structure is required. The second is the imposition of a progressive estate and gift tax system, which is intended to equalize wealth within society by preventing the passing of large accumulations of wealth between generations, free of taxation. Side by side with the progressive tax are the many transfer programs that also had their legislative origins in the 1930s. These include unemployment benefits, Social Security, disability payments, family leave, and much more, all of which started small, received emphatic judicial benediction when challenged constitutionally, and grew steadily and inexorably larger thereafter.

In its most explicit form, this redistributive rationale for taxation assumes such paramount importance under the progressive mindset that taxation necessarily has a key role to play in the operation of the economy even if the government by some miracle no longer had to play any role in the creation of public goods. Securing, not prohibiting, the orderly transfer of wealth from A to B, based on wealth differentials, is the raison d'être of the program. The contrast between the modern progressive and classical liberal agendas could not be more explicit.

On the second point, government interference in private business relationships is, according to the progressive mindset, regarded as an essential government function in order to overcome perceived differentials in economic power. The first of these differences involves employers and employees. The second is between banks and their borrowers. The older notions of free and voluntary exchange that captivated Adam Smith may have applied to a nation of small shopkeepers and manufacturers but were assumed to have no relevance to the complex and divisive process of industrialization that started in earnest after the Civil War. Looking first to the labor side, the progressive agenda came into full flower with the maximum-hour, minimum-wage, and workers'-compensation laws of the early 1900s, which had passionate defenders in such notables as Louis Brandeis, Herbert Croly, John Dewey, and Felix Frankfurter.

Their arguments do not go unnoticed, for they supplied the intellectual rationale for the National Labor Relations Act of 1935, dealing with unionization, and the Fair Labor Standards Act of 1938, dealing with overtime and minimum wages. Both these statutes have spawned huge administrative structures that to this day exert an immense influence over the operation of labor markets, especially for lower-income workers. The third generation of labor regulation involved the passage of the employment discrimination laws under Title VII of the Civil Rights Act of 1964, which was extended and strengthened over the next 45 years, chiefly by covering key areas like discrimination on the basis of age, disability, and sexual orientation. As is often the case, these measures enjoy a fair measure of bipartisan support, given that neither major party today is prepared to offer a steadfast defense of freedom of contract. They only differ on the reasons that principle should be disregarded in particular cases.

A similar approach exists with respect to mortgage markets. The mortgage moratoriums, whereby the defaulting homeowner is allowed to remain in possession of his or her property, is at root a modern variation of earlier forms of debtor relief, which Madison denounced during the founding period but which elicited a sympathetic judicial response in the 1930s. The progressive mindset has no patience for strict foreclosure, under which the owner is quickly removed before the value of the property declines further. The common thread that links the progressive attitude to employment and lending is the emphatic rejection of the principle of freedom of contract.

* * *

The Downward Progressive Cycle

I have outlined the differences in approach to make it clear that these differences in worldviews go to our core understandings of the relationship of the individual to the state. There is, therefore, no way to paper over these deep differences. As the next election comes ever closer, this nation faces a fork in the road. Does it continue with the progressive policies of the past several years, dating back to the first years of the second Bush administration, or does it return to the classical liberal model? The blunt truth is that this nation can no longer afford to hew to the progressive agenda on either matters of public finance or private arrangements. The progressive agenda supplies this one-two punch. First, it shrinks the size of the stock of financial wealth by a sustained program of ill-advised regulation of primary conduct. Second, it imposes extensive and counterproductive programs of redistribution that cannot be supported by a stagnant economy and a shrinking productive wealth base. As that base gets smaller, the demand for a stronger safety net induces yet another round of transfer payment and makes the tax burden heavier and the rate structure more progressive. The new redistributive tax regime in turn exerts greater negative pressures on production levels. In the midst of this uncertainty, there are fervent calls to create a stronger safety net. But that is a self-defeating game. The safety net can only be strengthened by offering greater protection against supposed exploitation of landlords, lenders, and employers. The economic downturn from these initiatives only puts more individuals in jeopardy, which then leads to further protectionist calls. And so the downward economic spiral continues.

The progressive effort to create short-term fixes against economic misfortune did not have its intended effect. In good times, to be sure, it insulated some individuals against certain *nonsystemic* adverse events. No one, however foolish, can waste 100 cents on the dollar for a government program. The mixed success of this program, however, carried with it this concealed consequence: a far higher level of *systematic* risk, for which neither federal stimulus dollars nor labor market regulation offers a suitable remedy. The impasse is now reflected in the deep and public divisions on the Federal Reserve Board, whose train of failed economic initiatives has led many of its members to think, rightly in my view, that it should withdraw altogether from the hapless task of using the latest refinements in monetary theory to heal the overall economy.

There is no elegant or costless way to break out of this deadly cycle. Some serious short-term dislocations will happen no matter what is done. Our national dilemma is similar to that faced by the surgeon who has to operate on a sick patient whose condition has been made worse by a previous botched operation. What is the least risky way to correct the errors that are properly put on the doorstep of some individual who, by reason of death, insolvency, or unavailability to suit, cannot be held personally accountable for past damage? The unhappy task is to avoid the greater dangers. Our economic doctors cannot unveil some no-risk policy capable of implementation on a grand scale. But high taxes and more job programs will preclude any return to higher growth and lower unemployment. A comparison of the two systems explains why.

* * *

The Stability of the Classical Liberal Model

The chief advantage of the classical liberal program is that, if faithfully applied, it creates long-term stability in social arrangements in both public and private transactions.

Start with taxation. The first component of the classical program stresses the limited role for taxation whose *sole* function is to provide those classical public goods that no system of market transactions can generate, such as infrastructure, police, and defense. Its underlying benefit theory is designed to benefit *all* individuals taxed, regardless of their wealth. To achieve this result, classical liberal thinkers all gravitate to the flat, or proportionate, tax on either income or consumption. This formula provides a single, clear metric that maximizes the chance of generating in-kind benefits – peace, security, infrastructure – to all in equal proportion to their wealth. Using a single tax instrument to collect general revenues has the critical advantage of limiting political competition for favorable tax rates by the select few seeking loopholes or by the large bulk of the population seeking wealth taxes or progressive rates. The restriction that tax revenues be spent solely for collective public goods reduces the likelihood that a skewed set of government payments will undermine the strict parity on the taxation side, a risk that looms large whenever any system of redistributive payments is made.

Properly constructed, a flat tax should *increase* overall social production. The ideal tax generates for each taxed individual a set of personal benefits (B), which are greater than the tax (T) that is levied on each person. If all persons are asked to make egoistic choices, the situation will lead to socially desirable results in which any improvement that is made will be shared pro rata by the entire population. An all-or-nothing vote on the tax should always generate unanimous support. Each self-interested person will vote in favor of a tax that generates him more in benefits than it imposes in costs. Moreover, so long as everyone moves in lockstep progression, the actual voting rule does not matter. To be sure, this condition is often highly artificial, for on some public expenditures (e.g., military operations), the public has to commit itself en masse notwithstanding deep disagreements on the wisdom of the effort – which is one reason the political dynamic of World War II was so different from that of the Vietnam War. But those cleavages cannot be removed by any system of taxation, which is why in the end, voting after collective deliberation offers the least-worst path to political legitimacy, which is certain to leave many people deeply aggrieved no matter what the collective outcome. It is for this reason, however, that where national necessities do not control, public expenditures should be narrowly focused on preserving domestic order and on supplying infrastructure and other public goods where systematic disagreements over the direction of public expenditures are likely to prove smallest. Yet even here, further tension is avoided if the costs of particular operations (e.g., public roads) are lifted from the general budget and financed by a set of user fees that can be used to repay long-term bonds that are needed to maintain these facilities over time. The borrowing mechanism (which should never be guaranteed by the general revenues) is critical, because the bond market will only back projects that meet revenue targets, which thus imposes a useful break on partisan political decisions.

With these special projects safely to one side, the

needed prescriptions are at war with the conventional wisdom. The proper course of action is to lower marginal tax rates on the rich in order to increase the investment that spurs new employment. Over time, national prosperity will do better if the government takes a smaller share from a larger pie than it does with a larger share of a (far) smaller pie. To see why, consider the idealized position of any random individual whose wealth is W prior to the imposition of an income tax. Once the tax is imposed, his new wealth (W^*) will be greater in all cases than his previous wealth (W) precisely because B is greater than T. Stated otherwise, for each person under the taxing regime,

$$W^* > W - T + B$$

Therefore, so long as this inequality can be maintained, the tax system has, by providing needed public goods, increased the return to private labor over what these people would enjoy in a zero-tax world. The willingness to work under a well-run tax system is thus greater than it would be in a world without any tax at all. The lockstep progression among individuals thus implies that even a democratic society would keep the rate of T down to the point at which the positive gap between B and T is maximized for all persons. Over time, as the aggregate wealth of the community increases, the total fraction of social resources should *increase*, as higher levels of wealth translate into insistent public demands for better roads and cleaner air. Nonetheless, the total fraction of wealth run through the tax system might well decrease or remain flat, which would leave even more wealth for private investment and consumption.

To be sure, the exact relationship between overall social income and the demand for public goods is hard to predict in the abstract. But the key point is that a fixed flat-rate structure is flexible enough to handle both cases, such that the uniform flat tax rate can move up or down, depending on the perception of public need. The stability of the tax structure in either case will, moreover, reduce the factional struggles for government favor by all groups within the system. The rigid assumption of perfect identity of interest for public expenditures is a conscious simplification, which is why this taxation regime remains vulnerable to factional intrigue. But the best should never be the enemy of the good. The overall system should be more impervious than any other taxation system to the risk that novel social challenges will disrupt the overall stability of the tax plan. That stability in turn should reduce the level of systematic risk of government misconduct that can lead to economic downturns. By not worrying about redistribution, the tax system improves the odds of securing high levels of growth, which should reduce the need in the first place for redistribution to levels that can be handled by charitable efforts (supported by a tax deduction) that meet the fewer cases of needy individuals left behind.

The political pressures to invoke ad hoc short-term arguments to deviate from the long plan are enormous, of course, which is why these provisions should be incorporated into the basic constitutional structure. No matter the revenue requirements of a given time, they can be generated by raising or lowering the single tax rate. Using this single instrument to control government revenue eliminates the huge jockeying that becomes a near certainty by allowing different forms of progressive taxes, special exemptions, or taxes on voluntary gifts during life or bequests at death. The simplicity of using a single tax instrument lowers the costs of compliance and reduces the likelihood that individuals will take tax-avoidance actions by "splitting" income or by creating fancy assignments, trusts, corporations, and partnerships in order to shift income from high- to low-bracket taxpayers in the same family orbit. More shenanigans, with more social waste.

A system of progressive taxation with a strong redistributive component has the exact opposite set of long-term consequences. No longer does the lockstep progression among all individuals put a break on factional intrigue. No longer is there any upper bound of wealth that can be funneled through the tax system, because the creation of public goods is only one rationale for taxation. Freed of that constraint, the progressive mindset specifically invites a majority of the population to vote for tax increases on others, which have no direct cost to themselves. The skewed distribution of benefits in favor of those who have paid little, if anything, in taxes only increases the demand for higher taxation whose incidence falls largely on the most-productive members of society. There is no obvious stopping point to this program. If some redistribution is good, why is more unwise? Indeed, in the United States today, the distribution of income tax burdens has become so skewed that close to half the adult population pays no income tax at all, while the top 1 percent with 1 percent of the income now pays 40 percent of the income tax and garners 20 percent of the income. It is unacceptable to let any elusive notion of tax fairness justify the current distribution of tax burden or indeed require a steeper system of progressivity. The theory has no obvious limits, for it depends critically on its application on the estimate of the diminishing marginal utility of wealth. In some models, that is thought to be exceedingly steep, such that a tenfold increase in wealth is thought to have only modest effects on happiness, which are measured by comparing exponents on the base 10. The increase from 10 to 10^2 (= 100) is thought to only double happiness from 1 to 2, while the increase from 10^2 to 10^3 (= 100) only increases it by 50 percent more, from 2 to 3. These estimates for money seem far too steep, but in the world of unobservables, any similar structure can justify huge differentials in rates that in turn feed into the political uncertainty.

It is often objected that any steep skew in the income tax may not be as ominous as it appears because less-fortunate people are still subject to payroll taxes for Social Security and Medicare. Most people also pay a variety of sales and property taxes at the state level and may also be subject to state income taxation. Those points are all true, and those taxation burdens do matter. But not for evaluating long-term stability. As with all economic transactions, critical tax decisions are always made at the margin. As long, therefore, as most voters know that they will pay no additional federal income taxes for any particular benefit program, they can vote for it with the confidence of receiving benefits without making any additional payments.

In reality, this position is an illusion. A shift in taxation or benefits in one actor is likely to be passed on to other actors within the system, whether they be employees in the form of lower wages, suppliers in the form of lower prices, or consumers in the form of higher prices. The predictable reduction in capital formation at the corporate level could easily lead to a reduction in investment that in turn reduces opportunities for new jobs, wages in established jobs, or both. The sinuous path that this unintended economic consequence will take in practice is impossible to pin down. Yet that is just the point. The level of instability is always higher when the degrees of political freedom are greater. Any given revenue target can be met with the flat tax. But teasing out the consequences of progressive taxes could easily be more difficult because the brunt of taxation is borne by the upper tail of the distribution, whose options, and vulnerabilities, to high tax are the greatest.

The first three years of the Obama administration illustrate the difficulties of running a program that seeks financial relief by taxing the nameless "millionaires and billionaires" who are said not to pay their fair share of taxes. Unfortunately, no fixed facts of nature make anyone a millionaire or billionaire for life. Unlike race, gender, age, and eye color, wealth is a highly mutable characteristic in an unstable political economy. Indeed, the general economic slowdowns after 2008 show the real danger in treating the wealthy as a fixed group whose income is invariant to economic conditions.

The first cut into this problem comes, ironically, from the commonplace but true observation that the United States is now a lightly taxed nation relative to earlier times. Federal tax revenues have dropped from their historic levels of around 18 percent to below 15 percent, from 2007 to 2010, with further declines in the offing based on the preliminary estimates for 2011. At the same time, federal expenditures have risen from around 20 percent of GDP to about 25 percent of GDP, a huge expansion in a short period of time. The regulatory burden has also risen as well, so that banks, for example, spend more on compliance than on lending. Put these three effects together, and it is all too easy to explain why the gulf between public revenues and public expenditures has risen to 10 percent of GDP, or 40 percent of the federal budget, which now can only be made up by deficit financing. The battle over the debt ceiling in July and August of 2011 was only evidence that the entire system was falling apart. The correct approach is to raise tax revenues, not chiefly by

Recession and the Rich

	2007	2009	Change
Tax Returns			
$200,000 and above	4,536,000	3,924,000	-13%
$1 million and above	390,000	237,000	-39%
$10 million and above	18,394	8,274	-55%
Taxes Paid			
$200,000 and above	$610 bill.	$434 bill.	-29%
$1 million and above	309	178	-42%
$10 million and above	111	54	-51%

increasing rates but by undoing the present regulatory morass. Examined closely, what triggered the downturn in income tax revenues is the radical decrease in the income of upper-income individuals, not any favorable rate break. This is evident in the table from *The Wall Street Journal*'s editorial piece "Millionaires Go Missing," which reveals, through public records, that the greatest decline in tax revenues hit those individuals whose income was more than $10 million per year.

The figures above do not get any better when put into perspective. One key measure of the burden of the deficit is its size relative to the gross domestic product, which is, roughly speaking, a measure of the capacity to bear interest and perhaps retire debt. During the presidency of George W. Bush, the federal deficit rose steadily in real terms. Nonetheless, the ratio of the deficit to the GDP did not rise sharply, given the expansion in the economy, in part attributable to the 2003 Bush tax cuts, which sparked an increase in overall growth. The far-larger increases in the national debt have come under the Obama administration. These have totaled about $3.8 trillion in less than three years and have occurred when overgrowth has either been negative or stagnant, which, in light of population increases, necessarily leads to the a consistent decline in average family income.

Today, total national debt has risen to close to 100 percent of GDP and will exceed that threshold in fairly short order. Those calculations hold as long as one takes into account not only the public debt that the United States owes to private individuals, corporations, and foreign nations, which constitutes about two-thirds the total, or close to $10 trillion. But it also includes intergovernmental debt, which is now close to half that amount (as of August 2011, $4.67 trillion), and is incurred now that much of the Social Security Trust is invested in government bills that will have to be redeemed once Social Security's current revenues are not, on a pay-as-you-go basis, sufficient to cover current program outlays.

It is easy to soft-pedal these interpersonal obligations with the amiable fiction that these treasury bills in the Social Security Trust are dollars that "we" only owe "to ourselves." That statement would be true only if all people held government paper in proportion to their share of public debt. But the moment the mix of those people who are in line to receive those payments varies from those who will have to pay it, the discharge of these obligations necessarily will shift money from one person to another. Accordingly, the more accurate statement of the intergovernmental debt is that it is owed, on net, by some of us to others of us. "Taxing each other" is a much more accurate way to look at the implicit wealth transfers. The comforting collective "we" drops out of the social calculations.

As might be expected, this stark situation in which we find ourselves has given rise to a deep division of opinion on how these multiple perils should be best addressed. On the blue side of the line, the Democratic Party, backed by many prominent economists such as Paul Krugman and Joseph Stiglitz, believes the best way to get out of the current economic and social malaise is through a Keynesian program that contains three key components.

The first key component is its fervent embrace of a system of progressive taxation (i.e., one that imposes high marginal tax rates on the "rich," defined variously as individuals who earn more than $200,000 or $1 million per year). Those additional tax dollars can be then be used to fund a financial-stimulus package to generate job opportunities for the 9.1 percent of Americans who are unemployed – up from 7.8 percent when Barack Obama took office. That tax increase was not imposed in late 2010 when the Bush-era tax cuts ran out, and many supporters of tax increases prefer to wait until the downturn has run its course before raising the rates, without knowing how to time that transition in the face of a double-dip economy. Other progressives think that there is not a minute to lose before they seek to redress the short-term misfortune of the many.

The second key component of the progressive solution calls for vigorous intervention in the employment relationship proper. One part of that initiative has been to extend the period for unemployment benefits to 99 weeks, far longer than it was previously. The third key component of the progressive platform has been various mortgage-relief proposals that allow persons who are in arrears to remain in their homes. None of these three proposals can work.

Start by examining the political dynamics in progressive taxes that can freely be used for any distributive purpose. Unlike the flat tax, the progressive tax is intended to create situations in which some people's direct benefits from taxation are lower by far than the taxes they pay. This occurs for two reasons. First, the amounts collected are higher, and second, the bulk of the taxes collected goes to transfer payments that offer no direct benefit to them. Put in terms of the relations above, T goes up and B goes down, so that the former dwarfs the latter. At this point, the net losses in wealth from taxation fall most heavily on the most productive members of society, although they are probably borne up and down the income system. One argument for these transfer payments is that they don't hurt the wealthy at all, for they should be seen as investments in programs that supply them with indirect benefits from improved public health and education. These indirect benefits are never zero, but it hardly follows that they are large.

Any decision to include indirect benefits in the social calculation, moreover, is defensible only if indirect detriments are included as well. These indirect detriments to the rich are substantial for several reasons. First, much of that money is invested in the passage and enforcement of new laws that have adverse impacts on the economic position of the well-to-do. How else should one treat, for example, rules that make more corporate activities subject to criminal sanctions or direct regulation? Second, much of the money raised goes to give wage supplements to unionized teachers, police, and firefighters. Their stronger financial position thus puts them in a better position to resist the kind of thoroughgoing reform of the public sector that is necessary to get out of the current financial crisis that engulfs it. Third, the success of these programs only reinforces the political rhetoric, which is likely to further tighten the regulatory noose.

Viewed as a whole, this entire package makes it pointless to gloss over the extensive level of wealth transfer introduced by new social legislation. These transfers will spark the factional activities that Madison so feared. The political forces will push hard on both sides of the ledger. The expenditures that seek to magnify transfers, like those intended to reduce it, are deadweight social losses. There is no single magic level of progressive taxation, either in theory or practice. There are only an infinite number of variations, some of which are so steep as to be ruinous and others so modest as to be futile. In that unwashed middle lies a range of possible alternatives between, say, 35 percent and 60 percent at the top rate, which presents more than enough wealth to fight over. Each gives private benefits to the parties who make them, but those benefits cancel out so that both sides are better off if they could avoid the arms race to begin with. In the end, the factional struggle could easily leave everyone worse off than they would be under the flat tax.

The story plays out in similar fashion for both employment and real estate markets. The key element of the classical liberal model is that stable relationships induce people to enter contracts because they cannot expect the gains from trade to persist over the entire life of the agreement. In contrast, the disruption of the contractual schemes by legislation has two baleful effects. First, it reduces the willingness to enter into voluntary transactions in the first place, which helps explain why large corporations continue to hoard cash in the current legal environment. Second, it creates incredible complications in sorting out business arrangements that fail.

Start with the observed state of today's employment markets. Chronic unemployment is a systematic risk. Today, some 44 percent of the people who receive benefits are classified as long-term, compared with about only 26 percent during the 1982–83 recession. As is often the case, these numbers speak with a forked tongue. One sensible interpretation is that moral hazard (whereby people stay out of the labor market to collect the benefits) has taken its toll so that people who are choosy about jobs decide to lengthen their stay on the public rolls. Yet that explanation does not square with one recent estimate that some 507,000 people in California alone have exhausted their 99-week benefit packages. The structural contraction of the workforce and the decline in marketable skills of the long-term unemployed has created a major social tragedy. The question is why.

The simplest model for understanding them rests on the proposition that these relationships will prove viable only when both sides are better off. Otherwise, these arrangements will not be formed. The question of whether these gains from trade will be realized depends critically on the relationship between the cost of putting these transactions and the gains from trade on the other. The deal will go forward only when the gains exceed the transaction costs. The classical liberal model of freedom of contract in the setting of wages and other terms has desirable effects on both dimensions. The parties can pick those terms that maximize the overall gains and then adjust the wage terms up or down to allow those gains to be shared by the other side. Similarly, the certainty of the legal rules reduces the cost of securing performance and compliance with these agreements in accordance with their original terms. The knowledge that these terms are binding then induces higher levels of care on both sides in deciding what those terms should be. Over time, we can expect gains from trade to increase and costs of enforcement to go down, thereby expanding the market.

The exact opposite is true under the progressive formulations. Therefore, every time the government imposes some restriction on how employment contracts are structured, it runs the risk that it will reduce these gains from trade, increase the transaction costs, or usually both. Perhaps the first government intervention that alters both gains and transaction costs will not make the latter greater than the former, but at some point they surely will, at which point jobs will either be lost or altered.

One example should be efficient to illustrate the point. A common attempt to increase overall levels of medical care is to give an employer this choice: If it wishes to supply a package of medical benefits, A, it must also supply a second package of benefits, B. It is this method that social planners hope will extend coverage for alcoholism, mental illness, or neonatal care. They often, however, fail to ask this simple question: If the added benefits were worth more to the employee than they cost the employer, why would not an employer supply it voluntarily if it could make both sides better? I know of no effective answer to that question. Hence, as the mandates pile up, the percentage of employees with health plans decreases, thereby fueling discontent with the health care system by swelling the ranks of the uninsured. Better it is to let water find its own level, without state interference.

The system of mandates reduces the net benefits from

the employment relationship in two ways. It forces people to buy what they do not want, and it imposes on them the not-inconsiderable costs of implementing that scheme. Conversely, cutting out the mandates reduces the private costs of compliance and the social costs of enforcement. It increases the employment rates. In so doing, it adds to the tax base and reduces unemployment levels. The new rules under the Patient Protection and Affordable Care Act only aggravate the situation in both dimensions, which leads to the strong prediction that private health care markets will continue to shrink in size, putting intolerable pressure on the public sector as firms shed both jobs and health care coverage simultaneously, albeit in different proportions.

What is true of mandates applies to every regulation from family leave to minimum wage. It is always a losing battle to reduce gains from trade while increasing transaction and compliance costs. The predictive implications are clear. Until there is a major relaxation of direct regulation of the employment markets, unemployment rates will remain high. Pulling the macroeconomic levers for monetary and fiscal policy will only exacerbate, not improve, the situation. The multiple initiatives that have failed in the past predict the failure of new gimmicks in the future, such as the reduction of tax deductions for charitable contributions or the addition of any tax on municipal bond income.

The progressive program is every bit as faulty on the question of mortgage foreclosure. Once again, the comparison to the classical liberal model that insists on strict foreclosure is instructive. The key virtue of the traditional law of mortgage is that its rules are sustainable over the long haul, just as was the case with employment relationships. It is easy to bewail the sight of people being carted from their homes. But this ostensibly harsh position has multiple long-term systemwide virtues insofar as it increases both the gains from trade and reduces the costs of compliance. Lenders and borrowers who know the situation can enter into a transaction with greater rapidity. The security of transaction is shared between the lender and borrower in the form of a reduced interest rate, which in turn increases the number of individuals who qualify for loans and the amounts that they can safely borrow. The quick foreclosure procedures then ensure that the bank can remove, if it chooses, the current owner from the premises before a combination of neglect and abuse reduces the value of the property. Yet in those cases when a voluntary renegotiation of the mortgage makes sense, it can be negotiated case by case, without the lender fearing that a concession made in one case will necessarily be binding in the next. Once the lender gets a clear title to the property, it can be resold at lower prices to a new owner who is in a position to keep current on the mortgage debt.

Viewed as a whole, the sale of distressed assets offers an explicit public recognition that the earlier transaction has failed. The great advantage of that ostensibly harsh approach is that these assets can now re-enter the market when they are accurately priced, so that future buyers and lenders need not bear the heavy burden of an unstable form of divided ownership. With that transaction completed, the former owner can enter into either the rental or real estate market, again at favorable prices. The loss of down payment is always a nightmare, but in the current situation, most tenants have paid only small down payments. The vast bulk of the decline in value is borne by the banks or the people to whom they sold the commercial paper in the secondary market, including Fannie Mae and Freddie Mac. A sound practice of foreclosure can reduce those losses and with them the risk of bank failure that could initiate yet another round of bailouts.

In contrast, the progressive program of mortgage relief has all the wrong consequences, which in recent years has heavily compromised the long-term stability of the mortgage market. Many excessive loans were made or guaranteed by the government. The combination of low interest rates and government guarantees induced banks to lend extensive sums to unqualified purchasers who bid up residential properties in order to gain access to cheap capital. Why should banks care if the government is willing to underwrite high-risk mortgages because public officials somehow think they know that a high level of homeownership is a proper end of national policy? The boom cycle, however, is inherently unstable, so that upward spiral can last only so long as some neophyte optimist waits in the wings. As long as the population of greater fools is finite – as it always is – this bubble had to burst. It did in 2008. Properties that were mortgaged to the hilt were now worth far less than the outstanding balance on the loan. Those failures inaugurated a second round of litigation as first state and then federal authorities sued major banks, claiming that they took advantage of Fannie Mae and Freddie Mac, thereby imposing additional strains on banks that are struggling to meet ever stricter capital requirements imposed by the Federal Reserve.

The long-term consequences of these new bailout and litigation strategies have introduced a sea change that is as unsustainable as it is catastrophic. Taken as a package, they induce lenders to hold back from the marketplace unless their borrowers have impeccable credentials. Deal volume goes down and interest rates go up – the double whammy of reduced gains from trade. By deliberately postponing the date of foreclosure, current mortgage practices ensure a reduction in the market value of the underlying land. That prolonged interim period in turn induces the federal government to throw good money after bad. It has been thoroughly documented today that at most a tiny fraction of underwater borrowers who have received funding under one notable government failure, the Home Affordable Modification Program, have been able to claw their way back to financial solvency. Jawboning banks to subsidize delinquent debtors is a waste of public funds. Blocking foreclosures for paperwork errors only compounds the problem when it is undisputed that the borrower is in default. The desire to avoid short-term hardships leads to major dislocations in these markets.

Conclusion

One of the central purposes of this brief monograph is to explain why the root failures in the current situation are a function of progressive policies at fundamental war with sound economic policy. The linchpin of that sound policy is this: Any society should like to encourage both government projects and private initiatives that can be described as "positive sum." The use of that term, drawn consciously from modern economic theory, means that as an matter of initial expectation, the project in question would provide for an overall social improvement that could in principle benefit rich and poor alike, even if in practice some of these projects will, as they always do, turn bad.

What differs is the strategies that are needed to improve the odds of getting positive-sum projects in the public and private space. In the public space, the need for government coercion is inescapable, so the challenge is to find funding devices and spending patterns that increase the odds of ferreting out losing public projects. The use of the flat tax, of borrowing on project assets for infrastructure projects and limiting the nature of public expenditures, are efforts in that direction. The effort is to make sure that no voting bloc is in a position to improve its own lot by hurting another. The common pleas that the progressives offer for participatory democracy are fine as far as they go, but they do not go far enough. The call for participation must always take into account the risk of faction by developing a variety of long-term constitutional protections to deal with the problem. The sense that just about anything goes with the collection of public revenues and the making of public expenditure has contributed mightily to the current malaise.

The preoccupation with positive-sum transactions exerts a different influence in private labor markets. Bracketing some important antitrust risks, the overriding objective is to find ways to increase gains and reduce compliance costs with voluntary arrangements. The principle applies to all private markets, including labor and real estate. The new move to fear exploitation, bargaining asymmetries, or imperfect information is said in fancy intellectual circles to justify this barrage of regulation. But in practice, the added complexity increases the risk of exploitation, magnifies bargaining asymmetries, and makes it ever more difficult to acquire reliable contractual information.

In light of these difficulties, the progressive system cannot sustain itself by its obsession with using fancy fixes at the macro and micro levels that only make everything worse. The great virtue of the classical liberal system is that it proves more productive for wealth increases and more resistant to political pressures. It is a one-two punch that is hard to resist. A return to a classical liberal system will meet with political resistance, and it will impose serious transitional difficulties. But make no mistake. Better that the nation tries to unravel its past mistakes. If it keeps going in the same progressive direction of the past decade or so, it will only compound its problems until the decline in economic well-being leads to genuine unrest at home and a major loss of influence abroad. Neither of these is a particularly appetizing prospect, no matter what anyone's political orientation.

PETER FERRARA

PRESIDENT OBAMA'S TAX PIRACY

STARTING ON JAN. 1, 2012, President Obama's economic recovery policy will begin implementing of comprehensive, across-the-board tax rate increases for every major federal tax. The top two income tax rates will effectively climb by nearly 20 percent, counting the phaseout of deductions and exemptions. The top capital gains tax rate is scheduled to soar by nearly 60 percent, counting the application of ObamaCare's new 3.8 percent tax on investment income. The tax rate on dividends is scheduled to nearly triple, from 15 percent to 43.4 percent, counting the ObamaCare tax as well. The ObamaCare legislation also increased the top Medicare HI payroll tax rate by 62 percent. On our current course, the death tax will also be reimposed next year with a 55 percent top rate.

Meanwhile, America suffers under the highest corporate tax rate in the industrialized world. The federal corporate tax rate of 35 percent is pushed close to 40 percent on average by state corporate income taxes, leaving American businesses and employers uncompetitive in the global economy. Yet the Obama administration refuses to consider any reductions in this corporate tax rate.

Ironically, however, much of the rest of the world has learned the lessons of Reaganomics. The average corporate tax rate in the European Union has been slashed from 38 percent in 1996 to 24 percent today. The federal corporate tax rate in both Canada and Germany has been reduced all the way to 15 percent. Ireland adopted a corporate tax rate of 12.5 percent in 1988, which caused per capita income in that longtime poor country to soar from the second lowest in the EU to the second highest. Our own Department of the Treasury has said Ireland raises more corporate tax revenue as a percentage of gross domestic product than we do with our much higher rates. Corporate tax rates in India and China, our emerging competitors, are lower as well.

Instead of lowering these stifling business taxes, President Obama and congressional Democrats are increasing them. President Obama insists on double taxing the foreign earnings of American companies with a $122 billion tax increase, further reducing the international competitiveness of American businesses. Then there's a $90 billion tax increase on banks and a $40 billion increase on oil, gas, and coal producers.

ObamaCare adds still more tax increases. A so-called Cadillac tax is imposed on high-value health plans equal to 40 percent of plan costs above certain thresholds, amounting to $32 billion in taxes on such health insurance during the first 10 years. But the thresholds are indexed only for general inflation, not health care inflation, so the tax will apply to more and more plans over time, eventually applying to average, ordinary plans. Less well known is that ObamaCare imposes a second tax on health insurance equal to $60 billion during the first 10 years. The health care takeover legislation also adopts new taxes on medical device manufacturers, prescription drugs, and even tanning salons, among others.

The individual mandate requiring individuals without employer-provided health insurance to buy government-specified health insurance is also a tax. Even with the budget-crushing health insurance subsidies provided in the ObamaCare legislation, the required insurance will be quite expensive, ranging up to 2 percent of income for people at 133 percent of the poverty level and up to 9.8 percent for those at 400 percent of the poverty level ($88,000 for a family of four). That is like a new payroll tax.

The employer mandate in the ObamaCare legislation is also an economically deadly tax. For companies that do not currently provide health insurance to their employees – mostly smaller businesses – the employer mandate will add substantially to worker costs, killing jobs. In addition, in my own recently released comprehensive study of the ObamaCare legislation, *The ObamaCare Disaster: An Appraisal of the Patient Protection and Affordability Act*, published by The Heartland Institute, I explain all the ways in which the legislation will increase the cost of health insurance. With the employer mandate, this will kill jobs even for employers that currently provide health insurance, as their employee costs will also rise as a result.

But even with this already enacted tax tsunami, President Obama and congressional Democrats are *still* not satisfied. Even though the Democrat-controlled Congress in 2009 and '10 refused to adopt the costly cap-and-trade legislation, President Obama is imposing the same policy through EPA regulation. That is effectively another tax on the economy that will cost trillions of dollars in future years. Former House Speaker Nancy Pelosi and other top Democrats also favor a new value-added tax (VAT), which is effectively another federal sales tax to burden working people and their families.

* * *

Tax Rates and Incentives

The key to understanding the impact of tax increases on the economy is to focus on tax rates, particularly the marginal tax rate, which is the tax rate that applies to the last dollar earned. The tax rate determines how much the producer is allowed to keep from what he or she produces. For example, at a 25 percent tax rate, the producer keeps three-fourths of his production. If that rate is increased to 50 percent, the producer keeps only half of what he produces, reducing his reward for production and output by one-third. Incentives are consequently slashed for productive activity, such as savings, investment, work, business expansion, business creation, job creation, and entrepreneurship. The result is fewer jobs, lower wages, and slower economic growth, or even an economic downturn.

In contrast, if the tax rate is reduced from 50 percent to 25 percent, what producers are allowed to keep from their production increases from one-half to three-fourths, increasing the reward for production and output by one-half. That sharply increases incentives for all of the above productive activities, resulting in more of them and more jobs, higher wages, and faster economic growth.

Moreover, these incentives do not just expand or contract the economy by the amount of any tax cut or tax increase. For example, a tax cut of $100 billion involving reduced tax rates does not just affect the economy by $100 billion. The lower tax rates affect every dollar and every economic decision throughout the economy. That is because every economic decision is based on the new lower tax rates. Indeed, the new lower tax rates affect every dollar, or unit of currency, and every economic decision throughout the whole world regarding whether to invest in America, start or expand businesses here, create jobs here, or even work here. All these decisions will be based on the new lower tax rates. Tax rate increases have just the opposite effect on every dollar and economic decision throughout the economy and the world.

Multiple Taxation of Capital

These incentive effects are compounded in our tax system through the multiple taxation of capital. Capital income is taxed not once but several times in our system. For example, consider a saver who invests a dollar in a corporate enterprise. Any dollar that corporation earns is taxed at the corporate income tax rate, totaling roughly 40 percent in America on average now. If the remainder of that dollar is paid to the investor in dividends, then it is taxed again through the individual income tax at the dividends tax rate. With President Obama increasing the dividends tax rate from 15 percent to 43.4 percent, applying that 43.4 percent tax rate to the 60 cents remaining after paying the corporate income tax leaves just 34 cents for the investor out of the original dollar earned. Don't expect much job-creating investment as a result.

But there is more. A third layer of taxation of capital income is represented by the capital gains tax. Consider an asset such as a share of stock. When the price of that asset increases, that reflects an increase in the expected value of the future income stream. That future income will be taxed by both the corporate income tax and the individual income tax when earned. If that asset is sold now, taxing the increased value by the capital gains tax is effectively taxing that future income stream a third time.

The death tax is still another, fourth layer of taxation of capital income. If the investor in our example above saves the 34 cents remaining on that dollar of corporate earnings after paying the corporate and individual income tax and leaves it to his children at death, applying the death tax to it would take roughly half of what is left, leaving his children just 17 cents out of the original dollar earned.

Our tax system further burdens capital income through depreciation rather than immediate expensing. Except for capital investment in plants and equipment, all other business expenses are deducted in the year they are incurred, because the income tax is supposed to be on net income after expenses. But deductions for the expenses of acquiring capital equipment must be spread out over many years under arbitrary depreciation schedules. Capital equipment is what makes American workers the most productive and hence the most highly paid with the highest standard of living, in the world. With such capital equipment, for example, workers can use mechanized, computerized, modern crane shovels rather than their bare hands for digging and building. Or they can use modern computers rather than just computing in their heads. The result of extended arbitrary depreciation schedules instead of immediate deductions or expensing is less of such capital equipment, slowing growth in jobs, productivity, and wages.

With President Obama and congressional Democrats increasing virtually all of these multiple layers of taxation on capital income, the interacting effects are compounded. That is why investing in America right now is like anchoring an unarmed cargo ship off the coast of Somalia. The natural results of the incentive effects of the tax increases are the capital flight and effective capital strike we are seeing in America right now. World capital, including capital from U.S. investors, is trending toward the more rapidly growing emerging economies and other economies recovering far faster and stronger than we are. That is the reason as well for American companies sitting on $2 trillion of capital right now and for banks sitting on a trillion dollars in excess reserves. The economy is poised to boom, and it can't wait to do so, but President Obama's tax piracy is barring the way.

President Obama's Tax Welfare

President Obama claims to have cut taxes for 95 percent of workers. But those "tax cuts" have all involved tax *credits* rather than reductions in tax *rates*. The centerpiece is a $400-per-year, $7.69-per-week "Making Work Pay" tax credit that is scheduled to expire soon.

Such tax credits do not work to stimulate economic growth, because they do not change the fundamental incentives that govern the economy. A $400 tax credit involves the government either explicitly or effectively sending you a check for $400. But after that, you and everyone else still face the same tax rates and economic incentives as before.

Tax cuts do not expand the economy by "putting more money in people's pockets," thereby leading to increased spending. Increased welfare benefits would put more money in people's pockets as well. But this is an outdated Keynesian rationale from the 1930s that does not work for two reasons. First, the government has to borrow or tax the money from someone else in the economy to give you the tax credit or increased welfare check. So, if it takes $400 out of the economy to give you $400 through the tax credit or increased welfare, it has not added anything to the economy on net. Second, again, there is no change in fundamental incentives.

Note also that Obama's tax credits are refundable, which means if you do not have enough income tax liability for the credit to offset, the government will send you a check for the difference. The tax credit in this case is entirely indistinguishable from welfare, which is never going to be the foundation for a booming economy. Obama's own budget documents show that 35 percent of his supposed income tax cuts go to people who do not pay income taxes; therefore, they are not tax cuts at all but welfare checks. This is why Obama's own budget accounts for this portion of his supposed tax cuts as outlays rather than revenue reductions. You can't *cut* income taxes for people who do not pay income taxes.

Just Taxing the Rich?

President Obama's apologists argue that his tax increases only apply to "the rich" who make more than $200,000 a year for singles and $250,000 a year for married couples. That affects only the top 2 percent of income earners and only 3 percent of small businesses, they contend. These rich "can afford" the tax increases, they say. They don't "need" the lower tax rates from the Bush tax cuts, which President Obama is going to let expire for them.

Note that except for the new 3.8 percent tax on investment and the Medicare payroll tax increase, all of the ObamaCare tax increases apply to those making less than $250,000 per year as well as to those making more than that arbitrary limit. This includes, most importantly, the individual mandate. Before passage of ObamaCare, President Obama argued on national TV that it would be ludicrous to consider the individual mandate a tax, regardless of what the dictionary says. After passage, his lawyers were in court arguing that the individual mandate is constitutionally justified because it is a tax. The cap-and-trade tax and the potential VAT also would apply to everyone, including those making less than $250,000 per year.

Moreover, as Kevin Hassett and Alan Viard explained

in *The Wall Street Journal* on Sept. 3, 2010, "The 3% [of small businesses] figure … is based on simply counting the number of tax returns with any pass-through business income. So, if somebody makes a little money selling products on eBay and reports that as income on Schedule C of their tax return, they are counted as a small business." Hassett and Viard explain the truly relevant data, saying:

> *According to IRS data, fully 48% of the net income of sole proprietorships, partnerships, and S corporations reported on tax returns went to households with incomes above $200,000 in 2007. That's the number to look at, not the 3%. Would Mrs. Pelosi and Mr. Biden deny that the more successful firms owned by individuals in the top income-tax bracket are disproportionally responsible for investment and job creation?*

In other words, the tax increases directly affect half of all small-business income, not just 3 percent, and those more successful small businesses are responsible for an even larger share of the employment that is created.

Moreover, tax rate increases impact not only those currently in the affected tax brackets but also those who expect or hope to be at those income levels in the future. An entrepreneur starting a small business may earn only $25,000 in the first year but may expect to make more than $250,000 once the business is successful, which is his incentive for starting the business in the first place. But higher tax rates that would depreciate the reward if he is successful may well stop him from even trying in the first place.

In addition, the venture capitalists and other investors essential for small businesses to succeed are directly affected by the higher tax rates, even if the small-business owner himself is not yet. Higher tax rates can and will prevent such small-business investments from ever occurring.

In the end, it is not about whether investors, entrepreneurs, or small businesses can "afford" increased taxes or "need" any tax cuts, which is a neosocialist argument. It is about what effect the tax rate increases will have on the economy, jobs, revenues, the nation's standard of living, and other factors. Through these effects, President Obama's comprehensive tax rate increases will harm everyone.

Kennedy and Reagan: What Worked

While President Obama and his hypnotized acolytes do not understand any of this, President John F. Kennedy did. Kennedy proposed legislation to reduce income tax rates across the board by 30 percent. Kennedy explained:

> *It is a paradoxical truth that tax rates are too high today, and tax revenues are too low and the soundest way to raise the revenues in the long run is to cut the tax rates.... [A]n economy constrained by high tax rates will never produce enough revenue to balance the budget, just as it will never create enough jobs or enough profits.*

Kennedy added:

> *Our true choice is not between tax reduction, on the one hand, and the avoidance of large federal deficits on the other.... It is between two kinds of deficits – a chronic deficit of inertia, as the unwanted result of result of inadequate revenues and a restricted economy – or a temporary deficit of transition, resulting from a tax cut designed to boost the economy, produce revenues, and achieve a future budget surplus.*

Kennedy explained further that the best way to promote economic growth "is to reduce the burden on private income and the deterrents to private initiative which are imposed by our present tax system – and this administration is pledged to an across-the-board reduction in personal and corporate income tax rates."

Kennedy's proposed tax rate cuts were adopted in 1964, cutting the top tax rate from 91 percent to 70 percent, as well as reducing the lower rates. The next year, economic growth soared by 50 percent, and *income tax revenues* ***increased*** *by 41 percent!* By 1966, unemployment had fallen to its lowest peacetime level in almost 40 years. *U.S. News & World Report* exclaimed, "The unusual budget spectacle of sharply rising revenues following the biggest tax cut in history is beginning to astonish even those who pushed hardest for tax cuts in the first place." Arthur Okun, the administration's chief economic adviser, estimated that the tax cuts expanded the economy in just two years by 10 percent above where it would have been.

In 1981, Reagan cut the top income tax rate of 70 percent to 50 percent, with a 25 percent across-the-board reduction in income tax rates for everyone else. Then, in the 1986 tax reform, he cut the top rate to 28 percent, with only one other rate of 15 percent for everyone else. Reagan also cut corporate income tax rates and, initially, capital gains rates as well.

By the end of 1982, just before the tax cuts were fully phased in, the economy took off on a 25-year boom, with just slight interruptions by shallow, short recessions in 1990 and 2001. As Arthur Laffer and Stephen Moore write in their book, *The End of Prosperity: How Higher Taxes Will Doom the Economy – If We Let It Happen*:

> *We call this period, 1982–2007, the twenty-five year boom – the greatest period of wealth creation in the history of the planet. In 1980, the net worth – assets minus liabilities – of all U.S. households and business ... was $25 trillion in today's dollars. By 2007 ... net worth was just shy of $57 trillion. Adjusting for inflation, more wealth was created in America in the twenty-five year boom than in the previous two hundred years.*

In 1984, the economy grew by 6.8 percent *in real terms*, the highest in 50 years. Nearly 20 million new jobs were created from 1983 to 1989, increasing U.S. civilian employment by almost 20 percent. Unemployment fell to 5.3 percent by 1989. Even with the Reagan tax cuts, total federal revenues doubled from 1980 to 1990, growing from $517.1 billion to $1,031 billion, or just more than $1 trillion. In Reagan's last budget year, fiscal year 1989, the widely overballyhooed federal deficit had declined to $152.5 billion, about the same as a percent of GDP as in 1980, 2.9 percent compared with 2.8 percent.

Contributing to the extension of this Reagan recovery into the 25-year boom were the tax cuts and other pro-growth policies adopted by the Newt Gingrich-led congressional majorities in the 1990s and the much-maligned George W. Bush tax cuts adopted in 2001 and 2003, which mostly followed in the steps of Kennedy and Reagan. Although the 2001 tax cut included some non-growth tax reductions, such as increasing the child tax credit, it also reduced the top marginal income tax rate from 39.6 percent to 35 percent, a reduction of only 11 percent that he had to fight for tooth and nail. Bush's 2001 tax cuts also reduced the rate for the lowest-income workers by 25 percent, from 15 percent down to 10 percent. In 2003, Bush cut the capital gains tax rate by 33 percent and the income tax rate on corporate dividends by more than half.

These tax rate cuts reversed the short, shallow 2001 recession and the negative economic effects of the Sept. 11, 2001, terrorist attacks, restoring growth. After the rate cuts were all fully implemented in 2003, the economy created 7.8 million new jobs, and the unemployment rate fell from more than 6 percent to 4.4 percent. Real economic growth during the next three years doubled from the average for the prior three years, to 3.5 percent.

Business investment spending, which had declined for nine straight quarters, reversed and increased by 6.7 percent per quarter. Manufacturing output soared to its highest level in 20 years. The stock market revived, creating almost $7 trillion in new shareholder wealth. From 2003 to 2007, the S&P 500 almost doubled.

Capital gains tax revenues had *doubled* by 2005, *despite the 25 percent rate cut.* In the last budget adopted by a Republican-controlled Congress, for fiscal year 2007, the budget deficit was $161 billion, only a small fraction of President Obama's budget deficits. The argument of some Obama propagandists that the Bush tax rate cuts caused the 2008 financial crisis has the same intellectual grounding as Soviet-era agitprop.

As Laffer and Moore write regarding the economy by 2007, "The economy in real terms is almost twice as large today as it was in the late 1970s." Steve Forbes summarizes:

> *Between the early 1980s and 2007 we lived in an economic Golden Age. Never before have so many people advanced so far economically in so short a period of time as they have during the last 25 years. Until the credit crisis, 70 million people a year [worldwide] were joining the middle class. The U.S. kicked off this long boom with the economic reforms of Ronald Reagan, particularly his enormous income tax*

> *cuts. We burst from the economic stagnation of the 1970s into a dynamic, innovative, high-tech-oriented economy. Even in recent years the much maligned U.S. did well. Between year-end 2002 and year-end 2007 U.S. growth exceeded the entire size of China's economy.*

In other words, the *growth* in the U.S. economy from 2002 to 2007 was the equivalent of adding the entire economy of China to the U.S. economy.

Peak Obama

Just as President Obama is following the opposite of President Reagan's economic policies in every detail, the result will be the opposite as well.

Instead of increasing spending with a trillion-dollar "stimulus" spending bill, Reagan came into office in 1981 with his much-derided budget cuts, cutting out close to 5 percent of federal spending right away. In constant dollars, nondefense discretionary spending declined by 14.4 percent from 1981 to 1982 and by 16.8 percent from 1981 to 1983. Moreover, in constant dollars, this nondefense discretionary spending never returned to its 1981 level for the rest of Reagan's two terms. By 1988, this spending was still down 14.4 percent from its 1981 level, in constant dollars.

Instead of the Fed madly gunning the money engines as today, Reagan's Fed pursued a historic tightening that wrung out the Great Inflation that had been accelerating at a frightening pace since 1968, with prices rising 25 percent during 1979 and 1980. The annual inflation had been cut in half by 1982 to 6.2 percent and in half again by 1983 to 3.2 percent, leaving inflation tamed for a generation thereafter.

Moreover, instead of President Obama's policy of mad reregulation, President Reagan pursued pathbreaking deregulation that ultimately saved consumers and the American economy trillions of dollars. Finally, as explained above in detail, while President Reagan enacted historic reductions in tax rates, President Obama is pursuing comprehensive, across-the-board tax rate increases for every major federal tax.

Reagan's second year was his rockiest in terms of overall economic performance because wringing out such high inflation so rapidly stifled the economy, a result that any college economics textbook will explain. Moreover, his tax rate reductions were phased in and did not become fully effective until Jan. 1, 1983. Arthur Laffer has long argued that the phasing in affirmatively delayed economic growth.

In mirror image, the second year of President Obama, as bad as it is, will be the best of his reign of error, unless new congressional majorities reverse his policies. The economy that year has benefited from what economists call "the slingshot effect," the natural tendency of the economy to snap back as smartly as the downturn was steep. That results naturally because every day, businesses scramble to rebuild themselves and workers seek new and better employment. That is why it is called the business *cycle.* That is also why the average recession since World War II has lasted only 10 months, with the longest previously lasting 16 months. By the next year, this slingshot effect was stale, and the stimulative effect of any snapback from the steepness of the downturn was spent.

President Obama's economy has also benefited from record-low interest rates of nearly zero and the Fed's enormously expansive monetary policy. But there is only one way for interest rates to go from here. (Note that in

Reagan's second year, interest rates were in long-term decline from historic highs, portending the coming boom.)

The positive effect of the enormous Fed monetary expansion will also soon be petering out, if it hasn't already. Monetary expansion does not create long-term economic growth. The Fed has to press the accelerator faster and faster to maintain the same stimulative effect. But if it does, then inflation starts to rise, accelerating faster and faster if the Fed continues. Indeed, the runaway expansion of the monetary base the Fed has already engineered will generate explosive inflation if the Fed does not pull it out in time.

Laffer has also emphasized that the specter of the comprehensive tax rate increases starting in 2013, precisely the opposite of the Reagan term, is boosting the economy this year, as producers scramble to produce what they can this year before the grim reaper arrives next year.

Yet despite all these favorable factors, the economy has been surprisingly weak this year, stunted by the fallacies of Keynesian Obamanomics. While the average recession since World War II has lasted 10 months and the longest previously has been 16 months, the August 2010 jobs report shows that *32 months* since the official start of the recession, scored by the National Bureau of Economic Research as beginning in December 2007, the economy is *still* losing jobs and unemployment is *still* rising. The Department of Labor reported another 54,000 jobs lost in August 2010, with unemployment rising to 9.6 percent. Major Obama voting blocs are being punished by Obamanomics. African Americans suffer a sustained depression reflected by 16.3 percent unemployment, and Hispanics are not far behind, at 12 percent unemployment. It is even worse for teenagers, with unemployment at 26.3 percent.

The total army of the unemployed remains stuck at nearly 15 million, with 42 percent of those classified as long-term unemployed – jobless for more than six months, the highest since the Great Depression. The number of additional workers employed part time for economic reasons was still rising in August, up by another 331,000 to nearly 9 million. The Bureau of Labor Statistics (BLS) defines these workers as those who "were working part time because their hours had been cut back or because they were unable to find a full-time job."

Another 2.4 million were defined as marginally attached to the labor force, stuck at that total for a year. The BLS explains that these individuals "wanted and were available for work, and had looked for a job sometime in the prior 12 months" but were not counted among the unemployed because they had not looked for work in the prior four weeks. These included 1.1 million discouraged workers, up 352,000 over the past year, not currently searching for work and therefore not counted as unemployed, because they believe that in the economy of hope and change, no jobs are available for them.

The army of the unemployed and underemployed consequently stands at 26.2 million Americans. That would add up to an unemployed and underemployed rate of 16.7 percent almost three years after the recession started. The full picture of hopelessness is measured by the precipitous drop in the civilian-employment population ratio, from 63 percent in 2007 to 58 percent today, fully reflecting the millions who have dropped out of the workforce altogether, giving up.

Moreover, the economic growth we have experienced recently has been less than half the growth we experienced after similarly severe downturns. The economy grew by almost 7 percent in Reagan's recovery in 1983 and 1984. Even under President Ford, real GDP grew by 6.2 percent in the year after the 1974–75 recession.

The accompanying graphs show what to expect in the next two years if the performance of the economy under President Obama is to be the mirror-image reverse of the performance under President Reagan. This would be the natural, logical result of following the mirror-image opposite of Reagan's economic program, including the above-discussed incentive effects of Obama's comprehensive federal tax rate increases, the costs and burdens of Obama's reregulation hitting next year, and the continued drain of private-sector resources caused by President Obama's supposedly stimulative spending increases and deficits. Laffer explained, before the effective date of these tax increases was delayed from 2011 to 2013:

> *[W]hen the U.S. economy comes to 2011, the train's going to come off the tracks. . . . The tax boundary that will occur on January 1, 2011 tells me that GDP growth in 2010 will be some 6 percent to 8 percent higher than GDPgrowth in 2011. A year on year decline from trend of some 6 percent to 8 percent in GDP growth would represent a larger collapse than occurred in 2008 and early 2009.*

We see signs of that already this year. Peak Obama economy. Economic growth is in a tailspin, falling from 5 percent in the fourth quarter of 2009 to 3.7 percent in the first quarter of 2010 to 1.6 percent in the second quarter. Unemployment is rising again, with the economy continuing to lose jobs every month. The stock market is stalled, mired 30 percent below its record highs over 14,000 in the Dow. This weak economy couldn't be a worse time to raise federal tax rates across the board.

* * *

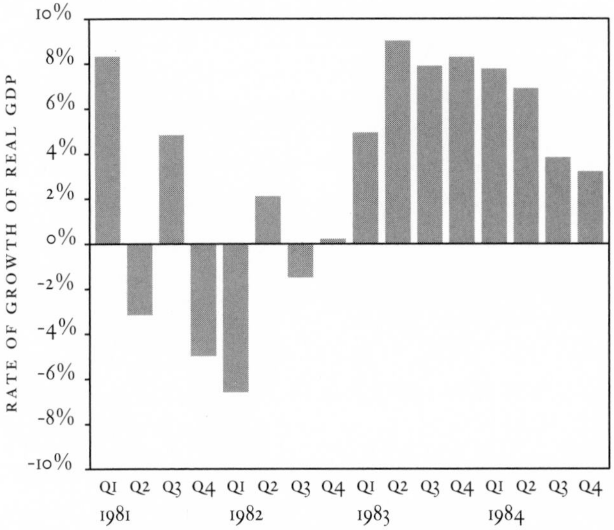

THE REAGAN RECOVERY

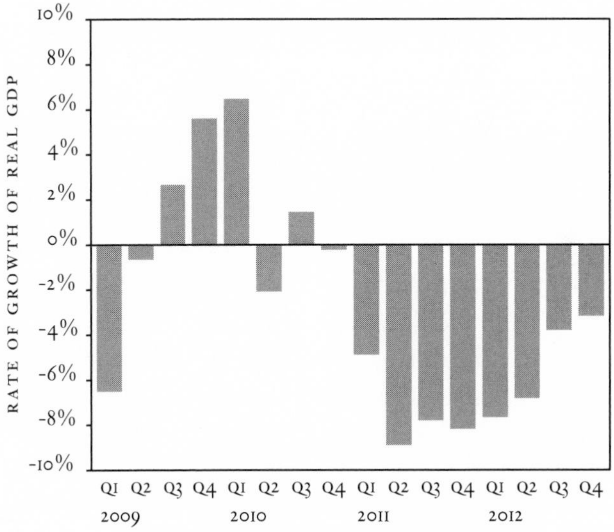

THE OBAMANOMICS RECOVERY
AS THE OPPOSITE OF REAGANOMICS

Peter Ferrara

President Obama's Revenue Gap

President Obama's budget projects that his tax increases on "the rich" (singles making more than $200,000 and couples making more than $250,000) would raise $678 billion in increased revenue during the next 10 years. The ObamaCare legislation projected another $210 billion from the increased payroll taxes on those workers, for a total of nearly $1 trillion. But these tax increases won't raise anywhere near the revenue projected. Obama will be lucky if this tax piracy doesn't result in *less* revenue.

For example, during the past 40 years, *every time* capital gains tax rates have been cut, revenues have *increased*, and every time capital gains tax rates have been increased, revenues have *decreased.* In 1968, a 25 percent capital gains tax rate generated real capital gains tax revenues of $40.6 billion, calculated in 2000 dollars. The capital gains tax rate was then raised four times in the next seven years, to 35 percent. By 1975, at the higher rate, capital gains revenues totaled $19.6 billion in constant 2000 dollars, less than half as much.

In 1978, the capital gains tax rate of 35 percent yielded $29.9 billion in 2000 dollars. The rate was then cut three times to 20 percent during the next four years. By 1986, the new rate, 43 percent lower than the 1978 rate, raised $92.9 billion in 2000 dollars, about three times as much. The capital gains rate was raised by 40 percent the next year, to 28 percent. Capital gains revenues fell to $56.2 billion that year and declined all the way to $34.6 billion by 1991.

In 1997, Congress cut the capital gains tax rate from 28 percent back down to 20 percent. Despite this almost 30 percent cut in the rate, capital gains revenues rose from $62 billion in 1996 to $109 billion in 1999. Revenues in the period of 1997 to 2000 increased by 84 percent over the projections before the tax cut.

Finally, Congress cut the capital gains rate from 20 percent to 15 percent in 2003. Capital gains revenues doubled from 2003 to 2005, despite this 33 percent cut in the rate. Revenues increased by $133 billion during the years from 2003 to 2006 as compared with pre-tax-cut projections.

President Obama's capital gains tax increases will only add to this historical record, resulting in less revenue rather than more.

Moreover, dividends paid soared after Bush cut the dividends tax in 2003, resulting in more revenue rather than less. President Obama's crushing dividends tax increase means that only 34 cents on average would be left out of a dollar of corporate earnings paid as dividends. That will result in a collapse in dividends paid, as corporations keep the cash to invest themselves, again resulting in less revenue rather than more.

The projections of higher revenues from the other tax rate increases all fail to take into account the negative incentive effects discussed above and the counterproductive interactions from all those effects. Since we know from experience that those incentive effects are powerful and real, the result at a minimum will be less revenue than expected, if not less revenue overall.

Even with all of Obama's tax increases and the increased revenue as projected, the CBO projects that by 2012, the national debt will have doubled in only four years, to $11.5 trillion. By 2020, it will have almost quadrupled since 2008 to $20.3 trillion. By the end of this year, the CBO projects that the national debt will reach 62 percent of GDP, higher than at any time in our history except for World War II and shortly thereafter. Indeed, as Brian

Riedl of The Heritage Foundation reports, the national debt is rocketing upward so fast that under current policies, more debt will be run up under eight years of President Obama than under all other presidents in history – from George Washington to George W. Bush – combined.

But since all of the tax increases on "the rich" won't raise nearly the projected revenue, federal deficits and debt will be even higher than this. The Obama budget already projects that net interest spending will soar to $840 billion by 2020, more than four times the current levels. Less revenue than now expected means this interest spending is also going to be higher, which translates into even more deficits and debt. If interest rates rise higher than the modest levels the Obama budget now projects, all of this tailspins into an even worse downward spiral.

Finally, if President Obama's comprehensive tax rate increases go through next year as planned, the probability of another double-dip recession will be more than 100 percent. That will leave the federal government with much less revenue overall, rather than more. Where will that leave the current deficit of $1.5 trillion? Well more than $2 trillion, making a mockery of the very notion of a federal budget.

Tax Piracy

President Obama's apologists argue that his tax increases on "the rich" are necessary just so the rich will pay their fair share. But even before President Obama was elected, official IRS data showed that in 2007, the top 1 percent of income earners paid 40.4 percent of all federal income taxes, almost twice their share of adjusted gross income. The top 5 percent paid 60.6 percent of all federal income taxes while earning 37.7 percent of adjusted gross income.

The top 10 percent paid 71.2 percent of all income taxes while earning 48 percent of adjusted gross income.

Meanwhile, the bottom 50 percent of income earners paid only 2.9 percent of all federal income taxes. Indeed, the bottom 95 percent of income earners paid 39.4 percent of all federal income taxes. That means the top 1 percent of income earners pay more federal income taxes than the bottom 95 percent!

This should lead you to ask regarding "the rich," just what would be their "fair share"?

IRS data also show that those earning more than $200,000 a year, on whom President Obama wants to increase taxes, constitute just 3 percent of taxpayers. Yet that 3 percent pays more in income taxes than the bottom 97 percent combined.

Given these facts, those who want to increase taxes on the top 1 percent of income earners, or the top 3 percent, in the name of "fairness" profess the morality of pirates or of gang rape. Moreover, the notion that still more revenues can be reaped from this narrow slice of taxpayers is daft. This is where the capital flight and capital strike is coming from.

The facts also demonstrate the falsehood of the charge made by Obama and the Democrats that Republicans cut taxes for the rich but haven't "given a break to folks who make less." The share of income taxes paid by the highest-income earners has basically doubled since 1981, when President Reagan brought his supply-side economics to Washington. That is because with the lower tax rates, incomes boomed along with the economy, and high-income taxpayers had the incentives to pull their money out of tax shelters and invest it in the real economy, fueling the boom.

But in 2007, again before President Obama was even elected, the bottom 40 percent of income earners as a group paid no federal income taxes. Instead, they received net payments from the income tax system equal to 3.8 percent of all federal income taxes. In other words, they paid negative 3.8 percent of federal income taxes. The middle 20 percent of income earners, the actual middle class, paid 4.7 percent of all federal income taxes.

This is the result of Reagan Republican supply-side economics that began with Reagan and Jack Kemp in the 1970s and 1980s, continued through Newt Gingrich and his Contract with America, and further played out with the Bush tax cuts of 2001 and 2003. Reagan and his Republicans abolished federal income taxes on the poor and working class. Moreover, they almost abolished federal income taxes on the actual middle class (the middle 20 percent).

It was, in fact, Ronald Reagan who first proposed in the 1970s the Earned Income Tax Credit (EITC), his alternative to welfare, which has done so much to reduce income tax liabilities for lower-income people. As president, he cut federal income tax rates by 25 percent across the board for all taxpayers. He also indexed the tax brackets for all taxpayers to prevent inflation from pushing workers into higher tax brackets.

In the Tax Reform Act of 1986, he reduced the federal income tax rate for "folks who make less" all the way down to 15 percent. That act also doubled the personal exemption, shielding more income from taxation for everybody.

Newt Gingrich's Contract with America adopted a child tax credit of $500 per child that reduced the tax liabilities of lower-income people by a higher percentage than for higher-income people. President Bush doubled that credit to $1,000 per child and made it refundable so that low-income people who do not even pay $1,000 in federal income taxes could still get the full credit. Bush also adopted a new lower tax bracket of 10 percent for the lowest-income workers, reducing their federal income tax rate by 33 percent. Again, he cut the top rate for the highest-income workers by just 11.6 percent, from 39.6 percent to 35 percent.

Many conservatives do not think it was a good idea to exempt so many from paying any income taxes at all. Nevertheless, the charge that the Republicans only cut taxes for the rich is factually groundless. Under Reagan Republican tax policies, the share of income taxes paid by the rich has soared to arguably excessive, even abusive levels, while income taxes were, again, abolished for the poor and working class and almost abolished for the middle class.

Taxes and Economic Freedom

Instead of judging taxes by the morality of tax piracy, the only reasonable way to judge taxes is by their impact on economic growth, prosperity, and economic freedom. Higher taxes mean less personal freedom because they reduce personal control over your income, and the government rather than you decides how it is spent or saved. Lower taxes mean more personal freedom because they increase personal control over your own income and leave you with more of your own income to choose to save, spend, or invest as you desire.

Therefore, taxes as a percent of GDP should be taken as a reverse indicator of economic freedom. Higher taxes as a percent of GDP mean less economic freedom; lower taxes as a percent of GDP mean more.

JOHN FUND

HOW THE OBAMA ADMINISTRATION THREATENS TO UNDERMINE OUR ELECTIONS

As a former community organizer who later taught classes in voting rights at the University of Chicago, President Barack Obama should be a fierce protector of the integrity of our electoral system. Indeed, as a U.S. senator from Illinois, he introduced a bill in 2007 to increase the criminal penalty for voter intimidation. "Both parties at different periods in our history have been guilty in different regions of preventing people from voting for a tactical advantage," he said at the time. "We should be beyond that."

He was right to be concerned. A Rasmussen Reports survey in 2008 found that 17 percent of Americans believe that large numbers of legitimate voters are prevented from voting. A slightly larger number, 23 percent, believe that large numbers of ineligible people are allowed to vote. That means 2 out of 5 Americans effectively believe our elections aren't free and fair.

Such cynicism is borne out by the widespread evidence that has accumulated over the past few years proving that the basic fairness of our elections is under assault from all sides:

- The radical organization ACORN (Association of Community Organizations for Reform Now) and other voter-registration groups have been frequently caught putting fraudulent names on voter rolls.
- A growing number of residents in states such as New York and New Jersey have homes in Florida and other states with milder climates and wind up registering and voting in both places.
- Legitimate and longtime voters sometimes find their names removed from registration lists by inaccurate purging.
- "Mickey Mouse," "Mary Poppins," and "Dick Tracy" are just some of the names showing up on registration lists along with many real individuals who are not eligible to vote.
- Arbitrary decision making is on the increase in very close elections, as the Florida 2000 presidential recount and the 2008 Senate race in Minnesota demonstrate. There is growing uncertainty as to who is entitled to cast ballots and whose ballots should be counted.

These and other problems cry out for repair. But now that he is in the White House, President Obama, far from using his new powers to restore Americans' faith in their elections, has moved in exactly the opposite direction. The full story of how this presidency has further undermined our election processes provides a disturbing look into one of the most significant threats our democracy faces today.

Justice Lets the New Black Panthers Walk

Bartle Bull couldn't believe his eyes. The former civil-rights lawyer had been arrested in the South during the 1960s. He once forced local officials in Mississippi to remove nooses that were hanging from tree branches outside polling places. But until election day 2008 in Philadelphia, he had never seen a man brandishing a weapon blocking the entrance to a polling place. And now he can't understand why the Obama Department of Justice has dropped its case against the New Black Panther Party, the hate group (according to the Southern Poverty Law Center and the Anti-Defamation League) whose thugs he saw threatening potential voters with truncheons when they tried to vote.

Bull, who was once Robert Kennedy's New York presidential campaign manager and is a former publisher of the left-wing *Village Voice*, has moderated his politics, going as far as to join Democrats for McCain in 2008. It was in that capacity that he traveled to Philadelphia on election day. When he visited a polling place at 12th and Fairmount, he found two men dressed in black combat boots, black berets, and black uniforms, blocking the door. One was brandishing a large police-style nightstick.

McCain volunteers called the police, and media filmed the whole incident. The police ordered the armed man to leave but did not take away his weapon. But one of his colleagues didn't go quietly. Minister King Samir Shabazz, head of the New Black Panther Party in Philadelphia, yelled at onlookers, "You are about to be ruled by the black man, cracker!"

In March 2009, Bull got a call from Christian Adams, an attorney with the Justice Department's Civil Rights Division, who asked him to provide an affidavit about the incident to support a civil-rights lawsuit against the New Black Panther Party and three of its supporters, one of whom, Jerry Jackson, is an elected member of Philadelphia's 14th Ward Democratic Committee and, as recently as spring 2009, has served as an official poll watcher in a local election. Bull said he would, provided that the Justice Department follow through on the lawsuit to the very end.

The lawsuit was filed, and when none of the defendants answered it, a federal court in Philadelphia rendered a default judgment against the defendants. Bull was astonished, therefore, when the government reacted by suddenly dropping charges against the New Black Panther Party and the two defendants. Another defendant was given only the mild sanction of being barred from displaying a weapon near a polling place for the next three years.

A Justice Department spokesman issued a terse statement saying only that the department made its decision "based on a careful assessment of the facts and the law." Career Justice Department attorneys told Bull that they were appalled by this inexplicable failure to enforce the Voting Rights Act. Those near the case believe that the decision was politically motivated – a signal sent, according to Bull, that "intimidation against poll watchers challenging the fraudulent voters registered by ACORN" may be permissible.

Hans von Spakovsky, a former official in the Justice Department's Civil Rights Division under President George W. Bush, told me he was shocked by the department's turnaround in the Philadelphia case: "Imagine if the defendants had been white and been intimidating voters and Justice had dropped the case. There would have been a political earthquake." In the wake of the Justice Department's action, the U.S. Commission on Civil Rights voted on Aug. 7, 2009, to send a letter to the department expanding its own investigation and demanding more complete answers. "We believe the Department's defense of its actions thus far undermines respect for rule of law," its letter stated.

Bull plans to keep the issue alive. "When he took office, Attorney General Eric Holder stated that America was a nation of 'cowards' when it comes to race and that he was going to make civil-rights cases a top priority," he told me. "But who are today's 'cowards' on race? This kind of double standard is not what Martin Luther King and Robert Kennedy fought for."

Indeed, Justice's behavior in the Black Panther case may have emboldened the radicals running the organization to think they had immunity.

In April 2012, the family of George Zimmerman, the neighborhood-watch member who shot a black teenager in Florida and came under fierce criticism from many minority groups, released a statement upbraiding the Justice Department for not responding to incendiary threats by the New Black Panther Party. They included ultimatums to the Sanford, Fla., authorities, saying they wanted Zimmerman arrested "dead or alive." The NBPP also placed a bounty on his head and called for an army of vigilantes to track him down and effect a citizen's arrest. It also said it planned to "suit up and boot up" and prepare for the next stages of the "race war."

"The Zimmerman family is in hiding because of the threats that have been made against us, yet the DOJ has maintained an eerie silence on this matter," the family's letter stated. "These threats are very public. If you haven't been paying attention just do a Google search and you will find plenty. Since when can a group of people in the United States put a bounty on someone's head, circulate Wanted posters publicly, and still be walking the streets?... Why, when the law of the land is crystal clear, is your office not arresting the New Black Panthers for hate crimes?"

Throughout all this, the Justice Department remained silent. At least its behavior toward the New Black Panthers appears consistent: ignore evil, see no evil, do not respond to evil.

Playing with the Numbers: The 2010 Census

The national census – supposedly an objective counting of every inhabitant of a country – has always taken place with politics lurking in the background. Jesus was born in Bethlehem because the Romans insisted that Joseph and Mary go back to the town of their birth to be counted for tax purposes. The 1937 Soviet census was annulled because it showed a sharp drop in population resulting from the famines and killings of the Stalin era; a "correct" census was held in 1939 after the administrators of the first one had been shipped to the gulag.

Obama began his term making clear that even the 2010 census was becoming a political football. In February 2009, GOP Sen. Judd Gregg withdrew his nomination to head the Department of Commerce partly in response to the administration's decision that the director of the Census Bureau would no longer report to the commerce secretary but to the White House. Gregg was upset at the prospect of political operatives using computer models and "sampling" techniques to adjust the census count upward on "underrepresented" groups. The *Philadelphia*

Inquirer called the proposed move "a threat to the fairness and accuracy of the census."

Liberal groups have long believed that up to 8 million members of minority groups and the homeless were not picked up in the 2000 census. To make up for these supposedly "missing people," sampling-based adjustments would be used to add people to the actual count all the way down to the neighborhood and block levels. Those "adjusted" numbers would have real political significance because they would redraw congressional and state legislative districts to allocate federal money.

In 1999, the Supreme Court ruled 5 to 4 that sampling could not be used to reapportion congressional seats among the states. But the court left open the possibility that sampling could be used to redraw political boundaries within the states. My sources inside the Census Bureau tell me that, assurances from Obama appointees to the contrary, sampling is about to make a comeback.

The problem with sampling-adjusted numbers is that they don't add up. In theory, statisticians may be able to generally identify the number of people missed in a head count, but they cannot then place those abstract "missing people" into specific neighborhoods, let alone blocks. Starting in 2000, the Census Bureau conducted three years of studies with the help of many outside statistical experts and concluded that "adjustment based on sampling" could damage census credibility. Rather than "enfranchising" minority groups, as its proponents piously claim, such a procedure exaggerates their numbers. "The adjusted numbers told us the head count had overcounted the number of Indians on reservations," former Census Director Louis Kincannon says. "That made no sense."

Robert Gibbs, the Obama administration press secretary, insists that "historical precedent" exists for the White

House to ride close herd on the census, but every living former Census director supports a pending bill in Congress to make the Census Bureau an independent agency and further insulate it from politics. Even the liberal *San Francisco Chronicle* was appalled at the White House power play: "Allowing Obama politicos like chief of staff Rahm Emanuel – a top House Democratic strategist in his prior life – anywhere near the census adding machine is . . . a Chicago-style setup that should worry any voter."

When President Obama met with Sen. Gregg at the White House the day before Gregg's withdrawal, Obama could have simply told him he hadn't known of the White House power grab and claimed that the Census Bureau would continue to report directly to the commerce secretary. But he didn't, and that refusal played a major role in Gregg's decision to withdraw. It was clear to him that in having to decide between his vaunted new "politics of transparency" and the left-wing pressure groups, Obama had chosen to side with the liberal base of his party.

Luckily, the political furor over the White House's takeover of oversight of the census seems to have had a beneficial effect. The census ended up proceeding along traditional paths, and no evidence surfaced of undue political influence over the process. But that doesn't excuse the Obama administration's initial ham-handed moves or nullify the concerns that were expressed early in the process.

Nullifying the Law

The Justice Department's charge – applying the law in an objective manner without political consideration – often involves a delicate balancing act, since political appointees set the department's policies and priorities. But the Obama Justice Department appears not even to have tried for balance and fairness in the brief time Obama has been in office. Instead, as its approach to voter registration shows, it has clearly and consistently chosen to misinterpret and misapply election laws for what appear to be political motives.

The federal 2002 HAVA requires states to coordinate their voter registration lists with other databases, such as Social Security records and driver's license lists, and to "verify the accuracy of the information provided on applications for voter registration."

Georgia, for instance, moved to comply with this federal requirement by passing a law in 2008 setting up a verification procedure that included checking to see if the potential voter was a citizen. (It is against both federal and state law for noncitizens to register or vote.) Georgia consulted with career Justice Department employees in 2008 in writing its rules.

Its program worked well. Using existing databases, Georgia flagged 4,000 potential noncitizens and sent them letters asking them to verify their citizenship status. More than 2,000 failed to comply, making it likely many were indeed not eligible to vote.

Minority turnout in Georgia was hardly affected by the new rules. In fact, from 2004 to 2008, Hispanic turnout increased by 140 percent, and black turnout increased by 42 percent. But on May 29, 2009, the Obama Justice Department used its power under the Voting Rights Act to veto Georgia's verification law. It claimed it would have a "disparate impact" on minority voters. The evidence? It cited findings that Asians and Hispanics were supposedly "twice as likely to appear on the list" of potential noncitizens as whites.

Of course, there is a ready explanation for this. Only 35 percent of Hispanics and 58 percent of Asians in Georgia are citizens. Although no evidence has been presented that anyone was prevented from voting in 2008 because they were improperly listed as noncitizens, the Justice Department's veto of Georgia's law held.

The Justice Department's about-face on citizenship requirements isn't the only case in which it has demonstrated a troubling double standard. Missouri, to use another example, has a long record of conflict with the federal government on the issue of bad registration records. At the time of the 2008 election, for instance, more than a dozen Missouri counties had more registered voters than the number of adults over the age of 18. Under the Bush administration, the attorney general had gone before the Eighth Circuit Court of Appeals and won a ruling to force the Missouri secretary of state's office to clean up its registration lists. But in March 2009, the Obama Justice Department dismissed this lawsuit – its own lawsuit – without explanation. As in the case of the New Black Panther Party voter-intimidation case it would abandon two months later, the Justice Department had effectively already won but nonetheless decided to surrender its victory. What kind of prosecutors act that way? The answer appears to be, highly political ones.

"The Justice Department is charged with securing the integrity of the voter registration process," notes von Spakovsky. "In just the first year of its time in office, this administration appears to be moving as fast as it can to evade those responsibilities."

Bullying a Small Town for Partisan Profit

In November 2008, the city of Kinston, N.C., voted to make local elections nonpartisan, meaning they didn't want candidates to be known by their party affiliations. Since all but nine of North Carolina's hundreds of jurisdictions follow the same procedure, the move was hardly controversial – until the Justice Department stepped in and overruled the voters' decision.

The move to nonpartisan elections clearly had minority support. It passed with a two-thirds majority in an election in which minority turnout was high because Barack Obama was on the ballot. Out of Kinston's 15,000 registered voters, 65 percent are black. A majority of the black-dominated precincts in the town voted for the change. Two of the five members of the City Council are black, as was the town's mayor until recently.

But none of that mattered to the Obama Justice Department. Even though there was no evidence that blacks faced *any* barriers to registration and voting in Kinston, Justice blocked the change to nonpartisan elections. Under the Voting Rights Act of 1965, Kinston is one of about 12,000 cities in the nation in which changes in voting procedures are subject to the Department of Justice's oversight.

Attorney General Holder's assistant attorney general, Loretta King, authored the DOJ's letter of dissent, arguing that the legislation's "effect" would be strictly racial and that removing the partisan cues in municipal elections would have a discriminatory effect on black voters because "it is the partisan makeup of the general electorate" that allows the winner of the Democratic primary to win in the general election. Justice was concerned that changing to nonpartisan elections would "likely eliminate the party's campaign support" for black candidates.

But the Voting Rights Act is supposed to protect *voters*, not particular political parties. The fact that blacks are a controlling majority in the city and can control election outcomes when they turn out to vote, as well as the fact that black voters themselves voted for the change, was essentially deemed irrelevant by Justice. It was no surprise that this racially biased decision was issued by King, who was instrumental in the dismissal of the New Black Panther Party case. (She has since retired from Justice.) Of course, the Civil Rights Division's action rests on the presumption that blacks simply cannot be trusted to make their own decisions as to which individual candidates to support and will be presumed to vote against their own self-interest unless candidates on the ballot have the "right" party label. In short, the Justice Department "knew" for whom Kinston's black community should vote, and it certainly couldn't be Republicans. This approach to enforcement stands the Voting Rights Act on its head and is anathema to all our constitutional requirements for fair elections.

As Abigail Thernstrom, a member of the U.S. Civil Rights Commission, put it: "Kinston reinforces the message to black voters and to potential black candidates, in order to be represented in this country, you have to be voting in the majority black district, and as a candidate, you have to be elected from a majority black district, because whites are too racist."

Several residents of Kinston and a candidate filed suit against the Justice Department in federal court in the District of Columbia, claiming that DOJ's objection was wrong and that parts of the Voting Rights Act are unconstitutional. They had to sue because Kinston's Democratic town officials, who could have contested the objection, failed to do so. As Democrats, they were happy that the citizen referendum had been voided. The citizens lost at the district court level and appealed the decision. In a very interesting development, however, the Civil Rights Division suddenly notified Kinston in January 2012 that it was "reconsidering" its objection to the nonpartisan referendum, even though there had been no request by the town of Kinston for reconsideration. Only a week later, it withdrew its objection, making a laughably false claim that there had "been a substantial change in operative fact."

One of the "changes" claimed by Justice was that the voter registration rate for blacks in Kinston was now 65.4 percent. Yet this was an increase of only 0.8 percentage points over 2008, when the registration rate was 64.6 percent and black voters overwhelmingly approved the referendum!

The only real "change in operative fact" was that it looked as if the Kinston lawsuit was headed for the Supreme Court. The facts in the case were so bad from the point of view of the Justice Department – and made the political manipulation of the VRA by the Civil Rights Division so visible – that Justice clearly wanted to withdraw its objection in order to convince the appeals court that the case has been mooted and should be dismissed, avoiding a decision on the constitutionality of the Voting Rights Act.

The original Justice letter has been exposed for being patronizing and self-serving, but it raises a larger issue. The cynical manipulation of federal power to benefit one political party over another underscores that the only real source of refuge from these political machinations is the Supreme Court. Here's hoping that the court will someday soon decide the fundamental issues involved in the Kinston case – the arbitrary power the Justice Department has over so many states and cities in which there is no recent evidence of racially discriminatory voting practices.

Blocking Voter ID by All Means Available

There is no question that every individual who is eligible to vote should have the opportunity to do so. It is equally important, however, that the votes of eligible voters are not stolen or diluted by a fraudulent or bogus vote cast by an ineligible or imaginary voter.

The evidence from academic studies and actual turnout in elections is also overwhelming that – contrary to the shrill claims of opponents – voter ID does *not* depress the turnout of voters, including minority, poor, and elderly voters. The real myth in this debate is not the existence of voter fraud, which is a real problem; the real myth is the claim that voters are disenfranchised because of voter-ID requirements.

Voter ID can prevent and deter not just impersonation fraud at the polls but also voting under fictitious voter registrations; double voting by individuals registered in more than one state or locality; and voting by illegal aliens. There are examples of all of these types of fraud that can be reduced or deterred with voter-ID requirements.

As the Commission on Federal Election Reform, headed by former President Jimmy Carter and former Secretary of State James Baker, said in 2005:

> *The electoral system cannot inspire public confidence if no safeguards exist to deter or detect fraud or to confirm the identity of voters. Photo IDs currently are needed to board a plane, enter federal buildings, and cash a check. Voting is equally important.*

Carter knows the issue of voter fraud well. His first election in a Democratic primary in Quitman County, Ga., in 1962 was stolen by voter fraud that local residents said "had been going on on election days as long as most people could remember." He had to go to court to get the election overturned and ended up winning the general election. The culprit responsible for stealing the primary election was later convicted of voter fraud in a previous congressional election.

As Carter learned, voter fraud exists, and criminal penalties imposed after the fact are an insufficient deterrent to protect against it. In *Crawford v. Marion County Election Board*, the 2008 case upholding Indiana's voter-ID law, the Supreme Court said that despite such criminal penalties:

> *It remains true, however, that flagrant examples of such fraud in other parts of the country have been documented throughout this Nation's history by respected historians and journalists, that occasional examples have surfaced in recent years ... that ... demonstrate that not only is the risk of voter fraud real but that it could affect the outcome of a close election.*

The denizens of the left were very surprised that the majority opinion in *Crawford* was written by Justice John Paul Stevens, a stalwart liberal, rather than one of the conservative justices. But the ACLU's cries that voter fraud is a myth did not find any acceptance with a justice who practiced law in Chicago, a city with one of the worst records of electoral malfeasance in American history.

Chris Matthews, a former staffer to Democratic Speaker of the House Tip O'Neill and current MSNBC host, knows the score.

When the topic came up on his show, *Hardball*, Matthews admitted that this type of impersonation fraud has "gone on since the '50s." He explained that people call up to see whether you voted or are going to vote, and "then all of a sudden somebody does come and vote for you." Matthews knows that this is an old strategy in big-city politics: "I know all about it in North Philly – it's what went on, and I believe it still goes on."

Given this record, the decision by the Obama Justice Department to block voter-ID laws in several states is deplorable and smacks of blatant partisanship. Over the course of the 44 presidents who have served this country, the U.S. attorney general has routinely been accused of playing politics, but the extent to which Eric Holder has practiced the art form is head-spinning.

Take his March 2012 decision to reject Texas's voter-identification law on grounds that it would hurt minorities.

Assistant Attorney General for Civil Rights Thomas Perez wrote to the Texas director of elections to inform him that the state's voter-identification law, which passed last year and requires voters to present *one* of several listed forms of ID at the polls, violates Section 5 of the 1965 Voting Rights Act. The decision follows Justice's rejection of South Carolina's voter-ID law in December, which the state is fighting. Texas will do the same.

The Justice complaint is based on a mind-numbing and arcane discussion of identification "datasets" used by the state. Texas, Justice says, didn't adequately explain its system's "disparate results" and "declined to offer an opinion" as to which data were "more accurate." Cross lawyers with statisticians, and what do you get? An endless morass, which will run past the November 2012 election.

When the Holder Justice Department objected under Section 5 to South Carolina's voter-ID law in December 2011, it very noticeably did not mention is prior approval of Georgia's more restrictive photo-ID law. South Carolina will allow an individual without an ID to vote if he has a religious objection or a "reasonable impediment" that prevents him from getting a free photo ID. In fact, DOJ was ignoring inconvenient facts and clear legal precedent in making its claim that South Carolina's law is discriminatory. Given its prior approval of Georgia's voter-ID law, it would have had a hard time explaining its objection to South Carolina.

The South Carolina objection was driven by the radical, left-wing ideology that has been behind almost all the law-enforcement decisions made by the Justice Department during the Obama administration. In fact, South Carolina's comparison of its voter-registration list to its DMV driver's-license records – once adjustments were made for individuals who were deceased, had moved to other states, or were mismatched – showed that only 1.2 percent of registered voters did not already have a driver's license. Yet the Justice Department still objected based on the nonsensical claim that minority voters were less likely to have a photo ID.

In 2008 in the *Crawford* case the Supreme Court ruled that a similar Indiana law requiring photo ID did not impose an undue burden on voters. The Justice Department approved a Georgia voter-ID law in 2005. But now Obama, Holder, Perez, the NAACP, and the American Civil Liberties Union claim that minority voters are being consciously suppressed and that Republicans are trying to gain a partisan advantage with voter-ID laws.

In a December 2011 speech on voter ID, Holder warned that "we will examine the facts, and we will apply the law." He called voter-ID laws "unnecessary" and said the fraud they are designed to prevent is almost nonexistent.

It's certainly true that in-person fraud at polling stations can almost be a perfect crime. If someone votes in the name of a dead person still on the rolls, that individual is unable to complain. No one would know what happened absent a confession on the part of a perpetrator. As Chris Matthews pointed out, in many voter-fraud "hotspots," a list of "usable" names that people can vote in the place of is often readily available to those tempted to commit fraud – along with cash payments to encourage the practice.

Just how easy voter fraud can be was demonstrated in April 2012, when conservative filmmaker James O'Keefe sent an assistant into a Washington, D.C., polling place where Eric Holder had been registered for 29 years. After establishing that Holder was on his list, a poll worker was ready to hand over his ballot and specifically told O'Keefe's assistant that no ID was needed. The assistant left before actually casting the ballot. O'Keefe has demonstrated the same vulnerabilities in state after state without ID laws.

In a sign of the hypocrisy that drives the Justice Department, anyone who wants to make an appointment with the attorney general or the head of the Civil Rights Division to discuss an objection to South Carolina's voter-ID law as "discriminatory" had better bring their government-issued photo-ID card. No outsider can enter the main Justice headquarters building, situated between Pennsylvania and Constitution avenues in Washington, *without* a photo ID. And to those who would argue that voting is a constitutional right, so is speaking to government officials. The First Amendment specifically protects the right of the people to "petition the Government for a redress of grievances."

For They Are Jolly Good Felons

Felony disenfranchisement laws keep an estimated 5.3 million Americans who have felony convictions from the polls, including 2.1 million who no longer are in prison. Here, the Obama administration has shown admirable restraint in not proposing its own federal legislation on the issue. But it has also steadfastly refused to take a position on bills pending in Congress that would do just that, and leading civil-rights advocates say they are convinced the Obama administration would quietly sign such a bill.

At present, standards regarding felons' access to the ballot box vary greatly. Maine and Vermont let jailbirds vote from their prison cells. A total of 34 states and the District of Columbia automatically allow felons who've served their time in prison to vote. Eleven states restrict the right of felons to vote after their sentences are served, while 35 states prevent parolees from voting. A total of 30 states bar those on probation from casting ballots. Legislation likely to be introduced would "rationalize" these disparate laws.

It's easy to understand why "felon enfranchisement" is a liberal issue. In a 2003 study, sociologists Christopher Uggen and Jeff Manza found that roughly a third of disenfranchised felons had completed their prison time or parole and would thus have their vote restored under such a bill. While only a bit more than a third of felons are African American, an overwhelming majority lean toward one political party – Democrat. In presidential races, the two scholars estimated that Bill Clinton won 86 percent of the felon vote in 1992 and a whopping 93 percent four years later. Voting participation by all felons, Uggen and Manza estimated, would have allowed Democrats to win a series of key U.S. Senate elections, thus giving the party control of the Senate continuously from 1986 to 2004.

There is some evidence that felons already swing elections even in states where many of them are barred from voting. The *Seattle Times* found that 129 felons in just two counties, King and Pierce, voted illegally in the photo-finish race for governor in Washington in 2004, which Democrat Christine Gregoire won, coincidentally, by 129 votes.

The issue of felon voting might be a little broken, but a

federal law won't fix it. We should leave the matter where the Constitution intended it be lodged – with the states. "If you're not willing to follow the law, then you can't claim a right to make the law for everyone else. And of course that's what [felons] are doing when [they] vote," says Roger Clegg of the conservative Center for Equal Opportunity. "Why should the federal government step in and determine a one-size-fits-all policy on felon voting?"

Conclusion

Americans are aware that their history includes painful examples of discriminatory hurdles to voting. They instinctively and justifiably resist anything that smacks of exclusion and oppose any attempt to create artificial barriers to voter participation. They also intuitively understand that when improperly cast ballots are counted or outright fraud countenanced, their civil rights are violated just as surely as if they were prevented from casting a ballot by a thug with a swagger stick.

Citizenship requires orderly, clear, and vigorous procedures to ensure that the integrity of our elections – and voter confidence in them – is maintained. "The more clearly rules are settled in advance, the better elections we will have," says Brad King, a former state elections director of Minnesota. "What we don't want is the designed sloppiness that a few politicians allow to seep into our system through ambiguity and vagueness."

We also don't want the unequal application of the law, something that the Obama administration's early actions signal might be happening. Shying away from pursuing election cases even when the evidence is literally handed to prosecutors on videotape (the New Black Panther Party case) is troubling. By not enforcing laws mandating accurate and complete voter-registration lists, the Obama administration is devaluing the most basic covenant between citizens and state. The impact on our system of self-governance is similar to what would happen to our economic system if the Treasury Department evinced no interest in containing the number of counterfeit bills circulating in the economy.

Nor is it only partisans making such claims. Chris Coates, a career Justice Department official who had been honored for his work in civil rights by the ACLU and the NAACP, was forced out as chief of the Voting Section of Justice by the Obama administration for insisting that the laws be applied without partisan or racial considerations. He found the record of Obama political appointees very troubling in that sense.

In 2010, Coates testified before the U.S. Civil Rights Commission that Deputy Assistant Attorney General for Civil Rights Julie Fernandes made it clear in meetings with his office that the Obama administration was interested only in filing "traditional types" of voting-rights cases that would "provide political equality for racial and language minority voters." Coates testified that everyone in the room understood what that meant: "No more cases like [the New Black Panther Party] case."

Coates also testified that in another meeting with Voting Section staff, Fernandes said the Obama administration was not interested in enforcing the provision of Section 8 of the National Voter Registration Act that requires states to maintain voter registration lists by regularly removing ineligible voters – for instance, the names of voters who have died or moved away.

Coates further testified to the U.S. Civil Rights Commission that he sent a memorandum to Fernandes and the Front Office in which he recommended opening investigations of eight states that appeared to be in noncompliance with the list-maintenance procedures of the National Voter Registration Act. He did not get approval for the project, and the Obama administration never filed a single suit to enforce this provision of the NVRA. Prosecutorial discretion does not allow prosecutors "to decide not to do any enforcement of a law enacted by Congress because political appointees determined that they are not interested in enforcing the law," Coates testified. "That is an abuse of prosecutorial discretion."

Coates testified that King, Fernandes, and other lawyers within Justice violated their oath to faithfully execute the law when they selectively enforced the Voting Rights Act based on the race of the victim and the perpetrator. "For the Department of Justice to enforce the Voting Rights Act only to protect members of certain minority groups breaches the fundamental guarantee of equal protection and could substantially erode public support for the Voting Rights Act itself," he told me. "Selective enforcement of the law, including the Voting Rights Act, on the basis of race is just not fair and does not achieve justice."

If we do not demand that the Obama administration and its allies in Congress abandon schemes and policies that further undermine confidence in our electoral system, we are headed for crises that will shake our electoral system and will make us look back on the disputed presidential vote of 2000 with something like nostalgia.

VICTOR DAVIS HANSON

HOW THE OBAMA ADMINISTRATION THREATENS OUR NATIONAL SECURITY

In his first year in office, Barack Obama has focused on "hitting the reset button" as the technique by which America will resolve conflict and craft policies that avoid the "arrogance of power" characteristic of past administrations. To accomplish this about-face, the president has sought to change the United States' role in the world from defender of the post-Cold War international order to apologist for its own misdeeds and agent of global change. We will be on the side of revolutionary governments, privileging the United Nations and hectoring allies in questions involving our system of defense, values, alliances, interests, and commerce.

The linchpin of Obama's foreign policy is the assumption that America is often disliked in the world today, not primarily because of intractable problems of long ancestry, but because of the aggressive nationalism of George W. Bush during the past eight years. "All too often," the president assured Arab journalists, "the United States starts by dictating."

Our reputation was further harmed, according to this narrative, by the inability of the prior president to have conveyed a sense of caring and goodwill abroad – despite Bush initiatives involving massive and unprecedented new infusions of American aid to curb AIDS in Africa and support for democratic movements in the former Third World.

In contrast, through empathy and competence, President Obama offers to transcend artificial divides and misplaced suspicions. And he can accomplish radical change not just through his singular charisma but also through his own unique personal story (e.g., "I have Muslim members of my family. I have lived in Muslim countries") and a more sophisticated, nuanced reliance on soft power and smart diplomacy. Thus, solutions will come from more international consensus and retiring the myth of American exceptionalism. ("I believe in American exceptionalism," the president explained, "just as I suspect that the Brits believe in British exceptionalism and the Greeks believe in Greek exceptionalism.")

The president will accomplish in a messianic fashion abroad what he also wishes to accomplish by similar techniques at home. There is a long-overdue need for change in helping the world's dispossessed and neglected. Just as poverty in America arises from the undue privilege of a few, so too are tensions abroad rooted in a system of global inequalities that the United States was crucial in establishing.

From Word to Deed?

Obama's application of his stated commitments to real-time situations so far has involved a realistic appraisal of relative dangers and expenses involved. To force concessions on vulnerable Israel is one thing; it's quite another to resist the bloodlust of the Iranian mullahs or the bullying of Vladimir Putin or commit the United States to trillions of dollars in expenditures to meet European-style cap-and-trade emission reduction.

A second constant in his approach has been an avowal of the power of partisan rhetoric. Often, Obama frames foreign-policy issues in terms of domestic politics rather than potential fundamental change abroad. A good example is the so-called war on terror, the bogeyman of the 2008 election. In campaign mode for both the Senate and presidency, and while overseas, candidate Barack Obama in varying ways criticized Bush-era renditions ("shipping away prisoners in the dead of night"); military tribunals ("flawed military commission system"); preventative detention ("detaining thousands without charge or trial"); the surge of troops into Iraq ("not working"); and the Patriot Act ("shoddy and dangerous").

As president, Obama has now grasped that at least some of these once constitutionally suspect policies were, in fact, essential tools in ensuring the ongoing absence of terrorist attacks on the American homeland since Sept. 11, 2001, and therefore must be continued. He likewise assumes that most of his supporters will be content with the symbolism of soaring civil libertarian rhetoric and forget the demand for changes in the Bush antiterrorism protocols that has kept them safe – especially given the multiple terrorist plots foiled by existing Patriot Act protocols in his first year of administration. Thus, the war on terrorism has undergone a cosmetic surgery of euphemism ("overseas contingency operations" aimed at "man-caused disasters") that will end "the politics of fear" without fundamentally altering existing antiterrorism methods.

Also clear in his early foreign-policy actions is a pattern of short-term accommodation without commensurate consideration of long-term consequences. Perhaps four years of engagement with Iran or concessions to Putin might soothe international tensions and resonate with global elites. Yet there is a good chance that displays of American accommodation to the mullahs of Tehran or a change of heart on missile defense that left the Czechs and Poles twisting slowly in the wind will be interpreted by Iran and Russia as symptoms of timidity to be manipulated, rather than as magnanimity to be appreciated – with dire results well down the road after the Obama presidency. Foreign-policy mistakes take time to mature; the serial tepid response to radical Islamic terrorism in the 1990s, for instance, did not bear bitter harvests until 2001.

At some future date, regional hegemons may decide to redefine their existing landscapes on more favorable terms to themselves (e.g., the Islamists and Western Europe; Putin and the former Soviet Republics; China with Taiwan; North Korea with the South; Iran with Israel; and Venezuela with its neighbors). They may well assume, as a result of Obama's early actions and international conversation, that the present government of the United States either would not object to these measures or would do nothing concrete to stop them – or perhaps even privately sympathizes with their particular grievances against the Western-inspired world order.

In other words, as Obamaism completes the transition from word to deed and from theory to practice in foreign policy, a more compliant and understanding America might find itself to be well liked as much as it is increasingly little-respected – as it gropes clumsily with world crises. A foreign minister who attended a Global Security Review conference in Geneva recently summed up Obama's sermonizing as "pointless rhetoric, no matter how elegantly expressed."

Yet we should not underestimate the resonance of "pointless" rhetoric with those who are sympathetic to world governance – as the recent awarding of the 2009 Nobel Peace Prize to President Obama attests. The European judges, in their citation, obviously delight in Obama as the anti-Bush sympathetic to their own particular utopian views. But he is seen as beleaguered at home by reactionary opposition that blocks his implementation abroad. He therefore is in need of both moral reinforcement through such an award and a strong reminder that Nobel Peace laureates do not pressure Iran, escalate in Afghanistan, occupy Iraq, tilt toward Israel, or keep open the gulag at Guantanamo. In 2002, Jimmy Carter finally grasped how the Nobel committee had morphed into a leftist lobbying organization intent on subordinating American foreign policy to international consensus. When he reacted accordingly in blatantly obsequious fashion by attacking President Bush on the eve of the Iraq War, he was rewarded with the prize after years of previous frustrating lobbying. But by then, Carter was largely irrelevant, not a sitting president at the reins of power. With Obama, the committee hit pay dirt and, in a new first, awarded a prize for "elegantly expressed" intentions rather than real achievement – in hopes of influencing ongoing American foreign policy.

The Middle East

In just nine months, relations with the Israelis have deteriorated more than at any time in our 60-year relationship. That Israel is an oasis of democracy in a vast desert of autocracy wins it no special consideration from Obama. In contrast, the Obama administration has hit the ground grasping for (in the fashion of the frantic diplomacy during the last days of both the Clinton and Bush administrations) the diplomatic coup that will magically end conflict in the region and provide an array of added dividends: oil security; a decrease in international Arab terrorism; better relations with the half-billion people in the Mideast; and closer diplomatic ties to a Europe that is increasingly busy with anti-Israel agendas.

The key to a "breakthrough" is seen largely in Israeli concessions. For the Obama administration, the cause of Mideast violence is not the absence of civil society or consensual government in the West Bank (or indeed among the Arab frontline states themselves), but rather lies with Israeli intransigence, particularly as embodied in its settlements.

For the Obama administration, pressuring a democratic ally is much easier than accepting the depressing fact there were as many Mideast wars before the 1967 "occupation" as after. It also ignores another reality – that the Israeli withdrawals from Lebanon and Gaza did not result in either peace or humanely governed Arab democracies in areas that Israel vacated but in continued tyranny and aggression.

Destruction of Israel remains enshrined as an ideal in the manifestos of both radical and "moderate" Palestinians on the West Bank. With Obama in office, they trust that such a visceral policy of hate will not affect support for their own envisioned frontline autonomous states. Meanwhile, Iran, in addition to acting through its proxies Hamas and Hezbollah, almost monthly boasts of obtaining nuclear capability, as its pathological leader denies the past Holocaust and supports the future one.

In short, Israel now finds itself on its own in a way that it never was in its past relationship with the United States. Should there be another Mideast war, intifada, or air strike on Iran, there is real doubt that the present administration would remain a reliable ally or, indeed, wish to continue as a supplier of key parts, military assistance, and foreign aid. Such apprehension is not paranoia: Zbigniew Brzezinski, Jimmy Carter's national security adviser and a foreign-policy adviser to the 2008 Obama campaign, recently said that the United States in the current climate might well shoot down any Israeli jets on their way to Iran as they passed near American planes in Iraq. "A Liberty in reverse," the conspiratorially minded Brzezinski added, in a tit-for-tat reference to a supposedly Israel-planned attack on a U.S. ship during the 1967 Six-Day War.

Iran

Obama's reaction to the mass protests over the rigged June 2009 Iranian elections that affirmed the rule of Mahmoud Ahmadinejad was at first silence. Only after violent government repression and world shock did the administration tepidly express concern.

It was not clear whether Obama, in realist fashion, assumed the protests would always fail and therefore did not wish to side with the losers. Or perhaps he felt that supporting an uprising on behalf of liberty in Iran might sidetrack his own scheduled October 2009 engagement initiatives with the theocracy. There, his charisma and postmodern foreign policies might bear fruit that has eluded other presidents, who have only found obstructionism in confrontational anti-Americanism and revolutionary zeal during 30 years of dealings with the mullahs.

In a variety of videos and communiqués, President Obama has reached out to Ahmadinejad. He does this without much concern about whether such state-to-state normality weakens Iranian democratic reformers at home or bothers Arab states in the region frightened by Iran's nuclear ambitions. He apparently believes instead that his own formidable charm and powers of persuasion can persuade Ahmadinejad to give up the nuclear option that, in fact, will bring Iran closer to the role it covets as regional superpower. As the Obama administration urges closer engagement with Tehran, new intelligence reveals that Iran has just finished the construction of a second, heretofore secret nuclear installation – making inoperative the 2007 National Intelligence Estimate that had claimed the theocracy abandoned efforts at bomb making in 2003.

In any case, as 2009 closes, there is now significantly reduced Western pressure for sanctions and embargoes to head off a nuclear Iran than in the past – given that the United States finds itself in the unprecedented position of moderating European states eager to press Ahmadinejad more aggressively. Yet through its increased distancing from Israel, American policy has ensured a greater likelihood of a pre-emptive, unilateral Israeli strike on Iranian nuclear facilities. An emboldened Iran, in turn, has dropped the diplomatic charade of a nuclear industry for peaceful purposes. Instead, it now boasts that its newfound nuclear capability will serve its own security needs as it sees fit.

Barring an Israeli strike, we should soon expect Iran to become a nuclear regional hegemon. As the Obama administration retreats to the flawed argument that the Western world can live with, or deter, a "nuclear Iran" in the fashion of present-day nuclear Islamic Pakistan, this breakthrough will spark a Mideast race among Sunni-dominated oil-producing states to acquire nuclear deterrence to counter Tehran's menacing new power.

* * *

"Good" and "Bad" Wars

Candidate Barack Obama in mid-2007 wanted the removal of "all combat brigades from Iraq by March 2008." At about the same time, he weighed in on the then new counterinsurgency strategies of Gen. David Petraeus with the conclusion that "the surge is not working."

Yet if he deemed Iraq the unnecessary and doomed "war of choice," he praised Afghanistan, relatively quiet back then, as the "war of necessity." There was the proper theater to confront al Qaeda and the Taliban, given their direct involvement in the Sept. 11, 2001, attacks: "We must refocus our efforts on Afghanistan and Pakistan."

Indeed, candidate Obama chest-thumped for more troops for the "good" war and even raised the possibility of hot pursuit after al Qaeda kingpins into Pakistan itself: "If we have actionable intelligence about high-value terrorist targets and President Musharraf won't act, we will." In fact, Obama often characterized our wrongful neglect of the necessary Afghanistan war in favor of the optional Iraq conflict as a critical policy failure: "We took our eye off the ball."

But by early 2009, the absolutely unforeseen had occurred. Iraq stabilized and became a quiet front. In contrast, the largely somnolent Afghanistan theater – where yearly fatality figures often had been less than monthly casualties in Iraq – suddenly heated up. The military unexpectedly called for more American troops and investment and for greater allied support.

The results of this odd development were twofold. First, Obama kept static the current American force level in Iraq (still more than 120,000 troops by autumn 2009). He assumed that the prior incessant media criticism of "Bush's war" would subside – as it did – and that there was no need to endanger a success there by following his earlier advice of precipitate withdrawal.

Second, the president immediately found that erstwhile supporters of the "good" war now wanted out from Afghanistan almost as quickly as they had from Iraq in its own dark days of violence. Accordingly, Obama found himself in another unprecedented position of being an antiwar figure burdened with commitments he had made to outflank his presidential opponent from the right on military affairs in a campaign season who was now deeply involved in an unpopular effort that was both escalating and requiring greater American investment.

Because the president had once broadcast that his own pro-Afghanistan war sentiment was in accord with the consensus of high-ranking military officers and sober statesmen, he now found it difficult to abandon a war that he supported in the past – even if it was largely to establish his national security bona fides during the campaign.

By late September 2009, Obama had not consulted with senior military leaders in the theater in Afghanistan, much less granted their requests for additional troops – although he did visit Copenhagen with an Illinois delegation to lobby for a 2016 Chicago Olympics bid.

The president had all but exhausted his serial tactic of blaming Bush for his present predicament in Afghanistan. Apparently, Obama lacks the confidence to seek the sort of stunning turnaround victory that an embattled Bush found in Iraq through supporting the surge of Gen. Petraeus in 2007–08 – a move that would polarize his left-wing base and not necessarily find majority support from the American public. In exasperation, the president thinks that he can either continue his inaction on Afghanistan and wait for a spontaneous Iraq-like American turnaround (a military solution he once scoffed at), or he must grant concessions to obtain an exit for American forces. That would entail inviting the Taliban to co-govern and would be tantamount to an American defeat, giving radical Islam a stunning military and psychological victory after their humiliating and costly setback in Iraq.

Radical Islam

If Obama entered office in a deep recession with two unpopular wars, he caught a break with the successful prior American effort to curb Islamic radicalism. Polls taken among the Mideast countries revealed a dramatic drop in Osama bin Laden's popularity. There were concurrent declines in support for suicide bombings. The United States had not been attacked in eight years. Al Qaeda was scattered. Thousands of jihadists who had flocked to Iraq had either been killed or captured – and their movement was seen on the Arab street as weak, incoherent, and in retreat.

Some 23 major domestic terrorist plots of some sort had been successfully pre-empted in their initial stages during the Bush presidency. An entire network of antiterrorism protocols was in place, and while they could facilely be caricatured as Bush's overreach, they could also quietly be left in place as proven safeguards against attack.

Unfortunately, however, Obama and his leftist base had made prior charges of Bush-administration illegality that required consummation even though they were sure to bring on complications. Obama had harangued so often that the Bush-era Guantanamo Bay detention facilities had resulted in a violent gulag that, upon taking office, he was boxed in by his own rash – and subsequently impossible – promises to close it down by January 2010. He made these promises without any plans to relocate the terrorist suspects who, in some cases, were unwanted even by mother countries that had lobbied for their release.

The frequent waterboarding of three terrorists – among them Khalid Sheikh Mohammed, the architect of the Sept. 11, 2001, attacks – was deemed unnecessary and of little intelligence value by Obama's Attorney General Eric Holder. Holder also said it was a proper cause to investigate, ex post facto, former CIA officials who supposedly engaged in an array of illegal "enhanced interrogation techniques." Augmenting the growing suspicions of his inability to stand the heat he makes in his own kitchen, Obama himself outsourced the problem to Holder – as seven former CIA directors of both parties lambasted the politically motivated attack on the agency.

With his own Muslim heritage on display, Obama chose to amplify his view of Islam in interviews with Arab journalists and in a much-heralded speech in Cairo in June 2009. In the Egyptian address, Obama, eager to appear culturally sensitive, made a series of astonishing historical statements, such as, "It was Islam – at places like Al-Azhar University – that carried the light of learning through so many centuries, paving the way for Europe's Renaissance and Enlightenment." (In fact, it was the flight of Byzantine scholars, threatened by the Islamic encroachment near Constantinople, that helped foster the rediscovery of classical wisdom in the West.) He also argued that much of the American tension with the Muslim world was due not to the unholy bargain between radical Islamists and failing and illegitimate autocratic governments, but to polarizing American attitudes during the Bush "war on terror."

In this new formulation, much of the current tension over radical Islam has been derived from mutual misunderstanding, including Western tendencies to deprecate Islamic historical achievement. *Jihad* was now to be defined not as a violent war against the West but a personal journey of rediscovery and internal moral struggle. Prior emphasis on the universality of freedom and American support for democratic reform was to be put aside – apparently seen either as improper interference into the internal affairs of Arab nations or unnecessary triumphalism about Western institutions.

If radical Islam actually did grow out of Western culpability, Obama's approach may well bring dividends. But if Muslim fundamentalist anger is largely self-induced and scapegoats the omnipotent and ubiquitous West for the Islamic world's own indigenous failures – from tribalism, gender violence, and apartheid to political autocracy, statism and religious intolerance – then the president's moral equivalence will send exactly the wrong message to terrorists and their state sponsors. In September 2009 alone, three major plots were broken up in Illinois, New York, and Texas that were aimed at causing mass murder.

Europe

The president enjoys ecstatic support among the European public – evident during his "Victory Column" speech in Berlin during the summer of 2008. European elites sighed in relief when the new administration immediately promised a dramatic American turnabout on climate change and the abhorrent war on terrorism. Nor did it hurt when Obama's federal government dramatically absorbed large elements of the private sector in a manner reminiscent of European statism.

Yet many European governments had enjoyed close relations with the Bush administration. In the past eight years, conservatives had come to power in France, Germany, Italy, and throughout Eastern Europe. For all of the public grumbles, they appreciated the American commitment to free trade, missile defense for Eastern Europe, and support for NATO and the European Union.

Europeans, therefore, may wish they had been more careful with what they wished for – a sentiment perhaps illustrated by an exasperated French President Nicolas Sarkozy, who scoffed at Obama's United Nations utopian nonproliferation rhetoric: "We live in the real world, not the virtual world. And the real world expects us to take decisions."

More generally, how do Europeans resist Obama's requests for more troops in Afghanistan – or his pleas for budget-breaking stimulus spending to spur the global economy? Does the decision to withdraw missile defense from Poland and the Czech Republic signal a new American inability or unwillingness to protect the now autonomous democratic nations freed from the sphere of the old Soviet Union? Can, or will, an American-led NATO really honor commitments to independent states on the border of Putin's Russia?

Russia

Prime Minister Vladimir Putin praised, with as much ecstasy as his dour persona could muster, the Obama administration when it aborted the Bush plans to deploy land-based antimissile defenses in the Czech Republic and Poland. These defenses were aimed at countering possible new Iranian threats – but they represented in Russia's eyes unacceptable new Western commitments to its former subject states. More ominously, Putin added, "And I very much hope that this very right and brave decision will be followed by others." And, no doubt, he has an array of further demands that Russia hopes to achieve through unilateral American backpedaling.

In fact, the foreign policy of Russia for years has been to oppose, regardless of the merits, whatever the United States is for. This obstructionism was not caused by Bush diplomacy on issues such as Georgia and the possible expansion of NATO into Russia's near abroad. Instead, it grew out of a perceived loss of global influence, anger at the confidence of autonomous former Soviet Republics and satellites, and gargantuan profits from Russian oil revenues.

Yet almost immediately upon coming to office, the Obama administration talked grandly of hitting the Russian "reset" button, as if the new antagonism were largely America's fault. Even if there was merit to reconfiguring an Eastern European-based missile defense against a possible Iranian threat – the issue is complex and defies easy answers – the unilateral manner in which Obama withdrew our commitment to the Polish and Czech governments had the effect of empowering a Russian autocracy while undercutting pro-American democracies that had taken real risks to align themselves with our initiatives.

Putin will not help corral Iranian nuclear proliferation, since he understands that such a theocratic bomb presents to the U.S. and its allies far more problems than it does to Russia. It is also likely that in the next energy crisis, he will increasingly use oil supplies to re-establish the old Soviet sphere of influence. Whether Putin moves militarily again into Georgia or uses force to obtain concessions from the Ukraine hinges not on the Obama administration's good faith or hope-and-change rhetoric but only on his own cost-to-benefit calculations of Russian self-interest. And the early actions of the current administration have not set any limits on the exercise of Russian international ambition.

* * *

Latin America

After 20 years of success for democratic governments in Latin America, Venezuelan President Hugo Chávez is trying to carve out a regional Marxist hegemony – fueled by oil-exporting revenues and revolutionary socialist rhetoric. Chávez desires to destroy freedom and capitalism in Latin America and establish a Cuban-style socialism in its place, with Venezuela in the center as the continent's revolutionary beacon for oppressed indigenous peoples.

Obama has reached out to Chávez – who entertained a near-pathological hatred for George W. Bush – ostensibly in hopes of curbing his regional ambitions. But such outreach has already backfired. Chávez has announced his intention to develop a nuclear-power industry in cooperation with Russia and Iran, with the obvious implication that he can become Latin America's first nuclear power.

Meanwhile, the administration has accorded our traditional ally, a democratic Colombia, little attention or appreciation for President Álvaro Uribe's stunning success in radically cutting back on the export of drugs and the power of drug cartels and in winning major battles against the communist FARC insurgency.

Currently, Latin America is roughly divided between center-left democracies invested to varying degrees in the American-led global order and a rejectionist cadre of Marxist revolutionary regimes in Nicaragua, Bolivia, and Venezuela. The latter are committed to stifling dissent, ending elections and establishing anti-American revolutionary states.

These fault lines were evident in the recent crisis in Honduras. There, in extra-constitutional fashion, leftist President Manuel Zelaya attempted to hold a nonbinding referendum – in essence, a slow-motion coup – in hopes of consolidating power in the manner of his ally and benefactor Chávez. Both the Honduran Congress and the Honduran Supreme Court ruled the election illegal. They ordered the military to arrest Zelaya, who was summarily exiled to the Brazilian embassy in Honduras and reduced to spewing anti-Semitic conspiracy theories. Unfortunately, the United States pressured his constitutionally appointed successor, Roberto Micheletti – the prior president of the Honduran Congress – to step down and recall Zelaya. The U.S. subsequently cut off foreign assistance to Honduras as it sought a sort of compromise that would return Zelaya to power.

The message to centrist Latin American governments, however, is that the United States has "flipped" and now is more sympathetic to revolutionary than to constitutional forces. As reported by *The Washington Post*, a senior Obama administration official's comments after a private meeting with Chávez, Bolivian President Evo Morales, Nicaraguan President Daniel Ortega, and other South American leaders may well give credence to such suspicions. "Inequity in this hemisphere is extreme, and a hemisphere blessed with a lot of resources should not be suffering the way it is. Race is a part of that in many cases."

The administration's policies in Latin America are, in fact, the natural complements to Obama's own ongoing domestic agenda that seeks to "spread the wealth around" and redistribute supposedly illegitimately obtained private capital. In that context, Obama has logically dispatched senior officials to Cuba to begin normalizing relations with Fidel Castro's dictatorship.

* * *

America's Enemies

During the first year of the Obama administration, those previously deemed hostile to the United States earned more attention than staunch allies. The pattern was quite remarkable. In the missile-defense controversy, the pro-American Czechs and Poles were rebuffed in favor of the anti-American Putin – the death of missile defense being announced on the 70th anniversary of the Soviet invasion of Poland, no less. Outreach to terrorist-sponsoring Syria and Iran was now a keystone of Obama's Mideast policy, coupled with growing pressure on traditionally loyal Israel. Britain provided troops and support in both Iraq and Afghanistan yet was snubbed in Washington through both shoddy protocol and insulting gifts. Hugo Chávez, not Colombia's Uribe, garnered American interest.

In an unparalleled exercise in vanity that assumes that enemies can be charmed into rethinking their enmity, Obama seems unaware that such international rivalries are based on long-standing animosities that preceded the Bush administration. The hostility is based not on misunderstandings or on our displays of "cowboy diplomacy" but on agendas that are not compatible with American, or indeed global, interests. The danger arises that our enemies see no obstacles to their regional ambitions, while our friends see no future support in times of crisis. Concession and appeasement might defuse tensions in the short-term, but this creates bills that will come due in the future when emboldened belligerents take risks that they otherwise might not have if the United States had refused to wear a "kick me" sign on the back of its foreign policy. It is no surprise that, almost simultaneously, China, India, Iran, North Korea, and Pakistan – in varying degrees –

either paraded new nuclear-weapons systems or announced long-range plans for stepped-up nuclear development.

Czars and the Secretary of State

The horde of "czars" – administrators not subject to Senate confirmation who are free to expand executive authority in the auto industry, the creation of green jobs, the absorption of the financial sector, AIDS, the stimulus, etc. – have a foreign-policy counterpart. Regional American kingpins, in the manner of Roman proconsuls, have been allotted extraordinary powers to "solve" crises at the expense of traditional State Department involvement. In the Mideast, there is czar George Mitchell. For the Central Region, we have czar Dennis Ross. In Afghanistan, Richard Holbrooke is our new czar who supersedes regional ambassadors and State Department section chiefs. There is even a Sudan czar, J. Scott Gration, and a weapons of mass destruction policy czar, Gary Samore.

The problem is not that prior administrations did not use special envoys or that the present cadre is unqualified. (Many, in fact, have a distinguished record of diplomatic service.) Rather, in our most urgent foreign-policy crises, we are relying entirely on senior statesmen who have not made their own initiatives known to the public, or perhaps even to the State Department, but who are empowered to make radical shifts in U.S. policy without institutional oversight.

As a result, Secretary of State Hillary Clinton in her inaugural year has devolved into an almost minor cabinet figure. Clinton seemed to be bypassed in the discussions on Korean and Iran proliferation, the accommodations to Putin, and most of the Mideast policy changes. Vice President Joe Biden, CIA Director Leon Panetta, and U.N.

Ambassador Susan Rice, in varying ways, have been observant of these turf battles and thus carved out additional spheres of influence that previously would have been part of the secretary of state's portfolio.

The position of secretary of state has been weakened before in traditional rivalries with the office of national security adviser – especially during the Richard Nixon and Ronald Reagan administrations – but never has its prestige been so rapidly diminished, ostensibly for partisan political advantage over a past and future rival.

The Bashing of George W. Bush

In the first year of the Obama administration, almost all foreign-policy officials prefaced their remarks with attacks on the Bush tenure. The world got the message: Everything in the past was bad; everything in the future would be good, as problems that Bush caused were now solved by Obama.

The party politics might be understandable, but the historical illiteracy is not. In the piling on, which shows no signs of abating even as Obama takes ownership of our foreign policy, there was to be no mention that the surge in Iraq had worked or that America had not been attacked for seven years following Sept. 11, 2001. There also was no admission that Obama himself had retained Bush-appointed Secretary of Defense Robert Gates and kept in place the majority of Bush's successful antiterrorism protocols, or that almost all European governments were pro-American. It was forgotten that that American AIDS relief to Africa had helped save millions; that relations with billion-person India and China were good; and that there were positive developments in the Middle East, from the end of the intifadas and the Syrian withdrawal from Lebanon to Libya's abandonment of its extensive WMD program and the Pakistani house arrest of nuclear proliferator Dr. Abdul Qadeer Khan.

The truth is that, by deliberately and mean-mindedly positioning himself in Manichean fashion as the anti-Bush, Obama has trapped himself in a variety of untenable positions, squandering a rare opportunity to build on Bush successes and use his undeniable charisma to advance bipartisan American foreign-policy agendas under his own brand.

The "reset" mantra itself was confusing. Allies are now unsure whether their own past pro-Americanism in the Bush years is to be reinterpreted by the present United States government as misdirected. And enemies are encouraged to believe that it was indeed logical to try to undermine the United States from 2001 to 2009.

Carter or Clinton?

The therapeutic view of the world abroad – that fundamental problems result from misunderstanding and thus are solved by greater empathy and conversation – is not new to Democratic administrations. Both Presidents Jimmy Carter and Bill Clinton mastered the art of apology and voiced American culpability as a way of winning international approbation on the cheap.

But the difference between the two is instructive for the future of the new Obama administration. Carter self-righteously scoffed at Cold War anticommunism. He turned on traditional allies, questioned American security commitments, and posed as a self-professed utopian advocate of human rights. For his sermonizing, Carter soon won a Soviet invasion of Afghanistan, communist entry into Central America, the takeover of the American embassy in Tehran, the rise of a virulently anti-American radical Islam, the contempt of Europe – and a one-term presidency.

Bill Clinton began his first year with similar claims on a radical new foreign policy, one to be far more humane than George H.W. Bush's calculating realism. But after initial stasis in the Middle East, the escalating violence in the Balkans, a series of domestic-policy disasters and the 1994 midterm correction, Clinton moved to the center at home and abroad and was re-elected in 1996 for his efforts.

In reaction to Saddam Hussein's violations of past accords, Clinton called for regime change in Iraq and enforced the no-fly zones. His perseverance in the Balkans led to quiet after the removal of Slobodan Milosevic. And while Clinton appeased radical Islam, his failure was no different than the equally naive Reagan and Bush Sr. administrations that likewise downplayed pre-Sept. 11, 2001, terrorist attacks.

By 2000, Clinton was not merely considered a centrist in domestic policy but was acknowledged abroad as more of a Harry Truman than a Jimmy Carter. Even conservatives who otherwise found him morally unpalatable had to acknowledge that this president was not out of the mainstream of a half-century of bipartisan foreign policy making.

At the end of his first year in office, Barack Obama seems to have chosen Carter's ideological path over Clinton's pragmatic one. As his foreign policy appears more and more ideologically driven, erratic, uncertain, and out of the mainstream, the president's response is to try to finesse the glaring contradictions in his initiatives by the power of his person. If there is no midcourse steering correction toward a more moderate appreciation of American interests, Obama might find that the people of this country will become disturbed by America's increasingly precarious position in the world and the messianic pretensions of their transnational commander in chief. If that happens, he could find his campaign slogan reformatted and shouted back at him: No We Can't; No We Shouldn't.

A 2012 Postscript

In August 2009, I painted a bleak picture of the first eight months of President Barack Obama's foreign policy – ending with the worry, "As his foreign policy appears more and more ideologically driven, erratic, uncertain, and out of the mainstream, the president's response is to try to finesse the glaring contradictions in his initiatives by the power of his person." Now after the first three years of the Obama administration, nothing has altered those initial apprehensions, and so I leave my original prognosis as written in 2009 unchanged: "America's in-creasingly precarious position into the world" still seems about right.

Reset with Russia failed. Vladimir Putin's autocracy opposes all Western efforts at the United Nations to check nuclear proliferation in Iran and atrocity in Syria. The former is now no longer the object of "outreach" but the target of a belated global boycott; the once loudly reopened American embassy in Damascus has now quietly reclosed.

The president ignored advice from his ground commanders in the theater to leave a small peacekeeping force in Iraq, then both surged and announced deadlines for withdrawal in Afghanistan. The latter remained the "good" war still in 2009, but by early 2012, there had been four successive senior American commanders, little presidential attention, and a serial array of czars and ambassadors in charge of diplomacy. The result was chaos. Riots broke out over burned Korans. Our Afghan allies murdered a number of American soldiers. An American rogue soldier gunned down innocent Afghan civilians – and there is now little public support for continuing the mission.

The administration was caught napping by the so-called Arab Spring, whose popular demonstrations and riots led to the removal of autocracies in Egypt and Tunisia in 2011. It then seemed further confused about what followed – given that either chaos or Islamism seemed as likely as constitutional government to replace dictatorship. Instead, far more confidently, still more administration pressure is applied to Israel to return to the 1967 borders. And in an embarrassing open-microphone session with French President Nicolas Sarkozy, President Obama shared his own anguish at Israeli Prime Minister Benjamin Netanyahu, who had been infamously snubbed at a White House meeting. In this regard, Palestinian diplomats have publicly claimed that they had received private assurances from President Obama that his policies in the Middle East would prove more flexible once he wins re-election.

The bright spot was the mission to kill bin Laden that succeeded in brilliant fashion. But even that triumph did not allay apprehensions that something is still not quite right with our "war on terror." In theory, the president still opposes the detention center in Guantanamo Bay, renditions, tribunals, preventative detentions, wiretaps, and intercepts. In fact, he continues to embrace or expand all these Bush-Cheney-era protocols, in an admission that they are both vital and constitutional. The president also continues to expand the once criticized Predator-drone targeted assassination program, surpassing the Bush number of such kills eightfold while including U.S. citizens among the targets – apparently on the theory that conservatives will be relieved by his expansion of prior policies, while liberals will not wish to hurt his domestic agenda by continuing their criticism of those once abominable protocols. Assassination by drone, however, does not seem compatible with a policy in which both *Islam* and *terror* are still officially politically incorrect terms.

More generally, the Obama administration has offered a new strategy of "leading from behind," in which the United States would cede leadership to NATO allies – should they choose to intervene abroad, as they opportunistically did against the oil-rich and dying Gaddafi regime in Libya. Breaking with recent precedent, President Obama asked the Arab League and the United Nations for authorizations to intervene in Libya while ignoring such requests to the U.S. Congress. This emphasis on a new multilateralism and internationalism is supposed to reflect both budgetary and political realities: America no longer has the financial wherewithal or desire to play a pre-eminent global role, as our defense budget is targeted for massive cuts and our strategic nuclear arsenal is seen more as provocative or dangerous than as a vital deterrent.

The president was also caught in yet another unguarded microphone incident, assuring then Russian President Dmitry Medvedev that he would be "flexible" after the "election," with a request to remind Vladimir Putin that in the present election year, he could not overtly state to the public what the future U.S. policy toward Russia might be in 2013. Observers worried that such private assurances either confirmed more concessions to come on missile defense and nuclear reductions or were the sorts of private promises that Obama might have also extended to other unnamed heads of state – or both.

Closer to home, reset with Venezuela and Cuba accomplished little; the Castro brothers and Hugo Chávez sound as anti-American as during the Bush years. And when

Nicaraguan President Daniel Ortega offered an anti-American rant in the presence of President Obama, Obama replied by shrugging that such scurrilous charges should not apply to his own person – given that he was just a child at the time of the supposed American crimes.

In Asia, North Korea is even bolder as it launches a new longer-range ballistic missile. Japan and Taiwan are more worried that they either are not under the American nuclear umbrella or that such guarantees may simply no longer exist as they had in the past. Both envision beefing up their own defenses. The huge national debt – $5 trillion borrowed in less than four years – has weakened influence with China, which more than ever resents lectures on human rights and fair trade from those who are simultaneously asking for hundreds of billions of dollars in loans.

The financial implosion of Greece and the subsequent fiscal earthquakes in Ireland, Italy, Portugal, and Spain have nearly wrecked the idea of the European Union – at precisely the time it seems to be distancing itself from the sort of statist policies that the United States wishes to embrace. In any case, the Obama administration's loud announcements of focusing on the Pacific and Asia and its relative neglect of traditional NATO agendas have left the Europeans with a sense of worry about now obtaining what they had once so wished for. President Obama realizes that his initial snub of the Anglo-American alliance was unwise, but he seems unable to reassure the public of its importance. The United States appears to be neutral about the "Malvinas" dispute in the South Atlantic and about unilaterally envisioning radical reductions in both our strategic forces and the defense budget in general.

Finally, the problem with the first three years of Obama's foreign policy is not just commission but errors of omission as well. Quite quietly, the known fossil-fuel reserves of the United States have expanded exponentially – thanks to new breakthroughs in horizontal drilling and fracking on private oil- and gas-rich properties. The result is that the United States could soon find itself self-sufficient in natural gas without much need to import oil from outside North America; in far better financial shape; and with far less worry about petroleum blackmail constraining its Middle East policies. Yet sadly, after hundreds of billions of dollars were squandered in failed federally subsidized wind and solar projects, the administration has still shown little interest in fast-tracking oil and gas exploration and production on federal lands. As gas prices hit record levels, the United States finds itself more, rather than less, straitjacketed by Middle East oil concerns, whether in its effort to embargo Iranian oil or to beseech the Saudi Arabians to put a few more barrels of their oil on the world market.

The theme of my original critique – that Barack Obama believed the world's problems had not antedated and, given his own unique profile and talents, would not postdate George W. Bush – seems confirmed by two more years of the Obama administration record. I also think my original comparison with Jimmy Carter's foreign policy of 1977–80 remains persuasive, but whether the similarity will be limited to a one-term duration, no one yet knows.

VICTOR DAVIS HANSON
Stanford, California
March 27, 2012

ANDREW C. McCARTHY

HOW THE OBAMA ADMINISTRATION HAS POLITICIZED JUSTICE

Foreword

President Obama had been in office for all of one year when this Broadside was published in January 2010, but even then, it was already clear that his was the most politicized Justice Department in American history. The ensuing years have featured enough corruption, cover-up, and raw political hardball to fill several new volumes. Indeed, the record is such that it is difficult to say which misadventure is the most scandalous. A few – for space limits us to just a few – bear noting.

For sheer shock value, "Fast and Furious" takes the prize. It was an inane investigation in which the Bureau of Alcohol, Tobacco, Firearms, and Explosives – in consultation with the Justice Department – knowingly armed savage Mexican drug gangs by encouraging arms dealers to make illegal gun sales to "straw purchasers," i.e., faux buyers whose true intention is to bulk-transfer weapons to aliens, convicted felons, and others barred by law. The idea was that the thousands of guns involved would lead investigators to violent criminals. What they predictably led to were innumerable violent crimes – including the murder of a U.S. border-patrol agent. The Justice Department brass is in its now familiar stonewall mode against congressional inquiries into who knew what, and when. Given the well-known antigun obsessions of top Obama officials, one can't help but suspect a political motivation to bolster the left's claim that America's "gun culture" fuels international violence.

Then there is the continuing war on state sovereignty, highlighted by the Obama/Eric Holder Justice Department's decision to sue Arizona over a law intended to *support* federal immigration laws by enabling police officers to inquire into a person's immigration status when there are reasonable grounds to suspect illegality – an inquiry that does not even require grounds for suspicion under Supreme Court precedent. The administration's rationale? States must enforce not *federal law* but *Obama policy* – which, in this instance, is to refrain from enforcing federal law. As the Arizona lawsuit proceeds, the administration continues to fight states that endeavor to crack down on voter fraud, particularly commonsense measures like requiring proof of identification. The election looms, and it is no holds barred. In the interim, on the national-lawlessness front, Obama makes recess appointments when Congress is not in recess; ignores First Amendment religious liberty by forcing observant Christian health care providers to supply abortifacients and contraceptives; and blithely ignores federal law requiring the president to address fiscal imbalances in Medicare once its trustees have sounded the alarm of imminent insolvency.

Nevertheless, most outrageous (which is saying something) is the mounting evidence that the Justice Department is immovably committed to a racially discriminatory policy on civil-rights enforcement. The New Black Panther Party gets a pass regardless of overwhelming proof of voter intimidation. Yet Attorney General Holder teamed up with race-grievance monger-extraordinaire Al Sharpton to pressure Florida officials to return murder charges against George Zimmerman – a young Hispanic man (dubbed a "white Hispanic" by Holder's fans at *The New York Times*) who shot to death a 17-year-old black male, Trayvon Martin. Zimmerman had called the police beforehand because he suspected Martin of drug use and criminal intent, and while there appears to have been no evidence of racial bias – the necessary trigger for a federal investigation – there is evidence that Zimmerman was being beaten by Martin when the shooting occurred. Investigators initially saw no basis for charges, but after weeks of agitation by Sharpton and Holder's throwing the DOJ's weight behind this campaign (while ignoring the bounty the New Black Panther put on Zimmerman's head), Florida appointed a special prosecutor who dutifully filed a murder indictment that legal experts on both sides of the ideological divide agreed did not pass the laugh test.

The point of enacting civil-rights laws was to uphold the Constitution and its bedrock principle of equal protection under the law for all Americans. In the age of Obama, the Constitution and its principles are an increasingly distant memory.

* * *

KHALID SHEIKH MOHAMMED realized the end was near. The legions of left-wing lawyers who'd volunteered their services to the al Qaeda Defense Bar had pulled out all the stops in their eight-year jihad against Bush-style counterterrorism. Their *bête noire* had been the military commission system, the time-honored procedure for trying war crimes. President Bush had attempted to reinstate it after the massacre of Sept. 11, 2001. The effort reflected America's determination that Islamic terrorists were not everyday criminal defendants to be swaddled in the Bill of Rights but military enemies to be captured, imprisoned, and executed.

For a while, the lawyers had derailed the effort, flooding the federal courts with challenges to the commissions' legitimacy. But the tide had turned. Judges had finally declined further obstructions. Commission trials had begun, and two al Qaeda operatives were quickly convicted. When KSM had been grabbed in Pakistan back in 2003, he smugly told his captors that he'd talk to them in New York ... with his lawyer. To his chagrin, though, the maestro of 9/11 soon learned that the lawfare party of the '90s was over. He found himself talking to the CIA. And now it was December 2008. Stuck in Guantanamo Bay and facing the imminent prospect of a military trial, KSM made an announcement: He and four fellow 9/11 plotters were prepared to plead guilty – to brag that they were guilty – and to proceed to execution and Allah's great orgy in the sky.

Meanwhile, in Washington a tectonic shift was under way. Barack Obama was blowing into town, fueled by a radical base that saw Bush, not KSM, as the real war criminal. Obama's campaign spokesman Eric Holder had fed the frenzy, promising the base a "reckoning." An Obama administration would hold Bush officials accountable for what he portrayed as serial transgressions against the Constitution and international humanitarian law. When that Obama administration became a reality, Holder was tapped to be its attorney general. He threaded his new Justice Department – particularly its upper tier – with veterans of the al Qaeda Bar. The reckoning was at hand.

With a lot of palaver about ending Bush's "politicization" of justice, Holder went banana republic, turning his vast prosecutorial powers against the Obama left's Most Wanted list. Investigations were pursued against Bush administration lawyers and CIA interrogators. Holder made commitments to assist foreign tribunals considering "torture" charges. He shoveled into the public domain previously classified information about CIA interrogations and other Bush counterterrorism initiatives. And finally, in November 2009, after pulling the plug on KSM's military commission – in a case that was on the verge of wrapping up – the attorney general made the stunning announcement that the 9/11 jihadists would be transferred to Manhattan for prosecution in the civilian justice system. Holder gave KSM his wish: a New York City stage where, after rifling through government intelligence files for the next two years, he gets to put the United States on trial for the stratagems that protected Americans from reprises of 9/11. It is the ultimate politicization of justice by a master of the game.

Real Politicization of Justice

During the tenure of Attorney General Alberto Gonzales, Democrats caterwauled about "politicization" at the Bush Justice Department. The hyperbolic allegation was largely based on Bush's firing of eight U.S. attorneys so they could be replaced by new appointees favored by influential Republicans. That sounds nefarious, but it is done by every administration. United States attorneys are executive branch officials who serve at the pleasure of the president and can be removed by the president for any reason – or no reason. The 93 U.S. attorney slots are coveted patronage, infused by political intrigue as senators and governors jockey to influence appointments in their states.

Indeed, at the start of his first term, President Clinton summarily fired all but one of the incumbents. Charging that justice is "politicized" due to the replacement of U.S. attorneys, an inherently political exercise, is no more sensible than claiming that the air we breathe is polluted by carbon dioxide. (Yes, yes, I know.) Still, the charge gained traction in Democrats' media-fueled campaign against the hapless Gonzales, a Bush confidant and thus a useful proxy for deriding post-9/11 national security policies.

The mantra that the Bush Justice Department had been "politicized" could not conceal the gaping hole in the left's indictment. There was no evidence of the only politicization that actually matters: the basing of *enforcement decisions in individual cases* on politics. A president's choice of lawyers and enforcement priorities is political by nature, and we wouldn't want it any other way in a democracy. But Americans have always drawn a bright line between staffing and enforcement. When it gets down to the brass tacks of real investigations, politics has no place.

DOJ's prosecution of individual legal cases must reflect our constitutional commitment to equal protection under the law. That is, it must not be corrupted by political considerations. The rule of law, part of the glue that holds a free society together, is dependent on evenhanded, nonpolitical law enforcement. That is why, routinely, trial judges instruct juries that cases must be decided strictly on the evidence, "without fear or favor." Furthermore, freedom itself hinges on robust political debate, a fundamental constitutional value. Law enforcement that targets political adversaries, criminalizes policy disputes, and shields political cronies is an aspect of tyranny.

When we talk about the bedrock principle that justice must not be politicized, it is this administration of justice that we mean. Yet it is precisely the administration of justice that has been hijacked by partisan politics in the Obama administration.

Past Is Prologue

Obama knew exactly what he was getting with Eric Holder. Holder had been Justice's No. 2 official for the last three years of the Clinton administration. He became the most influential actor in the most unabashedly politicized Justice Department in American history. He was the prime mover behind the infamous pardon of Marc Rich, one of the FBI's "most wanted" fugitives. Rich had been sought since the 1980s for millions in fraud, tax evasion, and trading with the America's enemies. In 1999, while Rich continued to evade capture – flitting across the globe to avoid prosecution, which is itself a crime – Holder flouted Justice Department protocols against negotiating with the agents of a fugitive. He advised Rich's chief attorney, the former Clinton White House Counsel Jack Quinn, on how to deal with federal prosecutors in New York in his effort to get the case dismissed. When that didn't work, Holder steered Quinn into position to lobby Clinton directly for a pardon – circumventing the rigorous Justice Department pardon process, which the deputy attorney general oversees. Holder kept New York prosecutors in the dark about the pardon application, ensuring that President Clinton heard only Quinn's specious claims. He then pushed the pardon over the goal line by recommending that it be granted during the frantic final hours of the Clinton administration.

The shocking Clinton pardons were politics at its crassest. An inveterate careerist, Holder extended his helping hand in hopes that Quinn, a top confidant of Vice President Al Gore, would look favorably on his quest to become Attorney General in a Gore administration. Holder had been tending carefully to that project since his arrival at DOJ in 1997, when he used his influence to block the appointment of a special prosecutor to probe Gore's black-and-white felony violation of campaign-finance laws. Holder also politicized the pardons process in 1999 for the benefit of Hillary Clinton's 2000 Senate campaign – acceding to his President's desire to pardon *terrorists*, specifically, Puerto Rican separatists, including members of the FALN, a group responsible for over 130 bombings in the United States.

The Clinton-era Holder sang the same paeans to "transparency" as the new but not-so-improved model. Back then, as now, he also dutifully stonewalled Congress – successfully claiming executive privilege to thwart attempts to get to the bottom of the FALN pardons. He was not as fortunate, though, in the Rich affair. A congressional committee aptly described Holder's conduct as "unconscionable"; inferred that Quinn's "key position to assist Holder's chances of becoming Attorney General" had been "a powerful motivation for Holder"; and implied that Holder had not been forthright in testifying that he had failed to inform himself about the nature and extent of Rich's criminality. That last condemnation would no doubt have been even stronger had the committee realized that in 1995, when he was the U.S. attorney for Washington, D.C., *Holder had actually targeted Rich* – going so far as issuing a press release to trumpet his office's successful suit against a Rich company (during the settlement of which Holder's subordinates had obtained an affidavit directly from Rich, the fugitive).

Though out of power in the Bush years, Holder had not run out of political chutzpah. When the country erupted in anger after 9/11, Democrats who'd failed to address al

Qaeda's provocations during the '90s knew they needed to project antiterrorist resolve. Holder rushed to the fore. In 2002, he admonished CNN that "we are in the middle of a war" and thus that captured terrorists should be detained without trial as "combatants." He explained that under governing "precedent," we could "detain these people until the war is over." And Holder was emphatic in rejecting the claim that al Qaeda had Geneva Convention rights: "One of the things we clearly want to do ... is to have an ability to interrogate [terrorists] and find out what their future plans might be, where other cells are located." Terrorists, he elaborated, "are not, in fact, people entitled to the protection of the Geneva Convention." But what about America's reputation in the world? Wasn't Holder worried about upsetting the Europeans? "Those in Europe and other places who are concerned about the treatment of al Qaeda members," he scoffed, "should come to Camp X-ray [at Gitmo] and see how the people are, in fact, being treated."

Time went by, the left evolved, and, true to form, Holder evolved along with it. Covington & Burling, the Washington law firm at which the former deputy attorney general was a senior partner, threw in its lot with the al Qaeda Defense Bar, seeking the release of the very prisoners Holder had earlier called for detaining. Simultaneously, the Obama campaign – viscerally antiwar and committed to the law-enforcement approach to counter-terrorism – caught fire. Sensing another chance to become attorney general, Holder signed on as a top adviser and spokesman.

That meant serving up red meat to the base, and the adaptable Holder rose to the occasion. In a June 2008 stem-winder at the left-leaning American Constitution Society, he inveighed against Guantanamo Bay, calling it "an international embarrassment." It had to be closed because "a great nation should not detain people, military or civilian, in dark places beyond the reach of law." The amnesia-stricken Holder was now theatrically horrified by Bush counterterrorism: Never had he believed he'd see a day when the "Supreme Court would have to order the President of the United States to treat detainees in accordance with the Geneva Convention." Nor was his revulsion confined to Gitmo. Bush officials, he summarized, had "authorized the use of torture, approved of secret electronic surveillance against American citizens, secretly detained American citizens without due process of law, denied the writ of habeas corpus to hundreds of accused enemy combatants, and authorized the use of procedures that violate both international law and the United States Constitution." Because of Bush's "needlessly abusive and unlawful" policies, Holder bleated that we had "lost our way with regard to [our] commitment to the Constitution and to the rule of law." As a result, we'd "diminished our standing in the world community" and rendered ourselves "less, rather than more, safe." It would not be enough for an Obama administration merely to reverse these policies. Holder titillated the crowd with a promise: "We owe the American people a reckoning."

Which Side Are We On?

The first thing one notices about the Justice Department's transition from Bush to Obama is the challenge involved in getting the highest-ranking lawyers engaged on the most significant cases. During the Bush years, national security was inarguably the nation's top priority, and Justice Department lawyers were fully engaged in the war on terrorism. By contrast, key Obama administration lawyers spent those years at law firms and institutions that enthusiastically provided *pro bono* legal representation and issue-advocacy for America's enemies. (Yes, American lawyers consider the representation of al Qaeda operatives who target the American public to be the noble work they provide free of charge under the haughty label *pro bono publico* – "for the public good.")

Under the profession's conflict-of-interest rules, this has rendered the Obama administration lawyers ineligible to work on cases in which their former firms participated. That includes Attorney General Holder, whose firm made the terrorists detained at Guantanamo Bay its most lavishly resourced no-fee project (3,022 hours in 2007 alone). Covington & Burling's website proudly boasts about the firm's success in urging federal judges to grant its "clients" – 18 enemy combatants – new "rights under the Fifth Amendment and the Geneva Conventions." Also touted is the firm's key role in the 2006 *Hamdan v. Rumsfeld* case, in which the Supreme Court invalidated the Bush military commissions. The lead counsel for Salim Hamdan – Osama bin Laden's personal driver and bodyguard – was Neal Katyal, a former Georgetown law professor who is now the Justice Department's deputy solicitor general. Holder's deputy attorney general, David Ogden – whose clients included child-pornography producers and pro-abortion extremists – worked at a firm that represented three enemy combatants and that figured prominently in *Boumediene v. Bush* (2008), in which the Supreme Court granted the alien detainees a U.S. constitutional right to challenge their detention in civilian federal court. The problems go well beyond Holder, Ogden, and their top staffers (drafted from these same firms). Similar conflicts plague, among others, Associate Attorney General Thomas Perrelli (DOJ's No. 3 official) and the chiefs of both the Criminal and Civil Divisions,

Lenny Breuer and Tony West. (The latter volunteered his services to represent John Walker Lindh, the so-called American Taliban, a U.S. national now serving a 20-year sentence after making war against his country.)

It bears observing that the leadership Obama and Holder envision for Justice is not yet fully in place. The Senate has blocked the nomination of an academic, Dawn Johnsen, to lead DOJ's Office of Legal Counsel. OLC is the lawyers' lawyer, driving the administration's legal policy by authoritatively interpreting the law for the attorney general. Its credibility is derived from its reputation for apolitical, academic discipline – informing policymakers of what the law is, rather than what staffers would like it to be. Despite the Democrats' filibuster-proof majority, Johnsen has been stalled because she is an unabashed political ideologue. Besides the obligatory tropes about Bush war crimes, she sees the law as a tool for enacting "the progressive agenda": "universal health care, public funding for childcare, paid family leave, and . . . the full range of economic justice issues, from the minimum wage to taxation policy to financial support for struggling families." The main impediment to her nomination, however, is her bizarre claim that abortion restrictions (e.g., the denial of public funding) are analogous to violations of the 13th Amendment's proscription against slavery – an argument she posited in a Supreme Court brief while serving as the legal director of the National Abortion Rights Action League. According to Johnsen, a pregnant woman "is constantly aware for nine months that her body is not her own: the state has conscripted her body for its own ends." The justices were unmoved, as they were by her equally startling theory that, absent government-provided abortion counseling, many women would be left without "proper information about contraception" – leaving them "losers in the contraceptive lottery [who] no more 'consent' to pregnancy than pedestrians 'consent' to being struck by drunk drivers."

Holder has a freer hand with posts that do not require Senate consent. That explains his hiring of Jennifer Daskal, a lawyer with no prosecutorial experience, to work in Justice's National Security Division. Her qualification? Daskal is a left-wing activist who advocated on behalf of al Qaeda prisoners while serving as the "counterterrorism counsel" (yes, *counter*terrorism) at Human Rights Watch. She has, for example, claimed that KSM may not be guilty of the unspeakable acts he can't stop bragging about because, after all, Bush may have tortured him into confessing. She lamented that another detainee, "a self-styled poet," suffered abuse in U.S. custody when he "found it was nearly impossible to write poetry anymore because the prison guards would only allow him to keep a pen or pencil in his cell for short periods of time." And she has been a staunch supporter of the terrorist detainee Omar Khadr, who was 15 when he allegedly launched the grenade that killed U.S. Army Sergeant First Class Christopher Speer. Daskal frets that a prosecution would violate Khadr's "rights as a child." Khadr recently turned 23.

Holder has assigned Daskal to help shape detainee policy.

With this cast of characters at the wheel, the Justice Department is pursuing three "national security" priorities: (a) repudiating Bush-era counterterrorism policies while reinstating the pre-9/11 law-enforcement model; (b) increasing the rights of terrorists; and (c) giving the left the "reckoning" against former Bush administration officials that Holder promised in June 2008.

The Justice Department has spearheaded the administration's conceptual attack on the war. The phrase "war on terror" is out, deemed too redolent of Bush, too suggestive that we are not adhering to the "rule of law" (i.e., to civilian judicial protocols), and, of course, too offensive to Muslims (i.e., it implies that the Koran may actually say things like "Strike terror into God's enemies, and your enemies" – Sura 8:60). So "war" has been replaced by "overseas contingency operation," and "terror" (thanks mostly to Janet Napolitano, Obama's homeland security secretary) is now "man-caused disaster." (So far "on" is still okay, but you never know.) The bellicose term "enemy combatants" has also been purged, replaced by "individuals currently detained at Guantanamo Bay." Unfortunately, that is the same formulation used to describe Cubans whom the Clinton administration detained when they tried to escape Castro's Workers' Paradise. To allay any confusion, Holder occasionally opts to call the combatants "individuals captured or apprehended in connection with armed conflicts and counterterrorism operations" – not quite as catchy.

Meanwhile, under the auspices of the so-called "global justice" initiative, DOJ has revived the Clinton-era framework that gave the FBI pride of place over the CIA in overseas counterterrorism cases. This entails the implicit assumption that hostile actors outside the United States are not alien enemies but criminal suspects vested with American constitutional rights. The bureau has expanded its extra-territorial role in questioning "suspects" (i.e., providing them with *Miranda* warnings that promise the assistance of free counsel during all questioning) and in the gathering of evidence. The goal is to facilitate prosecutions in the civilian justice system – with its criminal-friendly due-process standards and requirements for disclosing government intelligence.

In the first full day of his administration, President

Obama promised his base that the detention center at Guantanamo Bay would be shut down within a year – a move Holder vigorously supports. But this strictly political gambit lacked any accompanying plan for dealing with those "individuals captured or apprehended in connection with armed conflicts and counterterrorism operations" – i.e., jihadists hell-bent on mass-murdering Americans, who cannot be tried in either civilian or military courts because the evidence against them is intelligence information (often gathered from foreign agencies on the condition that it not be exposed). There is an obvious legal solution to this self-imposed problem: Gitmo should remain open, consistent with the views Holder flaunted in 2002. Alas, that would prompt mutiny on the left, for which there is no war, only war crimes – by Bush, with Gitmo near the top of the list.

So it is Holder's task to empty Gitmo gradually, while the administration quietly concedes that Obama's one-year deadline will not be met. Much to his chagrin, the attorney general has discovered that Europe's vilification of the detention camp did not mean it would be rolling out the welcome mat for the detainees. Our allies' recalcitrance prompted a Holder brainstorm: Our government should set a good example by relocating several of the detainees – i.e., terrorists trained in al Qaeda camps – *in the United States.* Dennis Blair, Obama's national intelligence director, even proposed that the alien terrorists receive welfare benefits from the American taxpayers they've been planning to kill, since "you can't just put them on the street." So far, Holder's flyer has been shot down by Congress – both Republicans and embarrassed Democrats who were roused by a furious public. Ever sensitive to bubbling anger on the left, the administration has also floated the possibility of moving detainees to U.S. federal prisons or even creating what critics aptly call "Gitmo North" – an old prison in economically depressed Standish, Mich. Unlike Gitmo, Standish is not ready to house terrorists and would thus need an infusion of stimulus money. Once thought a national security challenge, jihadism is now a shovel-ready public-works project.

Obama and Holder stress that no prisoners have escaped from federal "supermax" prisons. That, of course, is not the issue. Once the detainees are physically in the United States, the chance that federal judges will order their release here increases exponentially. Historically, moreover, incarcerated terrorists have plotted and directed attacks, urged their confederates to forge escape plots that endanger the public, and brutally assaulted prison guards in escape attempts.

Further, given the Obama DOJ's intimacy with the ACLU, there are other shenanigans to consider. Holder assures the public that terrorists will be securely detained in federal custody because he is empowered to order "special administrative measures." SAMs are enhanced restrictions on a terrorist inmate's ability to meet with other prisoners and communicate with the outside world. Yet, while making his pitch, Holder didn't see fit to mention that his department was simultaneously abandoning the SAMs in the case of convicted terrorist Richard Reid, the "shoe bomber" who tried to blow up a trans-Atlantic flight with nearly 200 people aboard. As Debra Burlingame explains, after a hunger-strike by Reid, the Justice Department capitulated to his risible contention that the SAMs violated the First Amendment – including Reid's asserted right to perform daily "group prayers in a manner prescribed by my religion" (the "group" in question includes the 1993 World Trade Center bombers and other convicted terrorists). Naturally, the ACLU is using the Reid precedent to challenge the SAMs on behalf of terrorists held in other federal prisons.

Holder, meanwhile, is finding other ways to clear out Gitmo. Despite the numerous known instances of detainees returning to the battlefield, the administration has "cleared for release" scores of the 200-plus remaining prisoners. They can leave the second a country willing to take them is found – meaning that if the administration succeeds in transferring the prisoners to U.S. jails, federal judges will have a stronger basis to release them here. Just how exacting is the Justice Department's "cleared for release" standard? Well, in February the administration sprang Binyam Mohammed. He'd been at Gitmo for six years because in 2001, Khalid Sheikh Mohammed tried to send him to the U.S. to be the accomplice of the "dirty bomber" José Padilla in a series of mass-murder attacks targeting U.S. cities. Mohammed is now living free and clear (and on public assistance) in Britain.

And then there's the military commission system, that burr under the leftist saddle. Its adoption was not just a thematic demonstration of seriousness about prosecuting a war as a war. As a practical matter, commission procedures lower the prosecution's bar for admitting hearsay evidence (which protects classified sources) and otherwise restrict the public disclosure of national-defense information. Though the al Qaeda Bar succeeded in persuading the Supreme Court's liberal bloc to invalidate the Bush-ordered commissions in 2006, Congress promptly authorized them later that year – underscoring the public will that jihadists not be granted the same judicial rights as the Americans they are sworn to kill. Holder and his ideologues wanted to end the system but reluctantly recognized that many combatants cannot be convicted under higher civilian court standards. So they are instead marginalizing commissions.

DOJ has worked with congressional Democrats to sculpt modifications that would force more cases into the civilian courts (e.g., removing the commissions' jurisdiction to try "material support to terrorism" offenses – a staple of terror prosecutions). Other face-saving tweaks will assure the left that Obama commissions are not like those bad Bush commissions. Especially rich is the administration's resolve on what it claims is the difficulty enemy combatants face in retaining counsel. Granted, staffing the Obama administration has left the al Qaeda Defense Bar somewhat depleted, but if anything in life remains certain, it is that America's enemies and American lawyers have no trouble finding each other.

The Reckoning

The most reprehensible undermining of our war footing, however, is the stunning transfer of KSM & Co. to federal court in New York.

Legally, the move makes no sense. The five jihadists were prepared to end the case by pleading guilty in the military commission a year ago. The transfer is proceeding despite the fact that the commission system is being maintained – indeed, Holder announced that the bombers of the U.S.S. *Cole* (who killed 17 members of the U.S. Navy) will be tried by commission, notwithstanding that a civilian indictment has been pending against them for years. By capriciously placing the worst war criminals in the civilian system, Holder gives the lesser jihadists consigned to military justice a powerful claim that they've been denied fundamental fairness. Worse, he makes a mockery of humanitarian law, which has strived for decades to civilize warfare. Wittingly or not, Holder's perverse message is: second-class justice for attacking military assets, gold-plated justice for mass-murdering civilians.

A civilian trial for KSM & Co. makes perfect sense only if it's seen as a political maneuver. The impatient Obama left has been champing at the bit for torture and war-crimes prosecutions against government officials who formulated and carried out Bush-era counterterrorism policies, particularly interrogation. This has created a political quandary for Obama. Though the war in Iraq became unpopular, Americans strongly approve of the Bush counterterrorism measures. Hence the resonance of former Vice President Dick Cheney's withering critiques of Obama's performance. The specter of investigations against Bush officials while terrorists are coddled appeals to Obama's base but galls most Americans. The president is thus walking a fine line: vaguely telling the public he prefers "to look forward, not back" but keeping the door open for prosecutions against any Bush official "shown to have violated the law" – something that, of course, cannot be "shown" absent the investigations the administration is saying it doesn't wish to conduct ... even as it conducts them.

Concurrently, because it is more palatable politically to publish the nation's secrets than to embrace the Third World practice of persecuting the ruling party's political adversaries, the Justice Department has pushed for disclosure of classified information. This increases the likelihood that the left will get its reckoning from some foreign tribunal – Holder in fact told the German press in April that he was open to cooperation with European investigations of Bush "war crimes." Resuscitating the case of KSM & Co. in a civilian setting perfectly fits this template. In civilian court, defendants have an unqualified right to represent themselves – they don't have to accept a military defense lawyer with a security clearance to screen them from top-secret intelligence. It is Defense 101 that when it's obvious that the accused is guilty and that the government's investigative methods are controversial, the accused shoots for jury nullification by putting the government on trial. A civilian KSM case will be an intelligence banquet for the left: new disclosures about coercive interrogations, "black site" prisons, renditions, warrantless surveillance, etc. – along with the identification of witnesses who can provide sworn testimony.

The civilian case is also the next logical step in the transformation of constitutional police powers into a political cudgel. Over strenuous objections from the Defense Department and the intelligence community, Holder released memos in which the Bush Justice Department's OLC provided guidance for the CIA's enhanced interrogation program. Transparently designed to inflame the public against Bush, the move backfired – just as the KSM gambit is backfiring. The release of the memos advanced no public interest but edified our enemies about how to improve their counter-interrogation training. Nor, despite the Obamedia's obsession with torture, did Americans miss the central point of the memos: the care taken by Bush DOJ lawyers to ensure that controversial tactics (e.g., waterboarding) steered clear from the legal line of torture.

Real law enforcement, though often challenging, is straightforward: you follow the evidence wherever it leads. Politicized justice, by contrast, is complicated – populist whim mixing uneasily with legal rigor. The DOJ memo disclosure is a case in point. Obama and Holder pandered to their base by sanctimoniously pronouncing that waterboarding is torture, no matter how and why it is administered. In reality, however, Congress intentionally made torture a difficult crime to prove, requiring not only heinous inflictions of pain but proof that the interrogator had a motive to torture his victim – as opposed to, say, a motive to obtain life saving intelligence. So the release of the memos prompted more salivating for indictments by Obama's base while simultaneously demonstrating that there is no case.

Holder's overtly political response to this dilemma would be comical were the stakes not so high. He has ordered investigations. This enables him to tell the left he is acting decisively while telling everyone else he hasn't done anything of consequence. So Bush administration lawyers are being probed by Justice's Office of Professional Responsibility to determine whether their guidance fell below norms of lawyerly competence. This finding could have profound professional and financial consequences for the lawyers, even though having OPR grade the scholarship of OLC is like having the Double-A batting coach critique Derek Jeter's swing. Remarkably, even as it investigates the Bush lawyers for their analysis of federal torture law, Justice has relied on that analysis in court to refute torture claims in other cases. And in astounding congressional testimony ignored by the press, Holder was forced to concede that waterboarding is not torture when government agents have a legitimate national security purpose other than inflicting pain (e.g., training intelligence operatives to resist interrogation).

More despicably, based on a 2004 inspector-general's report, Holder reopened an investigation of six-year-old allegations against CIA interrogators – an investigation that had been closed because professional career prosecutors (i.e., not Bush political appointees) had determined that no crimes had been committed. This is as cynical as it gets: the new party in power doesn't like the objective result, so it demands a do-over. Nor is the witch hunt cost-free: The CIA officers must endure additional expense and anxiety, while the intelligence community recedes into the ethos of risk aversion that allowed 9/11 to happen.

The same political gamesmanship is at play in the administration's mishandling of classified photos depicting instances of prisoner abuse. The ACLU is endeavoring to pry them loose in a Freedom of Information Act (FOIA) lawsuit. Although no one disputes that the photos will be used by the enemy to inflame jihadis and endanger Americans, the administration wants them to be released (to appease the left) but wants to blame disclosure on the courts as if its hands were tied (to avoid offending most Americans). Thus Holder initially declined to appeal a disclosure order, relenting – at Obama's direction – only after outcry from the public and the military. But as this theater now moves to the Supreme Court, we should see it for the farce that it is. FOIA empowers the president to seal information whose revelation would endanger lives and harm national security. Obama could end the case today simply by issuing an executive order. He hasn't done that because of politics. And as ever Holder is carrying his boss's water.

That is DOJ's new leitmotif, even outside the politically charged national security realm. The plug, for example, was recently pulled on a corruption investigation of New Mexico Gov. Bill Richardson, the influential Democrat who was Obama's original choice for Commerce Secretary – a nomination derailed by the probe. Though the grand jury investigation was being conducted by the U.S. attorney in New Mexico, the Associated Press reported that the case was "killed in Washington" – that is, by Main Justice.

Even if you didn't know about Holder's handling of the Gore case in 1997, the Richardson whitewash should come as no surprise. In one of his first official acts as attorney general, while our ears still rang from his pious confirmation testimony about honoring DOJ processes and keeping the Department above politics, Holder overruled his OLC's well-founded opinion that the controversial D.C. Voting Rights bill pending in Congress is unconstitutional. The bill is strongly favored by Democrats because it would give the heavily Democratic District of Columbia a representative in the House of Representatives (and lay the groundwork for eventual Senate seats as well). The infirmity, however, is blatant: the District is not a state: the Constitution plainly says House members must be chosen "by the People of the several States." When Holder didn't like this answer from OLC, he blithely ignored DOJ protocols and turned to his friends at the solicitor general's office (who represent the government in the Supreme Court but are not generally consulted on unenacted legislation). To them, he put a very different question – Could the Solicitor General defend the DC Voting Rights bill in court? – and got the desired answer. Of course, Justice is supposed to give us the *right* answer, not a wrong answer it supposes might be posited without too much embarrassment.

Embarrassment, however, abounds in the area of greatest political consequence to the Obama administration: voter fraud. As the president plummets in the polls and the Democratic Congress achieves record low approval ratings, the Justice Department has a message for those who would undermine the integrity of our elections: Have at it!

In 1993, as Democrats in Congress pushed to loosen voter-registration restrictions, Republicans insisted on a provision that required states to remove ineligible voters (people who had died or moved away) from their rolls.

The Bush Justice Department used it to lodge an enforcement action against Missouri – numerous counties there sport many more registered voters than voting-age residents. Holder's Civil Division, however, has quietly dismissed the suit despite the state's non-compliance.

The Department is also using the 1965 Voting Rights Act (an outdated vestige of Jim Crow) to bar states such as Georgia from using Social Security numbers and driver's license data to validate the U.S. citizenship of prospective voters, nattering that these commonsense measures have a "discriminatory effect" on minority voters. The Voting Rights Act gamesmanship achieved ludicrous heights in September. The voters of Kinston, N.C. – a small, predominantly black town – had voted to remove party affiliations from ballots in local elections. The DOJ has told them they can't. Holder's minions "reasoned" that this could deny African Americans their newfangled constitutional right to representation by Democrats – or, better, deny the Democratic Party its apparent right to be elected by blacks. In sum, Justice figures that without the right label (meaning the "D" label) next to a candidate's name, black voters cannot be trusted to decide which candidates to support.

Most astonishing, however, is the case of the New Black Panther Party. On Election Day 2008, Philadelphians were intimidated at polling stations by combat-clad Panthers. These Obama supporters shouted racial epithets while menacing voters, one with a nightstick. The hijinks were caught on videotape. One of the men, Jerry Jackson, was a credentialed Democratic Party poll-watcher whose MySpace page brayed about "Killing Crakkkas." The Bush Justice Department filed a civil-rights suit against three of the men. The Panthers contemptuously ignored the suit and defaulted. Yet before damages could be assessed, Holder's Civil Rights Division withdrew the case after the government had already won. The case was ultimately dismissed outright against two of the defendants. As to the third – the nightstick-wielding Samir Shabazz – DOJ fecklessly agreed to an injunction prohibiting him from displaying a weapon at a polling place for the next three years. (That's like settling a bank-robbery case by getting the robber to agree not to rob any more banks for three years). The U.S. Civil Rights Commission is demanding disclosure of DOJ's deliberations and rationale for abandoning the case. Despite his promise of a new era of transparency, Holder is doing what Holder does: He is stonewalling, just as he ignored the efforts of congressional Republicans to obtain the same information. It's not a complete stalemate, though. Thanks to the dismissal, Jerry Jackson has gotten his poll-watcher credentials back. Next election season, he'll be right back in business.

By then, while CIA agents and Bush officials mortgage their homes to pay legal fees, KSM will be settled in New York, with a team of lawyers combing through American intelligence files to prepare for his trial. That's politics ... but it's not justice.

BETSY McCAUGHEY

OBAMA HEALTH LAW: WHAT IT SAYS AND HOW TO OVERTURN IT

The Obama Health Law: Dangerous to Your Health and Freedom

The Obama health law is a bruising blow to American freedom and medical excellence. But the war is not over. It cannot be. There can be no negotiation between freedom and coercion.

The White House has launched a 50-state public-relations campaign to convince the public that the law enacted against their will is to their benefit. We cannot falter now. With the U.S. Constitution on our side and the hearts and minds of the American people with us, freedom will prevail. Please use the information contained in this Broadside to alert your fellow patriots to the dangers of this new law. It will lower your standard of care, put the government in charge of your care, and take away something as precious as life itself: your liberty.

There are better ways to improve health insurance and help the uninsured. Congress should rip up the 2,700-page Obama health legislation and enact a 20-page law in plain, honest English – a law that members of Congress can actually read before voting on it.

Will the New Obama Health Law Affect Me?

Yes. The law requires almost everyone to enroll in a one-size-fits-all "qualified" health plan, beginning in 2014. When you file your taxes, you must attach proof that you are enrolled. The law gives the IRS new powers to track you down and penalize you if you don't comply.

The law also empowers the Secretary of Health and Human Services to make the important decisions: what "qualified" plans cover, how much you will be legally required to pay, and how much leeway your doctor will have.

The Obama health law also transfers decision-making power from your doctor to the federal government. Even if you are insured by Aetna, Cigna, or another private company and pay the premium yourself, the government is still in charge. You are required to be in a "qualified" plan, and qualified plans can pay only doctors who implement whatever regulations the Secretary of Health and Human Services imposes in the name of improving health care "quality." That covers everything in medicine – whether a doctor should use a stent or do a bypass surgery or when to perform a cesarean section.

Your doctors' decisions will be monitored for compliance with federal guidelines, and your doctor may have to choose between doing what is right for you and avoiding a government penalty. Never before in American history has the federal government attempted to standardize medical practice.

This is a huge loss of medical privacy and freedom. Never before has the federal government dictated how doctors treat privately insured patients, except on narrow issues such as drug safety. The Constitution does not permit it.

* * *

Betsy McCaughey

Welfare Reform in Reverse

President Obama promised to solve the problem of the uninsured by making private health plans more affordable. That is not what the law does. Instead, the law vastly expands Medicaid, the public program for the poor. The number of people with private insurance inches up only 3 percent when the law goes into effect, but Medicaid enrollment soars. Nearly one-third of Americans (31 percent) below age 65 will be on Medicaid or CHIP (the children's version), moving America toward a Medicaid nation. States customarily determine eligibility and benefits under Medicaid, based on what their own state taxpayers and budgets could handle. Under the new law, the feds take control.

Medicaid must cover anyone with an income below 133 percent of the poverty line (roughly $33,000 for a family of four when the law goes into effect) regardless of their assets. Medicaid enrollment is expected to shoot up 57 percent in Texas and 42 percent in Virginia, for example, with similarly huge increases in a dozen other states.

The law also creates a brand-new entitlement – subsidies for people buying government-designed private health plans on state insurance exchanges. Households earning up to $92,200 (in 2014) and an amazing $100,000 (by 2019) will be eligible. All in all, these two new entitlements – the Medicaid expansion and the subsidies – will cost an estimated $917 billion through 2019 and possibly twice the cost in the second decade, according to the Congressional Budget Office.

Half of the price tag for these new entitlements is paid for with tax hikes, but the other half comes from slashing future funding for Medicare by $575 billion through 2019. People who have paid into the system their whole working lives and are counting on it will get less care because the money is being shifted to support a vast expansion of government dependents.

Most Americans currently get their health insurance through a job – their own, their spouse's, or a parent's. But if the Obama health law remains in effect, you may lose it in 2014. In fact, despite the law's employer mandate, federal authorities already admit that fewer people will be getting health insurance on a job than if the law hadn't passed. Providing the mandatory package will be so expensive for employers – adding an estimated $1.79 an hour to the cost of hiring a low-wage worker – that many employers will opt to pay the penalty instead. If your employer makes that decision, you will have to sign up for Medicaid or buy a plan on the state insurance exchange.

Treating Seniors Like Clunkers

Everyone knows that if you don't pay to maintain and repair your car, you limit its life. The same is true as human beings age. We need medical care to avoid becoming clunkers – disabled, worn out, and parked in nursing homes and wheelchairs. For nearly half a century, Medicare has enabled seniors to get that care.

The Obama health law reduces future funding for Medicare by $575 billion over the next decade, just when 30 percent more people will be entering Medicare as the baby boomers turn 65. Those numbers don't add up. Baby boomers who are counting on Medicare will get less care than seniors currently get.

Most of the Medicare cuts are made by slashing what hospitals, home care services, and other institutions are paid to care for elderly patients. Cuts are even made to hospice care and dialysis care, opening an express lane to the cemetery. Defenders claim the Medicare cuts will eliminate fraud and abuse, not care. If this were true, wouldn't the government have eliminated the fraud and abuse already? In truth, only 1 percent of the cuts will come from fraud and abuse, the Congressional Budget Office estimates.

Slashing Medicare payments will force institutions to cut back on the standard of care. Hospitals will operate in an environment of scarcity, with fewer nurses on the floor and more waits for high-tech diagnostic tests. Richard Foster, chief actuary for the Centers for Medicare & Medicaid Services, warned Congress on April 22, 2010, that the cuts in payments to hospitals will likely force 15 percent of hospitals into the red, and some hospitals may have to stop taking Medicare. Where will seniors go when their local hospital stops accepting Medicare?

Simply cutting what hospitals can be paid for treating seniors is a deadly way to "save" money. New data from all the hospitals in California show that seniors treated in hospitals that provide more intense care and spend more have a better chance of recovering and resuming their lives (*Annals of Internal Medicine*, February 2011). Seniors with pneumonia, congestive heart failure, strokes, and hip fractures were more likely to die from these conditions at the low-spending hospitals. Reducing care at the very end of life may be wise, but across-the-board reductions in Medicare payments to hospitals, rehabs, and nursing homes also reduces care for patients who are capable of surviving their illness and going home. That's the goal of health care.

In the past 40 years, hip and knee replacements, bypass surgeries, angioplasties, and cataract operations have transformed the experience of aging. Older people used to be trapped in wheelchairs with crippling arthritis or stuck in nursing homes with clogged arteries. But these procedures have significantly reduced disability among the elderly, as a September/October 2007 *Health Affairs* study shows. Elderly people are more active – volunteering, shopping, and enjoying their grandchildren. The Obama health law will undo this progress by reducing access to care.

The new law also expressly authorizes the Secretary of Health and Human Services to modify or eliminate preventive services for seniors based on the recommendations of the U.S. Preventive Services Task Force, the group that recently raised public outrage by saying women ages 40–49 and older than 74 should no longer get routine annual mammograms. A half-page later, the law empowers the secretary to increase preventive services for Medicaid recipients. The agenda couldn't be clearer.

Beware of more Medicare funding cuts to come. The law establishes an Independent Medicare Advisory Commission to make further reductions while shielding members of Congress from public outrage.

Driving this evisceration of Medicare are dangerous misconceptions, misuses of scientific data, and a dismissal of older people as not worth the upkeep.

Less Care Is Not the Answer

President Obama and his budget director, Peter Orszag, have told seniors not to worry about the funding cuts, claiming that Medicare spending could be cut by as much as 30 percent without doing harm. They cite the *Dartmouth Atlas of Health Care 2008*, which tries to prove that patients who get less care – fewer hospital days, doctor's visits, and imaging tests – have the same medical "outcomes" as patients who get more care. But read the fine print.

The Dartmouth authors arrived at their dubious conclusion by restricting their study to patients who died.

They examined what Medicare paid to care for these chronically ill patients in their last two years. By definition, the outcomes were all the same: death. The Dartmouth study didn't consider patients who recovered, left the hospital, and even resumed active lives. It would be important to know whether these patients survived because they received more care.

The journal *Circulation* addresses that question in its Oct. 20, 2009, issue and disputes the Dartmouth conclusion. Examining patients with heart failure at six California teaching hospitals, doctors found that hospitals giving more care saved more lives. In hospitals that spent less, patients had a smaller chance of survival. That's the opposite of what Obama claims.

Most Doctors Do Not Knowingly Waste Money on Dying Patients

Newsweek's cover story on Sept. 21, 2009, "The Case for Killing Granny," published at the height of the debate over the Obama health care bill, argued that "the need to spend less money on the elderly at the end of life is the elephant in the room in the health-reform debate." Politicians pressing for "reform" frequently implied that money was being poured into treatments for dying patients who would not benefit.

Numerous studies prove that this is generally false. In 2006, Emory University researchers examining the records of patients in the year before they died found that doctors spend far less on patients who are expected to die than on patients expected to survive.

The Emory researchers said it's *untrue* that "lifesaving measures for patients visibly near death account for a disproportionate share of spending." They also found that doctors often can't predict when a patient is in the last year of life. The most expensive patients are those who showed every sign of being able to recover and then didn't.

In any case, the Obama health law's across-the-board reductions in funding for Medicare won't simply reduce end-of-life care; they will also reduce care for patients who are perfectly capable of surviving their illnesses and going on with life.

Increasing Longevity Is Not Bankrupting Medicare

Access to medical breakthroughs has resulted in huge improvements in longevity and quality of life. Life expectancy at age 65 has jumped from 79 years to 84. The harshest misconception is that this improvement in life expectancy is a burden on society. Wrong. Medicare data show that a patient who dies at 67 spends three times as much on health care at the end of life as a patient who lives to 90. Medicare data also prove that after age 70, patients tend to spend the same amount cumulatively on medical care whether they live another five years or another 25 years. Patients who live longer tend to spend far less per year and much less at the end of life.

What is costly is when seniors become disabled. Fortunately, access to care is not only lengthening life but also reducing disability. And nondisabled seniors use only one-seventh as much health care as disabled seniors. As a result, the annual increase in per capita health spending on the elderly is less than on the rest of the population.

It's true that Medicare is running out of money, but the medical breakthroughs that are enabling people to live longer are not the problem. There are too many seniors compared with the number of workers supporting the system with payroll taxes. This temporary imbalance is due to the post-World War II baby boom. To remedy the problem, the Congressional Budget Office has suggested inching up the eligibility age by one month per year (with an almost imperceptible impact on people nearing retirement) or asking wealthy seniors to pay more. These are reasonable solutions; reducing access to treatments is not. Medicare has made living to a ripe old age a good value. ObamaCare will undo that.

The cuts in future Medicare funding – which Obama calls "savings" – will mean less help in coping with aging and possibly shorter lives. Do we as a nation really want to treat seniors like clunkers?

Ripping up Your Constitutional Rights

The Obama health law robs you of your constitutional rights. Several provisions fail the constitutionality test and reveal Congress's disrespect for the public and the rule of law. To halt this attack on your liberty, we must advance to the next battlegrounds – the U.S. courts and the voting booth.

Making Health Insurance Compulsory

Twenty-six states went head-to-head with the Obama administration in an epic three-day U.S. Supreme Court showdown in March 2012. The marquee issue was whether the federal government can compel Americans to buy a product – in this case, health insurance – claiming it solves a national problem. Challengers warned that if the federal government can force you to buy insurance, it can force you to buy a burial plot, or a GM car to prop up Detroit, or stocks and bonds to prop up Wall Street. The states challenged the Obama administration to show any limit on what the federal government can force you to do or buy if the mandate were upheld. No limit, they warned, means no liberty.

Sen. Orrin Hatch (R-Utah) agrees. Before the law was enacted, he cautioned his Senate colleagues, "[I]f Congress may require that individuals purchase a particular good or service ... [w]e could simply require that Americans buy certain cars.... For that matter, we could attack the obesity problem by requiring Americans to buy fruits and vegetables."

Some members of Congress claim the "general welfare clause" of the Constitution empowers them to impose an insurance mandate. But they're taking the phrase out of context. The Constitution gives Congress power to tax and spend consistent with the general welfare, not to make other kinds of laws solely because they are for the general welfare.

The Obama health law expressly claims that the interstate commerce clause of the Constitution gives Congress the authority to force everyone to buy insurance. But for half a century, states have regulated health insurance. In fact, individuals are barred from buying a health plan in any state except where they live, the antithesis of interstate commerce.

In the past, congressional majorities frequently resorted to the commerce clause to try justifying expansive lawmaking. They did not always succeed. In President Roosevelt's first term, Congress enacted the National Industrial Recovery Act (NIRA), claiming the power to micromanage local businesses, set wages and hours, and even regulate how customers selected live chickens at the butcher. Four Brooklyn brothers, owners of Schechter Poultry Corp., a kosher chicken market, challenged the NIRA. The Schechters said Congress had no authority to interfere with their local business – that there was nothing interstate about it. The brothers took their case all the way to the U.S. Supreme Court and won. Their victory proves that in extraordinary times, it takes ordinary people to stand up for freedom.

Since the Schechter decision, the Supreme Court has stretched the meaning of interstate commerce to allow Congress to intrude in many areas. Yet in 1995, the high Court struck down a federal ban on guns in school zones, admonishing Congress that its power under the commerce clause still has limits, no matter how good the intentions. Congress was told to leave it to the states to police school zones.

Ten years later, congressional health "reformers" hoped that the U.S. Supreme Court's 2005 decision in *Gonzales v. Raich*, defining *interstate commerce* very broadly, would give them a constitutional E-Z Pass to enact national health care. In that 2005 case, the Supreme Court ruled that the federal government could stop Angel Raich from consuming homegrown marijuana for medical purposes, even though it was permitted in her state and advised by her doctor. Amazingly, the Court said her homegrown supply – six stalks in all – amounted to interstate commerce because it could have a "substantial effect on supply and demand in the national market for that commodity."

In September 2005, Sen. Patrick Leahy (D-Vt.) grilled John Roberts, then the nominee for chief justice, demanding assurances that he would stand by the *Raich* ruling instead of trying to restrain congressional lawmaking on health care. The surprise came in the Supreme Court's next term, when in the words of Justice Clarence Thomas, the court made a "hasty retreat" from *Raich.*

This is the setting for the states currently suing to

challenge compulsory insurance. Although the smart money is usually on the court upholding an act of Congress, Congress's claim that *not* purchasing a product (health insurance) affects interstate commerce may be too implausible for the justices to accept.

Medical Autonomy and Privacy

As important as these state challenges to compulsory insurance are, they gloss over an issue that is more consequential to our health and longevity: Can the federal government dictate how doctors treat their patients?

During the past half-century, the Supreme Court has established a zone of privacy protected by the Constitution. It includes a couple's choice to use contraception recommended by their physician (*Griswold v. Connecticut*, 1965) and a woman's choice to have an abortion provided by her physician (*Roe v. Wade*, 1973). How can freedom to make these choices with your doctor be protected but not freedom to choose a hip replacement or a cesarean section? Either your body is protected from government interference or it's not.

The Obama health law requires that nearly everyone enroll in a "qualified" plan, then it says plans can pay only doctors who implement whatever regulations the Secretary of Health and Human Services imposes to improve health care "quality" (Section 1311). That covers everything in medicine. If challenged, this provision is likely to meet disapproval from a pro-privacy court.

Consider how the high Court ruled one year after the *Raich* decision. Oregon had passed a Death with Dignity Act that set standards for doctors to administer lethal drugs to terminally ill patients who request them. The

Bush administration argued that assisted suicide was not "legitimate" medical care; therefore, federal agents could halt the use of the drugs.

The Supreme Court ruled 6–3 against the Bush administration's interference in *Gonzales v. Oregon* (2006). Such intrusion, the Court said, "would effect a radical shift of authority from the States to the Federal Government to define general standards of medical practice in every locality." That's what the Obama health law does.

For example, it requires doctors to record patients' treatments in an electronic medical database and monitors doctors' decisions. Dr. David Blumenthal, the Obama administration's national coordinator for health information technology, explained in *The New England Journal of Medicine* in April 2009 that "embedded clinical decision supports" – his euphemism for computers telling doctors what to do – will manage the quality of doctors' decisions. The Supreme Court is likely to view these controls as a "radical shift" in authority from the states to the federal government – and even more important, a threat to privacy rights.

Before the current health care debate, the public discussed government interference in medical decisions largely in one context: abortion. When a lower federal court struck down the Partial-Birth Abortion Ban Act in 2004 (a decision later reversed by the Supreme Court), Planned Parenthood President Gloria Feldt said, "This ruling is a critical step toward ensuring that women and doctors – not politicians – can make private, personal health care decisions." During the litigation, federal authorities requested access to medical records to determine whether the partial-birth procedure was ever medically necessary. Privacy advocates defeated nearly every request.

Advocates for women's rights need to reassess the

impact of the new health law. Whether you are a man or a woman, pro-choice or pro-life, you lose freedom and privacy under this law.

Deficit Reduction Is a Shell Game

President Obama's health law creates $917 billion in new entitlements through 2019 and twice that figure in the second decade. But when the ink was barely dry on the new law, the president called for deficit reduction and fiscal responsibility. He is calling for entitlement reform. The best way to reform entitlements is to not create new ones.

If your spouse went on a spending binge and came home laden with shopping bags, then announced it was time for the family to go on a budget, what would you do? You'd insist that the latest purchases go back before the rest of the family is made to sacrifice anything.

Step one toward fiscal responsibility is repealing the Obama health law. Americans don't have to tolerate unfair insurance practices. Barring these practices takes up about 24 pages of the 2,700-page health law. These reforms can be enacted separately. Repealing the health law would mean sending back the big-ticket items – those brand-new entitlements with the price tags still on them – before they go into effect in 2014.

Amazingly, the president crisscrossed the country claiming that the new health law is "paid for" and "reduces the deficit." He omitted to say that it was paid for by raising taxes by $500 billion *and* eviscerating Medicare.

Expanding federal programs and paying for them with a half-trillion dollars in new taxes is not deficit reduction. It is freedom reduction.

When Rep. Paul Ryan of Wisconsin said the focus should be on reining in government spending, Rep. Steny

Hoyer, (D-Md.), majority leader of the U.S. House of Representatives, wrote in *The Wall Street Journal* on April 28, 2010, that the commission should take a more "balanced approach that shares the burdens fairly," meaning raising taxes.

Hoyer treated reducing spending and increasing taxes as morally equivalent options. They are not. Raising taxes reduces individual liberty.

The national sales tax already being discussed – a VAT – would affect everyone. In Europe, VAT stands for "value-added tax," a sales tax collected at each stage of a product's production and distribution. Although the phrase "value added" has a positive connotation, there is nothing positive about it. In the U.S., a VAT should be called a Vanishing America Tax, because it would erode our freedom and standard of living.

In many European countries, VATS started small but now add as much as 25 percent to the cost of an item, such as a car. The tax is hidden in the price – not added at the cash register – so when the government raises taxes to satisfy new demands for revenue, few shoppers realize tax increases are to blame for higher prices. VATs have diminished the purchasing power of European families and would do the same to American families.

Even before the health law was enacted, the government was growing beyond the consent of the governed. In fiscal year 2009, local, state, and federal governments together spent 40 percent of everything produced in the U.S. In many European countries, government spending consumes half or more of everything produced to support government-run health care and government intrusions into many other aspects of life. When the government spends so much, less is left for people to spend as they choose.

Only once before in American history did government spending cross the 40 percent line – to wage World War II. Nothing today justifies a similar confiscation of nearly half of people's resources.

Amazingly, although the 40 percent mark was crossed, Congress plowed ahead and enacted the huge health care entitlements, claiming they were fine because of the tax hikes. That makes it clear that the cause célèbre in Washington – deficit reduction – is a shell game. In plain English, it means raising your taxes to keep pace with government spending.

Members of Congress need to be reminded that government spending should not consume 40 percent of all we are capable of producing. If they can't remember that number, they should write it on their palms. Americans don't want to be Europeanized.

U.S. Health Care Still Tops

Advocates for overhauling American medicine try to bamboozle the public into believing that other countries offer better care at a lower cost. On *Meet the Press* in August 2009, Tom Daschle, designated by President Obama to be his Secretary of Health and Human Services, said that Americans were spending too much and getting poor-quality care. "The World Health Organization listed us 37th, just below Costa Rica and above Slovenia," said Daschle, arguing for an immediate overhaul. Daschle was referring to a report issued in 2000 by the World Health Organization.

That WHO ranking – 37 – became a compelling statistic in the national debate. It was cited on NPR's *Morning Edition* on Aug. 18, 2009. A *St. Louis Post Dispatch* editorial on Sept. 4, 2009, cited it as proof that action was needed. The *St. Petersburg Times* used it to rebut Sen. John McCain's claim that the U.S. has the best health care in the world.

Then, on April 22, 2010, just a month after Obama's law was signed, the truth came out about the number 37. Dr. Philip Musgrove, editor in chief of the WHO Report 2000, announced in *The New England Journal of Medicine* that it was "long past time for this zombie number to disappear from circulation." He called the ranking "meaningless." "This is not simply a problem of incomplete, inaccurate, or noncomparable data; there are also sound reasons to mistrust the conceptual framework behind the estimates. . . ."

Well said, Dr. Musgrove, although a bit tardy. The WHO deemed the U.S. No. 1 for "responsiveness to the needs of patients." But the U.S. was demoted to 37th for "overall performance" because the WHO report gave far more credit overall to countries in which government finances all health care, calling it fairer than a market system.

Also influential was a bag-of-tricks report from The Commonwealth Fund, an organization that favors government-run health care and tailors its research conclusions to support that view. During the Senate debate over health reform, Sen. Kent Conrad (D-N.D.) pointed to a large blue chart showing the United States in last place in health performance. "All of these countries have much lower costs than we do," he said, "and they have higher quality outcomes than ours."

Conrad was duped by a Commonwealth report published in *Health Affairs* in 2008 that puts the U.S. in 19th place due to diseases that are curable if treated soon enough.

Yet most of these deaths are caused by heart disease and circulatory diseases. The United States has a high incidence because for 50 years, Americans were the heaviest smokers and now are among the most obese. Bad behavior, not bad medicine, is to blame. Our health care system treats these diseases very effectively.

As the National Bureau of Economic Research concluded, "It seems inaccurate to attribute … high death rates from these causes to a poorly performing medical system."

Plus, while the Commonwealth researchers claimed to consider curable diseases of all sorts, they conspicuously omitted malignant prostate cancer – where U.S. care is stunningly successful. An American man diagnosed with it has a 99.3 percent chance of surviving it – far higher than in any Western European country. It's not a death sentence here, but in Scotland, only 71 percent survive, and in Germany, only 85 percent.

Conrad also trotted out another "pro-reform" statistic, pointing to a "shorter [U.S.] life expectancy compared with other industrialized countries." Again, demographers are quite clear on this. The causes of reduced U.S. life expectancy are our higher rates of auto fatalities and violent crime, plus half a century of excessive smoking – not bad medicine.

Setting the record straight, the National Bureau of Economic Research cautions that "the low longevity ranking of the United States is not likely to be a result of a poor functioning health care system."

The best measure of any nation's medical care is how likely *you* are to survive a serious illness and resume your previous active lifestyle. Cancer survival rates are unambiguous evidence of American achievement. Yet during the debate over health care reform, even National Breast Cancer Awareness Month was misused to promote the White House's agenda. If cancer runs in your family, this political propaganda could be dangerous to your health.

First Lady Michelle Obama stood with breast cancer survivors at a White House ceremony on Oct. 22, 2009, and claimed that American health care is "a system that only adds to the fear and stress that already comes with the disease."

The truth is, a woman diagnosed with breast cancer in the U.S. has a 90 percent chance of surviving it. In Europe, a woman's chance of survival is below 80 percent on average. These statistics, from the National Bureau of Economic Research, reflect the experiences of all women, not just those with insurance.

According to the bureau's research, women fare better in the U.S. because breast cancer is diagnosed earlier and treated more aggressively. Death rates from breast cancer have declined faster in the U.S. than anywhere else.

In the American system, there is a premium on the development of new detection methods and therapies. In other countries, government health programs delay adopting innovations in order to keep treatment costs down.

President Obama's Nobel Prize captured headlines in October 2009. But if breast cancer is a worry for you, three other Nobel Prizes awarded that month are more important. Scientists working in the U.S. took the Nobel Prize in Medicine for their research on how cancer cells continue to divide and duplicate far longer than healthy cells. Their research may hold the key to stopping the relentless growth of cancer.

Only one of these three Nobel scientists, Dr. Carol Greider, was born in the United States. The others were born in countries with government-run health care but chose to relocate to the U.S. to pursue their careers in medicine. Dr. Elizabeth Blackburn emigrated from Australia to the U.S. in the 1970s because, she told *The New York Times*, this country was "notably attractive" as a place to do research. Dr. Jack Szostak came from London.

The unrivaled pace of medical discovery in the U.S. is largely responsible for higher cancer survival rates here, according to the research bureau. Innovation is also responsible for about two-thirds of the annual increase in American health care spending, according to presidential adviser Blumenthal, writing in *The New England Journal of Medicine* in March 2001. Blumenthal and other advocates of ObamaCare want to slow down the adoption of new technologies. But no one battling cancer wants to settle for what oncologists had to offer a decade ago, and 10 years from now, no one will want to settle for 2010 treatments. The pace of innovation does add to costs, but it also gives families reason to hope.

Since 1950, the U.S. has won more Nobel Prizes in medicine and physiology than the rest of the world combined. If someone in your family is dealing with an illness still considered incurable, this is the nation of hope. Highest cancer survival rates and fastest development of cures – compelling reasons this is the fight of our lifetime.

The Dangerous Ideas of the President's Medical Adviser in Chief

The new Obama health law puts important decisions about your care in the hands of presidential appointees. They will decide what insurance plans cover, how much leeway your doctor will have, and what seniors get under Medicare. Chief among these advisers is Dr. Ezekiel Emanuel, brother of White House Chief of Staff Rahm Emanuel. Dr. Emanuel has already been appointed to two key positions: health policy adviser at the Office of Management and Budget and member of the Federal Coordinating Council for Comparative Effectiveness Research.

Dr. Emanuel says that health care reform will not be pain-free and that the usual recommendations for cutting medical spending (often urged by the president) are mere window dressing. As he wrote in the Feb. 27, 2008, issue of the *Journal of the American Medical Association*, or *JAMA*: "Vague promises of savings from cutting waste, enhancing prevention and wellness, installing electronic medical records, and improving quality are merely 'lipstick' cost control, more for show and public relations than for true change."

True reform, he argues, must include redefining doctors' ethical obligations. In the June 18, 2008, issue of *JAMA*, Dr. Emanuel blames the Hippocratic Oath for the "overuse" of medical care: "Medical school education and postgraduate education emphasize thoroughness," he writes. "This culture is further reinforced by a unique understanding of professional obligations, specifically the Hippocratic Oath's admonition to 'use my power to help the sick to the best of my ability and judgment' as an imperative to do everything for the patient regardless of cost or effect on others."

Dr. Emanuel chastises physicians for thinking only about their own patients' needs: "Patients were to receive whatever services they needed, regardless of its cost. Reasoning based on cost has been strenuously resisted; it violated the Hippocratic Oath, was associated with rationing, and derided as putting a price on life."

"In the next decade, every country will face very hard choices about how to allocate scarce medical resources," Emanuel predicted in the Sept. 19, 2002, issue of *The New England Journal of Medicine*.

"You can't avoid these questions," Dr. Emanuel said in an Aug. 16, 2009, interview in *The Washington Post*. "We had a big controversy in the United States when there were a limited number of dialysis machines. In Seattle, they appointed what they called a 'God committee' to choose who should get it, and that committee was eventually abandoned. Society ended up paying the whole bill for dialysis instead of having people make those decisions." Emanuel obviously feels more comfortable than most of us do with the notion of a panel or committee playing God.

In *TheLancet.com* on Jan. 31, 2009, Dr. Emanuel and co-authors presented a "complete lives system" for the allocation of very scarce resources, such as kidneys, vaccines, dialysis machines, and intensive care beds. Dr. Emanuel makes a clear choice: "When implemented, the complete lives system produces a priority curve on which individuals aged between roughly 15 and 40 years get the most substantial chance, whereas the youngest and oldest people get chances that are attenuated."

Dr. Emanuel concedes that his plan appears to discriminate against older people, but he explains, "Unlike allocation by sex or race, allocation by age is not invidious discrimination.... Treating 65-year-olds differently because of stereotypes or falsehoods would be ageist; treating them differently because they have already had more life-years is not."

The youngest are also put at the back of the line: "Adolescents have received substantial education and parental care, investments that will be wasted without a complete life. Infants, by contrast, have not yet received these investments."

Dr. Emanuel urged the president to push forward with the Obama health law, no matter how intensely Americans opposed it. On Nov. 16, 2008, he recommended that the president use Chicago-style arm twisting if necessary. "If the automakers want a bailout, then they and their suppliers have to agree to support and lobby for the administration's health care reform effort."

That's how the Obama health law got passed.

Medicare's Proposed Rationer in Chief Donald Berwick

On April 19, 2010, President Obama nominated Dr. Donald Berwick to head the Centers for Medicare & Medicaid Services. Berwick is a dangerous choice for seniors and baby boomers who will be depending on Medicare.

Berwick confesses to having a love affair – a "romance," he says – with the British National Health Service. In a speech commemorating the NHS's 60th anniversary, he praises its orderliness, frugality, redistribution of wealth, and explicit rationing. "Behold the mess – the far bigger, costlier, unfair mess" that is health care in the U.S., he says.

Berwick has radical plans to transform American medical care. He laid them out in his "Triple Aim" plan published in 2008 in *Health Affairs*. He concedes the "pain of the transition" will entail "the disruption of institutions, forms, habits, beliefs, and income streams in the status quo...." The new Obama health law will allow Berwick to transform Medicare without any further approval by Congress or the American public. The law authorizes the executive branch to create pilot programs – reorganizing how and where patients are treated, what choices they have, how their doctors are paid, and what medical services they can get – and then expands these programs on a nationwide basis as quickly as possible.

When the president campaigned for his health legislation, he told people with insurance not to worry. If you like your doctor and your coverage, you won't have to change, he repeatedly promised. Americans didn't vote for the pain of transition. Yet Berwick's writings indicate the large changes in store for Medicare patients.

First, expect an environment of medical scarcity, meaning fewer MRIs and other equipment and longer waits to be treated. Applauding the British system at its anniversary, he said, "You [the NHS] plan the supply; you aim a bit low; historically, you prefer slightly too little of a technology or service to much too much; and then you search for care bottlenecks and try to relieve them."

Second, expect that your own health choices will be "managed" by a "medical home." You will no longer be the one deciding when to see a doctor or consult a specialist. Medical home is this decade's version of HMO-style medicine, according to the Congressional Budget Office, with a primary care provider to oversee your access to costly services such as visits to specialists and diagnostic tests. In his "Triple Aim" plan, Berwick says not to expect your primary care provider to be a physician. Many, perhaps most, will be nurses or physician's assistants. Currently, Medicare patients can decide to see a doctor and Medicare pays. Not in the future.

Worse still, if you do get to a doctor, don't expect the doctor to be able to make decisions based on your individual case. Physician autonomy is a thing of the past, argues Berwick, who wrote an essay called "The Epitaph of Profession" in the 2009 *British Journal of General Practice.*

Berwick earned accolades for his 100,000 Lives Campaign, a superb effort to codify and disseminate guidelines to keep patients safe from infections, bedsores, and other unintended consequences of medical care. In the area of patient safety, guidelines should be rigorously enforced. There are no disagreements about the need for clean hands. Patient safety rules are like the rules a pilot follows in the cockpit. But beyond patient safety, in fields from cardiology to obstetrics, there are numerous disagreements on what are best practices. Yet Berwick argues aggressively for almost eliminating physician leeway.

In his "Triple Aim" plan, Berwick deplores the American heath care system as "designed to respond to the acute needs of individual patients." His plan is to "anticipate and shape patterns of care for important subgroups." Subgroups could be defined by age, affliction, or socioeconomic status. Woe to you if you're not in a favored subgroup or part of the plan. In his beloved British National Health Service, those decisions are made by what he lauds as the "maddening, majestic machinery of politics." The elderly fare poorly in that system, as you can see by visiting a ward reserved for their care in a British hospital. You will find long rows of beds, sometimes even without a privacy curtain, and cancer survival rates far lower than current survival rates in the U.S.

Second Opinions from America's Leading Physicians

Many physicians understood the dire consequences of the Obama proposals for their own patients. President Obama didn't consult with them. But on Oct. 19, 2009, a group of highly regarded physicians assembled at the Grand Hyatt hotel in New York City. Here is what they had to say on the fundamental issues:

On Treating the Elderly

Dr. Seymour Cohen, oncologist, named to "America's Top Doctors": "When we went to medical school, people used to die at 66, 67, and 68. Medicare paid for two or three years. Social Security paid for two or three years.

We're the bad guys. We're responsible for keeping people alive to 85. So we're now going to try to change health care because people are living too long. It just doesn't make very good sense to me."

Shifting Resources From Specialty to Primary Care

Dr. Jeffrey Moses, interventional cardiologist, named to "America's Top Doctors": "If you have heart failure or heart attack or coronaries in general in the hospital, you need to be treated by a cardiologist. Study after study shows that ... when you have an illness and you want to have an accurate diagnosis and the most up-to-date and accurate treatment, you want a specialist."

Patient Privacy

Dr. Samuel Guillory, ophthalmologist, refractive and orbital surgery, named to Castle Connolly's "New York's Top Doctors": "We're being asked by the executive branch ... to break the code with patients and deliver all their records into electronic medical records...."

Cost-Cutting Methods

Dr. David Fields, obstetrician and gynecologist, Lenox Hill Hospital, New York: "Government is in the process of duplicating everything that managed care did for the last 15 years that was reviled by everybody and which we fought very hard to overcome.... Capitation was the worst thing that ever happened to medical care."

Dr. Tracy Pfeifer, plastic surgeon, former president, New York Regional Society of Plastic Surgeons: "When physicians graduate from medical school, we take an oath, the Hippocratic Oath, to do no harm to our patients.... These government programs that are being proposed I think are very scary in the sense that physicians could be induced to violate the Hippocratic Oath."

Dr. Joel Kassimir, dermatologist, Mount Sinai Hospital, New York: "We're now being told by physicians advising the president that we take the Hippocratic Oath too seriously."

A 20-Page Bill in Plain English to Reduce Premiums and Help Laid-Off Americans

This Bill Is Not Dangerous to Your Health or Your Freedom

Contains No Mandates Forcing Individuals or States to Do Anything

Every day, Americans tell me they want a bill written in plain English. They want members of Congress to read the entire bill before voting. They want a bill anyone can inspect. A 20-page bill means that pork projects, secret deals, and exemptions for Washington insiders cannot be slipped between the pages. The language in this bill does not give the American people the runaround.

Twenty pages should be enough. The framers of the Constitution established the entire federal government in just 18 pages.

This bill recognizes that states have regulated health insurance for more than six decades, consistent with the McCarran-Ferguson Act of 1945. Some states have taken smart approaches to lowering costs and expanding access, especially for people with pre-existing conditions. This bill copies what works.

Title 1: Liberates consumers to buy policies from

other states and puts consumers on notice that the products they buy out of state may have different consumer protections than those imposed in their own state. This title also imposes federal consumer protections on plans sold interstate, ensuring that those plans prohibit rescission and protect consumers who have paid their premiums from being dropped. An HMO plan costs a 25-year-old California male $260 a month, while a New Yorker has to pay $1,228 for a similar plan. Free the New Yorker to shop outside his state.

TITLE 2: Provides federal incentives for states to establish medical courts, ensuring quicker, fairer verdicts in medical liability cases and at the same time preserving every litigant's right to trial by jury. Medical courts will be presided over by a judge who knows the issues, has the experience, and can identify honest expert witnesses. (The judge will also reduce the impact of those who are not honest. Tort law has always been a matter left to states.) This bill does not mandate that states establish medical courts or attempt to federalize tort law. It does provide block grants to states to impose caps on damages and, more importantly, to establish medical courts. Why just cap unjust damage awards when you can eliminate them by having expert judges?

TITLE 3: Provides federal incentives for states to establish or improve subsidized high-risk pools to help consumers with pre-existing conditions and poor health. (This concept is similar to what is also proposed in the Patients' Choice Act, supported by Sen. Tom Coburn (R-Okla.). No state is required to establish these pools.)

TITLE 4: Extends the current 65 percent COBRA subsidy, established by the American Recovery and Reinvestment Act of 2009. The president's fiscal year 2011 budget also contains such an extension. Republicans are likely to find this an important common ground. COBRA subsidies are not a permanent entitlement but rather a temporary helping hand to those who have been laid off. The average COBRA annual premium for a family of four is $13,322, a big price tag when you've lost your job. For more than half of uninsured Americans legally in this country, being uninsured is a temporary problem. They find another job and are insured again in less than a year. We need to help them in between jobs. The 10-year cost of Titles 1, 2, and 3 of this bill is $27 billion. The COBRA extension is already included in the president's fiscal year 2011 budget. Funding this COBRA subsidy could cost $24 billion per year and provide coverage for an estimated 7 million people.

You can read the entire bill at:

www.defendyourhealthcare.us.

When you're told that "something had to be done" and the "Obama health law is better than nothing," you have the answer: Here is a 20-page bill that will help make insurance affordable and help the uninsured. It can be done without lowering your standard of care, putting the government in charge of your care, or taking away your freedom.

The American people should be calling on the president and Congress to repeal the ObamaCare law.

STEPHEN MOORE

HOW BARACK OBAMA IS BANKRUPTING THE U.S. ECONOMY

Barack Obama's chief of staff let the cat out of the bag when, shortly after Obama was elected president, he said, "A crisis is a terrible thing to waste." Washington loves a crisis because it justifies the existence of bureaucrats, politicians, federal agencies, and edicts. Government becomes the savior – even, as now, when government policy mistakes created the crisis in the first place. This is why government in Washington always expands and very rarely recedes during a national security or economic crisis.

So when the stock market crashed by 1,200 points, big banks like Lehman Brothers, Bear Stearns, and Citibank teetered on the brink of bankruptcy and the financial system seemed on the verge of a 1929-style collapse, the answer proposed by politicians and bureaucrats was the greatest experiment in Big Government in 50 years.

Did it work? Ask Vice President Joe Biden, and the answer is, it worked – as he put it in September 2009 – "beyond my wildest dreams." But for most Americans, this is a nightmare, not a dream come true. In fact, the $2.8 trillion experiment in government that began tentatively in George W. Bush's first three years and continued with arrogant enthusiasm during Obama's first months has been a depressing failure. For all of President Obama's cheery talk of "necessary government intervention to prevent a depression," the statistics tell a demoralizing tale:

- The dollar stands at only 60 percent of its value in 2007, as our paper currency continues to deteriorate in purchasing power.

- The U.S. gross domestic product fell by a breathtaking 9 percent. Some $7 trillion of wealth had evaporated from the start of the recession through autumn 2009.

- In 2012, there were still 5 million more Americans unemployed before the September 2008 crash, and all the job stimulus bills. After four years of Obama policies, the unemployment rate has remained above 8 percent for 36 straight months.

- The debt has already widened by $5 trillion, and the hands on the debt clock can barely swirl fast enough to keep pace with the voracious borrowing of the present Congress.

- The Census Bureau reports that personal incomes and wealth of Americans took their worst tumble in two decades as the poverty rate increased – *after* the government fix.

As we stare at these facts through the haze of Obamanomics, we can see certain truths. We know, for instance, that a major trigger point for our depressed economy was too much debt and too much spending that we couldn't afford.

Households accumulated too much credit-card and mortgage debt. Businesses took on too much leverage (think of Bear Stearns and Lehman Brothers, with debt-to-asset ratios of more than 30-to-1). And the federal government took on more debt than any other institution on the face of the planet, most of it to finance absurdly wasteful spending. Some of this spending took place under Republicans, as Rep. Nancy Pelosi, Sen. Harry Reid and the rest of the Democrats who now run Congress never tired of telling us when their party did not control the White House. But when Pelosi became speaker of the House, the deficit was $160 billion. It went to $400 billion in one year, and, another year later, the deficit reached $1.5 trillion.

So if the Democrats were telling us that all of this excessive debt under Bush caused the economic crisis, how is more debt supposed to get us out of it? The idea of borrowing more and more money today to pay off all the people we borrowed money from in the 1990s and 2000s is a debt-based Ponzi scheme – Bernie Madoff economics.

Cash for Policy Clunkers

The excruciating history of a year's worth of relentless policy mistakes can be retold in a hurry. First came the bailout of Bear Stearns, the Wall Street investment bank. That cost an estimated $29 billion – a jaw-dropping figure at the time that would soon seem like loose change.

Then came the $400 billion federal bailout of Fannie Mae and Freddie Mac, the quasi-governmental home mortgage guarantee agency. Rep. Barney Frank, the chairman of the House Financial Services Committee, had condemned editorials in *The Wall Street Journal* for calling these agencies houses of cards with huge and mounting systemic risk. Frank told us that they didn't need adult supervision. He even said that when it came to Fannie Mae, he wanted to "roll the dice." Uncle Sam did just this, and we all had to pay when the dice crapped out.

But Congress was just getting started. Two weeks later came the AIG insurance company bailout, another $182 billion when all was said and done. But this was just a warm-up for the $700 billion bailout of the banks. The Troubled Asset Relief Program, or TARP, took money from taxpayers and sound banks and handed it over to banks that took on excessive risks with subprime mortgages. Some banks might be in better shape a year later, but we've allowed others that should have failed to keep operating, rewarding bad risks and excessive leveraging and sanctifying a new doctrine in finance called "too big to fail."

Some of the best economists I know believe that the bailout of the banks was absolutely necessary to prevent a collapse of the financial system. They worried that we might have had a domino effect of failing banks without the infusion of tax funds to keep the banks solvent. Perhaps that is true. We did, thankfully, avert a 1930s-style bankruptcy contagion of the banks. One big problem, however, is that the bank-rescue plan has become an excuse in Washington to bail out any large firm that is facing bankruptcy. We now have a de facto "too big to fail" doctrine in Washington, where nearly every major corporation has an implicit federal taxpayer safety net to protect them from the repercussions of their bad business decisions or their financial gambles that don't pay off.

As the Obama administration took power, White House Chief of Staff Rahm Emanuel, embellishing on his comment about not wasting a crisis, told a liberal audience that they could, in fact, use the financial crisis to "do things that they normally could not do." And President Obama quickly acted on that insight by asking Congress to enact a $1 trillion spending plan that went to items that had been jotted down on the liberal wish list, without much hope of ever coming to pass, over the previous 40 years.

There would be money for the National Endowment for the Arts, for Head Start, for unemployment insurance, for renewable energy subsidies, for a new fleet of cars for bureaucrats. There would be a bailout of the pork industry (how appropriate!), tens of billions for new labor union jobs and housing aid that would be ciphered through corrupt left-wing "welfare lobby groups," like ACORN (Association of Community Organizations for Reform Now).

This was supposed to result in "shovel-ready infrastructure," like roads, bridges, and school construction. But only 15 percent of the money was for such brick-and-mortar projects. Most of the rest of the money lined the pockets of the groups that made the 2008 election possible. Even Congress, though, couldn't stomach a $1 trillion program when the budget deficit was already headed to $1 trillion – nearly double the all-time record. So the price tag was shaved to $800 billion and passed with pompous pronouncements about how the public weal had been served.

The president noted that amid this spending free-for-all, families would be getting tax-rebate checks of $500 to $1,000 to help make ends meet. What a deal, responded Brian Riedl, budget expert of The Heritage Foundation. Tax cuts of $1,000 for a family, but $13,000 in new debt.

The Obama budget is filled with more than three dozen tax credits and new spending programs allegedly designed to help stretch the incomes of middle-class families – including Obama's signature tax cut of a $400 credit per household. But to get the $400 tax credit, each family in America will have to bear nearly $100,000 of its share of the new debt on the federal credit card. No wonder so many Americans have come to recognize the Obama giveaways as a kind of fool's gold!

But the Obama administration was just getting started. A few weeks after the stimulus came the president's new 10-year budget blueprint, a decadelong socialist fantasy that read as though ghostwritten by Hugo Chávez. It called for $40 trillion of government spending over the next decade, financed by tax hikes on the rich (more about that later) and an ungodly level of new debt, projected at $9 trillion – which surely was an underestimate. Under Obamanomics, the government would borrow more money in 10 years than it had in the first 225 years.

Government Motors

The Obama administration wasn't finished completing the nationalization of industry that began with banks, mortgage companies, insurance firms, and Wall Street investment houses. Next on the debt assembly line was a multibillion-dollar takeover of the auto industry allegedly designed to save Chrysler and General Motors but actually created to rescue the United Auto Workers. With a potential price tag of $100 billion for the two companies, it would have been cheaper for taxpayers to write a $300,000 check for every autoworker at GM and Chrysler in return for their promise never to make another car.

In the unconstitutional bankruptcy that was designed by shrewd UAW lawyers and the White House, the federal government essentially stole $3 billion to $5 billion from the companies, which was rightfully owned by the GM and Chrysler creditors, and reassigned the money to the unions. This overrode hundreds of years of corporate contract law that says creditors are first in line – before stock owners, workers, and other stakeholders – to claim the assets of a company. The Obama administration ripped up those creditors' contracts and strong-armed the bondholders to take pennies on the dollars they were owed. Lost in the shuffle was an obvious and enduring truth: America is a rich nation, after all, precisely because we believe in the sanctity of contracts and property rights.

GM and Chrysler emerged from a trumped-up bankruptcy owned jointly by the United States government, the Canadian government, and the autoworkers union. Given the congenital incapacity of government to run enterprises at a profit, the likely result is that U.S. taxpayers will be shoveling tens of billions of dollars into these car companies year after year until Government Motors finally goes out of business. Think Amtrak.

Obama says the bailouts were a success, but the federal government still hasn't paid back all the money it had loaned to the auto industry – and it probably never will. Meanwhile, Ford is financially healthy and took no taxpayer dollars.

An even more unprecedented seizure of power was the Fed's decision to buy up failing assets in the U.S. – especially subprime mortgages. The Fed more than doubled the assets it holds on its balance sheet, from $1 trillion to roughly $2 trillion. The collateral standing behind thousands of these mortgage-backed securities are subprime homes that have already been defaulted or foreclosed on. They are junk-quality bonds, bought by taxpayers to further bail out banks and homeowners. The Fed even began to buy up more than $1 trillion of treasury securities under a program called QE2.

* * *

A Debtfare State

It is hard to believe today that in 2006, when Democrats took over Congress, Pelosi stated, "Democrats are committed to no deficit spending. We will not heap mountains of debt onto future generations."

It wasn't hard to claim the mantle of fiscal responsibility back then, because the Republicans had created half-trillion-dollar deficits. So in 2006 and 2007, Pelosi preached to us from the Gospel According to St. Robert Rubin that the Bush budget deficits are evil and immoral and driving up interest rates; we need to atone for those sins by repealing the Bush tax cuts; and we must install pay-as-you-go budgeting so big deficits never happen again.

But once they took power and the economy wavered, the Democrats discovered the irrelevance of fiscal discipline. No lesser an authority than Rubin himself declared in early September 2009 that deficits aren't so bad after all: "Fiscal stimulus can give the economy a timely boost in the face of great uncertainty and concern with the short-term economic outlook." In other words, go out and run up the federal credit card, and you can still feel good about yourself in the morning, although there will ultimately come a morning that is the morning after.

As the current recession has worsened, Congress and then Obama have kept bidding up the price of a stimulus. First, it was $40 billion. Then Secretary of State Hillary Clinton said $60 billion. On the eve of the financial meltdown, Pelosi was talking $100 billion. Then Obama proposed his $1 trillion spending bomb. But the Congressional Budget Office forecast was that we were already scheduled to borrow $1 trillion in 2009 – without any further stimulus. This was already twice as much borrowing as in any year since World War II.

A few weeks later, the Obama budget was delivered into our laps. That budget increases government spending by $817 billion over the next five years, and those numbers are lowball estimates. The debt grows by more than $1 trillion a year for the next five years, settling at $11.5 trillion in 2013. Over the decade, the debt rises by $9 trillion. It creates major new entitlements for health care, welfare, and unemployment benefits that could blow another $2 trillion hole in the already $50 trillion unfunded liabilities crisis. The roughly 8,000 domestic agencies of government receive a $50.9 billion budget hike. That's a 9.3 percent spending hike over last year, which is spectacularly generous, given that many federal agencies already received more than 70 percent increases in their budgets, thanks to the $800 billion stimulus plan passed earlier this year. The president also proposed a $150 billion line of credit for new foreign aid programs, almost three times more than ever spent.

Yet only a few days after this budget was released, the president promised a return to "fiscal responsibility." He told the country that his agenda of bailouts, budget deficits, and runaway spending is motivated "not because I believe in bigger government – I don't." You could have fooled me.

In the Ronald Reagan, George H. W. Bush, and Bill Clinton years, when Democrats wanted to raise taxes, they argued that the deficit must be brought down to lower interest rates. But now they propose to raise the deficit exponentially, exposing the deficit phobia of the Rubin wing of the Democratic party as a hypocritical ruse for Democrats to pay homage to "fiscal responsibility" when Republicans want to cut tax rates to grow the economy. When Democrats want to grow government spending, deficits don't matter so much after all – even when they are in the trillions of dollars.

In a public-relations ploy to pretend to prove that the president really does want a "new era of fiscal responsibility," the Obama budget office scrubbed line by line through the budget to find waste, fraud, and abuse. It discovered $16.7 billion of budget savings by cutting 121 programs. This is about how much the feds spend every three days, or, to be more exact, 0.45 cents of savings out of every dollar Uncle Sam will spend this year.

By all means, get rid of the Denali job training program (savings: $3 million), USDA public broadcasting grants (savings: $5 million), and payments to high-income farmers (savings: $58 million). But compared with the moonshot approach needed to deal with debt, this was a bottle rocket. Three-quarters of the budget savings come from the national defense budget, not from domestic agencies. Of the 10-year savings of $71 billion in entitlement programs – which are now a mind-numbing $62.9 trillion in debt over the long-term – one-third of the cutbacks are not cuts at all: They are tax increases, mostly on the oil and gas industries.

This left $4.7 billion of cuts from programs like agriculture subsidies and Medicare, which sounds like a lot, but at the very moment Obama was announcing these cuts, the Democrats in the Senate were pushing forward a new universal health care program that will add between $1 trillion and $1.5 trillion of *new* unfunded costs over those same 10 years.

It's hard to take $17 billion of savings seriously when the government spent more than 10 times that much money to bail out one company, AIG. At the pace Obama is setting, with $16.7 billion of savings a year and assuming no new debt, the budget will be balanced by around 2110.

The Obama administration and congressional Democrats defend their record deficits and debt by pointing the

Federal Outlays by Category, 2001–2008

(*Inflation Adjusted*)

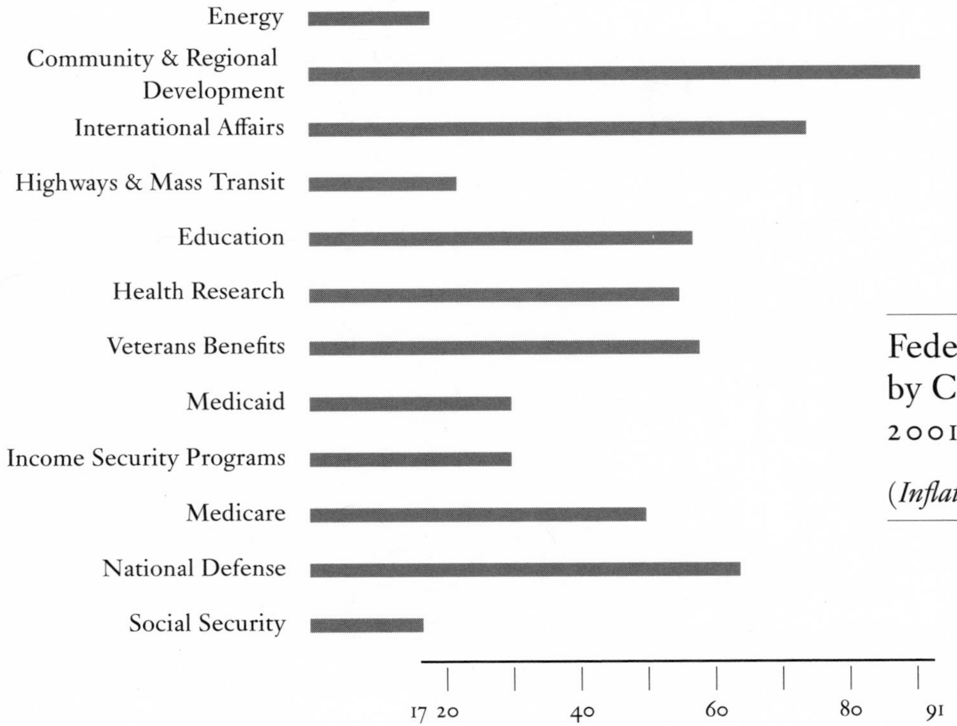

finger at Bush. And, in fact, spending in the eight years before Obama came to power expanded from $1.789 trillion in 2000 to $2.979 trillion in 2008. That's a 67 percent increase. How many Americans saw *their* incomes grow by 67 percent? Quick, raise your hand.

Now that they are in power, the Democrats claim that the spendthrift Bush years were pinched and niggardly, intentionally starving vital infrastructure and social services. But this idea is confounded by the chart below, which compares government spending with the major areas of "investment" that liberals insist need more funding. Most of these areas grew during the Bush presidency by four, five, or six times the rate of inflation.

In Obama's first half-year in office, these budgets rose another 54 percent – or 30 times the rate of inflation – according to the House Committee on the Budget. In 2012, Barack Obama's budget called for $8 to $10 trillion of new debt over the next decade.

The Soak-the-Rich Fallacy

High tax rates are a staple of the Obama agenda. As the president has put it, the people who made money in the past two decades of Bush-enabled greed should pay more to cover the cost of health care, unemployment insurance, foreign aid, and bridges to nowhere.

The tax increases he has proposed would bring tax rates on the productive and job-creating class in America to their highest levels since the 1970s. Obama would raise the capital gains tax rate to 23.8 percent from the current 15 percent, the dividend tax to 43 percent from 15 percent, and the income tax rate to 42 percent from 35 percent. He also wants a "Buffett rule" applied to millionaires and billionaires. Combined, this would raise the highest tax rate to the 45–50 percent range. The table below shows the impact of all of these tax rate hikes.

Since roughly two out of three of tax filers who fall into this income category are small-business owners, operators, or investors, these taxes are aimed straight at the balance sheet of the American entrepreneur and job creator. Can higher tax liabilities entice this group to hire more workers? (It's worth noting that in the first four years that Bush cut these tax rates, tax payments by Americans with an income of more than $1 million doubled, and jobs increased by 8 million.)

There is another problem with the notion that soaking the rich will balance the budget. Even if the federal government were to take every penny from those who are in the richest 1 percent of income, this would only yield a little less than $2 trillion. That is what the government spends in eight months. So even a 100 percent tax wouldn't raise enough. The Congressional Budget Office says that tax rates would have to rise to 75 percent or 80 percent to balance the budget in the coming years. Even many liberals agree that tax rates that high would destroy the U.S. economy.

Obama Tax Plan

	Current	Obama Proposal
Income Tax Rate	35%	42%
Capital Gains	15%	23.8%
Dividends	15%	43%
Estate Tax	35–45%	55%

Barack Obama, Meet Christina Romer

One person whose research shows that higher taxes can be chaotic and destructive is Christina Romer, the president's chief economic adviser. Here is what she said about taxes, back when she was teaching at the University of California, Berkeley: "Tax increases appear to have a very large, sustained, and highly significant negative impact on output."

Romer and her husband, David Romer, who were professors of economics at the University of California, Berkeley, wrote this in an exhaustive 2009 study on U.S. tax policy changes over the past 100 years. The Obama economics team should pay closer attention to one of its own. Christina Romer's findings are a tutorial on why raising tax rates, especially during a time of economic crisis, can be highly destructive.

Perhaps most relevant to the current economic policy debate is Romer's analysis of the Herbert Hoover income-tax-rate increases at the start of the Great Depression. She writes, "The revenue act of 1932 increased American tax rates greatly in an attempt to balance the budget, and by doing so dealt another contractionary blow to the economy. . . ." Repeating that mistake would be a grievous error.

Raising tax rates for the rich is simply a futile way to raise government revenues. Back in 1980, when the top tax rate was 70 percent, the richest 1 percent paid 19 percent of all income taxes. Today, with a top tax rate of 35 percent, the richest 1 percent pay 40.1 percent of income taxes. Cutting the tax rate in half *doubled* the tax contribution from the rich. If you want a growing economy, more investment, more jobs, and a lower deficit, cut tax rates, don't raise them.

Even the Congressional Budget Office admits that the new "Buffett rule" will raise less than $5 billion a year. That is 0.5 percent of the deficit. The budget deficit is $1.2 trillion. Where will the other $1.195 trillion come from? This brings us to the greatest myth of all, that 95 percent of Americans will be spared the agony of tax cuts. It was Obama's most memorable promise. But now, Democrats are starting to see they can't pay for all their spending and get the money from the richest 1 percent, 2 percent, or even 5 percent of our citizens. So, for example, the $1 trillion health care reform bill includes seven new taxes on the middle class, including a $3,000 income tax penalty on working families who don't purchase health insurance.

Middle-Class Tax Bomb

After 3½ years in office and the wildest spending binge in history – already $3.4 trillion of new federal spending has been enacted or proposed for the next decade – the Obama administration concluded that for the government to pay its bills, taxes are going to have go up – way up. And not just on the richest 1 percent, 2 percent, or 5 percent, but on everyone – not with an income above $250,000 but above $2,500.

It's not hard to figure out how they've come to this conclusion. The Chinese, among others, have warned that Obama's $10 trillion of deficits over the next decade could upend the entire world financial system. But this White House isn't remotely interested in cutting spending. Its top priority is to hatch a new 10-year, $1 trillion health care charge when the existing health care programs are already $30 trillion in debt.

No responsible economist believes the Obama fairy tale, that this deficit can be brought down substantially by taxing the rich. It is the middle class, which the president admits is living paycheck-to-paycheck in this recession, that will ultimately have the privilege of paying for his administration's unpaid bills for an $880 billion stimulus plan, $200 billion in industry bailouts, the trillion-dollar health care expansions, and hundreds of billions for renewable energy subsidies.

Now we need to worry that in a second Obama term, we will be hit with the tax the American left has secretly coveted for decades: a European-style national sales tax, or value-added tax (VAT). A 5 percent national sales tax would be a cash cow for Uncle Sam, raising $250 billion to $500 billion a year, depending on exemptions. This is, of course, a highly regressive tax and blows to smithereens once and for all the idea that the middle class gets a net tax cut under Obama. (The experience of Europe is that VATs have not lowered budget deficits but instead have given politicians money to underwrite the socialists' cradle-to-grave welfare state expansions.)

The Democrats have long wanted to install a Swedish-style gold-plated welfare state in America, and all that has been missing is the Swedish-style tax on families to pay for it. To get from here to there, the left will have to tax the middle class, as the Europeans do, because, as Willie Sutton famously replied when asked why he robbed banks, "That is where the money is." So thanks to the $9 trillion of debt spending that we have in the pipeline, one thing is certain about paying for Obamanomics: Taxes are going up not just for the rich scapegoats but for everyone.

The Road from Serfdom

We are in the midst of one of the great ideological battles in the history of America. The left has seized on an economic crisis, largely created by its own money machine programs, to vastly expand government power well beyond anything before seen in America. It is no exaggeration to say that we will not recognize our country in 10 years if all of the spending, the cap-and-trade climate-change measures, the government takeover of the health care system, the higher tax rates, and the spectacular debt bubble endure.

We have become one nation with two wholly divergent views of how to grow a prospering economy that lifts all boats. No wonder there are massive protests among Americans all over the country marching against a not-so-slow road to socialism and tyranny.

George Washington warned against what we now face when he said, "Government is ... a fearsome master." Ronald Reagan, godfather of the alternative vision of low taxes, limited government, and individual freedom to choose, put it another way: "A government big enough to give you everything you want is big enough to take everything you've got."

At times like this, I become more nostalgic for the indispensable missing voice in this debate: Milton Friedman's. No one could slice and dice the sophistry of the left's government-market interventions better than Friedman. Imagine what he would have to say about the arrogance of the U.S. government's owning and operating the car companies or managing the $2 trillion health care industry. "Why not?" I can almost hear him ask. "After all, they've done such a wonderful job delivering the mail." (USPS, by the way, just posted a $4 billion loss, even as service deteriorates. And these are the people we are going to allow to run our health care system?)

I've been thinking a lot lately about one of my last conversations with Friedman, when he warned that "even though socialism is a discredited economic model and capitalism is raising living standards to new heights, the left intellectuals continue to push for bigger government everywhere I look." He predicted that people would be seduced by collectivist ideas again. He was right.

In the midst of this global depression, not only are rotten ideas all the rage, like trillion-dollar Keynesian stimulus plans, nationalization of banks, a government takeover of the health care system, and confiscatory taxes on America's wealth producers, but Friedmanesque principles of global free trade, low tax rates, and deregulation are being accused of murdering global prosperity. When The University of Chicago wanted to create a $200 million Milton Friedman Institute, Sen. Bernie Sanders of Vermont, a proud and self-admitted socialist, snarled that the university must never "align itself with a reactionary political program supported by the wealthiest, greediest, and most powerful people and institutions in this country." Then he finished his rant by fuming, "Friedman's ideology caused enormous damage to the American middle class and to working families here and around the world."

The indisputable truth is just the opposite, of course. Professor Andrei Shleifer, who has written a just-in-time tribute in the prestigious *Journal of Economic Literature* aptly titled "The Age of Milton Friedman," writes, "The last quarter-century [from 1980 to 2005] has witnessed remarkable progress of mankind. As the world embraced free market policies, living standards rose sharply while life expectancy, educational attainment, and democracy improved and absolute poverty declined." He documents that Deng Xiaoping in China, Margaret Thatcher of Britain, and Reagan in the U.S. led the charge toward free markets, and "all three of these leaders professed inspiration from the work of Milton Friedman."

Even the United Nations recently conceded that thanks

to the expansion of free trade and globalization, the number of people in the world living in abject poverty (on less than $1 a day) fell by almost half in the past 25 years. Friedman's ideas on capitalism and freedom, in other words, did more to liberate humankind from poverty than all of the New Deal, Great Society, welfare state, and Obama economic stimulus plans stacked on top of each other.

Perhaps the idea of Friedman's that is most in disrepute is deregulation of industries. The Obama administration is convinced that a new era of regulatory shackles on hedge funds, money managers, and banks will restore prosperity. One time, I watched a debate between Friedman and James Tobin, the Keynesian Nobel Prize-winning economist from Yale. Friedman recalled traveling to an Asian country in the 1960s and visiting a project where the government was building a canal. Friedman was shocked to see that instead of modern tractors and earth movers digging the canal, the workers had shovels. He asked why there were so few modern machines, and the bureaucrat responded, "You don't understand – this is a jobs program." Friedman responded, "Oh, I thought you were trying to build a canal. If it's jobs you want, then you should give these workers spoons, not shovels."

My hunch is that if Friedman were alive today, he would be telling whoever had the wisdom to listen to him that everything our government has done in response to our economic crisis has been exactly the wrong thing to do.

What would Milton Friedman, architect of our past 25 years of prosperity, tell Americans who are fearful of the dark economic trough in which they now find themselves? I once asked him, if he could make three policy changes to increase economic growth, what would they be? He unhesitatingly replied, "One, promote free trade; two, create a competitive model in education; and three, cut government spending." How much should we cut spending? He said, "As much as possible."

There is a ready answer to liberals who wring their hands at the high passions and raw emotions that dominate the public square today: It's the economy, stupid. We are now witnessing, even if we don't quite realize it, a battle for the soul of America. The stakes are about as high as they have ever been. You can't tax, borrow, and inflate your way to prosperity. Government power grabs will not make us freer. And they certainly won't make us any richer. If we don't learn these lessons very soon, our children will be much the poorer for our economic ignorance and selfishness.

MICHAEL B. MUKASEY

HOW OBAMA HAS MISHANDLED THE WAR ON TERROR

Foreword

This Broadside was written in 2010, and obviously events have occurred since, but I do not think it has been in any meaningful sense overtaken by them. Osama bin Laden has been killed, as has Anwar al-Awlaki, but the failures described in the Broadside are failures of commitment and strategic vision that cannot be made up by one or two tactical successes. For example, when the president announced with justified triumph the killing of bin Laden, he announced also that we had seized a trove of intelligence from bin Laden's hideout and even disclosed the detail that the trove included the location of al Qaeda safe houses. Long-term success was sacrificed to a moment of self-indulgence. The attorney general defended the drone strike on al-Awlaki by pointing out, among other things, the requirement that capture had to be found unfeasible – which raises the interesting question of what we would have done with al-Awlaki had he been captured and specifically how valuable intelligence might have been gathered from him, interrogation protocols being limited to the Army Field Manual.

And of course, the administration is engaged in yet another attempt to get Iran to forswear nuclear weapons, when it has built nuclear facilities hardened against attack, has developed rockets that can deliver such weapons, has endured sanctions rather than permit its facilities to be inspected, and has continued to proclaim its intention to excise Israel from the Middle East.

In sum, the administration continues to live in a fantasy world in which choices have no consequences, and it invites the nation to do the same.

* * *

EARLY ONE AFTERNOON in the mid-1990s, a then colleague of mine, Judge John Sprizzo of the U.S. District Court for the Southern District of New York, and I were returning from lunch, and as we walked up Pearl Street in lower Manhattan, he surveyed the scene – a dump truck blocking vehicular access to the street; concrete barriers in front of the courthouse; deputy U.S. marshals brought in from other districts around the country, clad in black SWAT uniforms and bulletproof vests and carrying firearms of a sort more associated with the battlefield than the cityscape. Sprizzo shook his head: "What the hell are we doing here? This is a military problem, not a legal problem." That casual comment has seemed, at least in retrospect, like lightning in the middle of the night, suddenly and starkly illuminating the landscape before darkness envelops it again. Of course, even the darkest night gives way to dawn, and it should by now be clear to all but the most obtuse that terrorism is substantially a military problem, and military means and measures, even military tribunals, are the appropriate way to deal with some or all of it.

The scene Judge Sprizzo was looking at and reacting to had been precipitated by the February 1993 bombing of the World Trade Center that killed six people; injured more than a thousand and caused tens of millions of dollars in damage; and led to the trial of four of the perpetrators. Among the plotters' announced goals was securing freedom for El Sayyid Nosair, who had been convicted in the state courts of New York in connection with the November 1990 murder of Meir Kahane, a right-wing Israeli politician shot by Nosair just after delivering a speech in a midtown New York hotel. Oddly, the prosecutors had presented so many overlapping witnesses with contradictory accounts of the shooting that Nosair was actually acquitted of the murder but convicted of using the weapon involved. At the time he committed his crime, Nosair had been dismissed as a lone misfit. The contents of his apartment, including jihadist literature and writings containing fantasies about attacking the United States by toppling tall buildings, had sat largely unexamined in a warehouse until after the 1993 bombing. Indeed, an amateur video of Kahane's November 1990 speech, examined in 1993, would show that present in the hall, in addition to Nosair, was Mohammed Salameh, who would later participate in the 1993 bombing to help free Nosair. Other evidence would show that Nosair was supposed to have made his escape by getting into a cab driven by Mahmud Abouhalima, another 1993 bomber, and was captured when he jumped into the wrong cab and eventually had to flee on foot.

There would be later plots, successful and unsuccessful. A partial list includes the plot in December 1994 and January 1995 to blow up airliners over the Pacific, which actually resulted in one bombing in December 1994 that killed a Japanese engineer on a flight from the Philippines to Tokyo. In addition, there were the 1998 car bombings, moments apart, at the U.S. Embassies in Nairobi, Kenya, and Dar es Salaam, Tanzania, that killed 224 people and wounded thousands, and the millennium plots that included a plan to blow up Los Angeles International Airport, foiled when Ahmed Ressam, betrayed by his nervous demeanor, was captured aboard a Seattle ferry with a bottle of explosives in the trunk of his car. An attempt to blow up the destroyer USS *The Sullivans* in Aden, Yemen, failed when the would-be suicide bombers overloaded their skiff with explosives and it sank. The follow-up of that attack, in October 2000, was the bombing of the USS *Cole* in Aden, Yemen, which killed 17 sailors.

And there would be other trials, including the trial of Ramzi Yousef, mastermind of the 1993 World Trade Center bombing and architect of the Pacific airliner bombings. There was also the trial of Omar Abdel Rahman, the so-called "blind sheikh," and several codefendants, including Nosair, for a wide-ranging terrorist plot that encompassed the Kahane murder in 1990; the 1993 World Trade Center bombing; and a plan to blow up various critical sites in New York City, including the Lincoln and Holland tunnels, FBI headquarters in Manhattan, and the United Nations. Finally, there was the prosecution of millennium bomber Ahmed Ressam.

The 1993 World Trade Center bombing was described at the time as a wake-up call to this country to take notice that it was dealing with something broader than random criminal acts. That something was Islamic violence to which this country was no longer immune. Unfortunately, our response to each subsequent act was framed in the argot of conventional criminal prosecution: a stern declaration that we would "bring to justice" those responsible. The ongoing assumption was that "justice" meant a trial in a federal court, with attendant discovery for the defendants and their supporters outside the courtroom of not only the evidence the government would introduce to convict them but also of some of the means and methods used to gather that evidence. This presented a trove of intelligence for those on the outside. For example, when the government followed the standard practice in conspiracy cases of disclosing to the defense the unindicted conspirators in the prosecution of Omar Abdel Rahman, the "blind sheikh," the list included Osama bin Laden; it was learned years later that that list found its way within weeks to bin Laden in Khartoum, Sudan.

Perhaps not unnoticed during all of this, but certainly not taken at face value, was the declaration by Osama bin Laden, first published in a London newspaper in August 1996 and reissued in 1998, that included a call to "every Muslim who believes in God and wishes to be rewarded to comply with God's order to kill the Americans and plunder their money wherever and whenever they find it."

After Sept. 11, 2001, the Bush administration made it clear that conventional criminal investigation and prosecution would no longer set the limit of the government's response. Although few had taken bin Laden seriously when he issued his call in 1998, Sept. 11 seemed to mark a turning point. To "bring them to justice" was added "bring justice to them." Relying on the Authorization for Use of Military Force issued by Congress in the days following the terrorist attacks, the administration went to war. That disconcerted many, not only those on the left, who may be expected to cringe at any assertion of executive power, particularly by a Republican administration, but even those actually engaged in the business at hand. Thus, for example, Islamic fundamentalism was not identified as the source of the problem. Indeed, even as he mobilized the nation in an address to Congress, President Bush assured us that Islam is a religion of peace and said that it had essentially been kidnapped by a band of extremists. To savor how far political correctness has carried us, and in what direction, imagine President Roosevelt telling Congress on December 8, 1941, that the peaceful Shinto religion had been kidnapped by a cabal of militarists. The Bush administration presented the war as "a war on terrorism." Anyone with a pulse knew who was supposed to be in the crosshairs. But "global war on terrorism" did not invite precise analysis of either the nature of the threat or who presented it. On the contrary, it gave an opening to those who opposed the whole enterprise. Some carped at imagined hypocrisy because the effort was directed only at Muslims and not at the IRA, Basque separatists, Peru's Shining Path guerrillas, etc. Others claimed derisively that it was at least misleading to speak of a war against a tactic rather than those employing it or their goal.

Like many disputes that engage the attention of lawyers (and the controversy over our response to terrorism has engaged lawyers to a degree never before seen in our history), this dispute turned as much heated attention on the label as on what was inside the package. The choice of label, it appeared, would determine the outcome of the debate. This was particularly so in a conflict in which the adversary did not follow the rules of war and should not have been able to invoke the protections of those rules. If the struggle legitimately could be called a war, then all the powers available to fight a war, including everything from intelligence gathering to the detention of captured combatants, would be available to us. Also, because our adversaries did not accept international conventions that had been put in place to try to civilize war to the extent possible – wearing uniforms, carrying arms openly, following a recognized chain of command, not targeting civilians – they could not reasonably invoke the protection of those conventions.

Despite its recourse to euphemism ("religion of peace," etc.), the Bush administration responded to 9/11 with a clear-eyed recognition that going to war was a difficult choice, fraught with difficult consequences, including difficult legal consequences. As long as the Bush administration remained in office, the legal norms of a struggle called "war" would prevail. For a good part of the period between September 2001 and January 2009, when the Obama administration assumed control of the executive branch, Congress gave at least grudging assent. The 2001 Authorization for Use of Military Force was followed by the USA Patriot Act. This authorized, for the investigation of terrorism, surveillance techniques and other measures that had been used before in conventional criminal investigations.

The involvement of the nation's courts in issues underlying this war, specifically the federal courts led by the Supreme Court, has been – to use a term dear to President Obama – unprecedented. Opponents of the Vietnam War tried to take to the courts in an effort to stop it, but they failed. Opponents of the government's tactics against terrorism have had far more success. One prisoner held at the U.S. military base at Guantanamo Bay succeeded in challenging the government's right to charge him before a military commission without congressional authorization. Congress responded with the necessary approval in the Military Commissions Act of 2006. But the Supreme Court would be receptive as well to the rights of detainees, even outside the United States at Guantanamo Bay, to challenge the lawfulness of their detention by requiring their jailer to meet the standards applicable to civilian prisoners exercising the historic right to petition by habeas corpus.

It was not always thus. During World War II, the United States held hundreds of thousands of German and Italian prisoners of war – the vast majority of whom fought in strict obedience to the laws of war, and tens of thousands of whom were confined at camps in the United States mainland – without even one of them being permitted to challenge his confinement by filing a habeas corpus petition in a federal court. In *Johnson v. Eisentrager*, an opinion handed down after the end of World War II, Robert Jackson, who served not only as attorney general and then as a Supreme Court justice but also as this nation's chief prosecutor at Nuremberg, derided the very idea that a prisoner of war could petition for a writ of habeas corpus:

> *The writ, since it is held to be a matter of right, would be equally available to enemies during active hostilities as in the present twilight between war and peace. Such trials would hamper the war effort and bring aid and comfort to the enemy. They would diminish the prestige of our commanders, not only with enemies but with wavering neutrals. It would be difficult to devise more effective fettering of a field commander than to allow the very enemies he is ordered to reduce to submission to call him to account in his own civil courts and divert his efforts and attention from the military offensive abroad to the legal defensive at home. Nor is it unlikely that the result of such enemy litigiousness would be a conflict between judicial and military opinion highly comforting to enemies of the United States.*

By contrast, in this struggle, lawyers who oppose either the government's goals or its methods or both have taken to the courts in an effort not only to blunt the weapons employed by the executive branch but also to overwhelm and prevail by sheer volume of litigation. One prominent practitioner of the self-congratulatory activity known as public interest advocacy has said frankly, and accurately, that there are thousands of lawyers ready and willing to overwhelm the federal courts with litigation on behalf of detainees, if only given the chance. And the courts have opened their doors to the effort. Explaining why that has happened would take many pages. But the willingness of the courts to step in where the legislative branch has abdicated means that the outcome of a deadly struggle is as likely to turn on who has more or better lawyers as on who has stronger forces.

Previous wars presented a far more straightforward path to victory than the war on terrorism did. In World War II, for example, the enemy was clearly defined. So was our objective: to smash the enemy's war-making machinery and, if necessary, some of its civilian infrastructure and compel a formal surrender. All of this could be accomplished with conventional armed forces fighting other conventional armed forces. Islamic terrorists do not present this tidy target. They do not occupy a particular geographic location and indeed hide among civilian populations. One of our most critical assets is intelligence. Unless we can find out who is planning what, there is nothing to do but await attack and rely either on good fortune or heroism to stop it, or on first responders to mitigate its effects.

There are essentially two ways to gather intelligence. One relies on technology – electronic intercepts of various kinds. The other relies on people. The former requires that we try to listen in on those planning to attack us; the latter requires that we elicit from those who directly participate in those plans the people who participated, what they plan to do, and how. The two are sometimes referred to with the shorthand "signals intelligence" and "human intelligence." When we investigate conventional criminal conspiracies like drug gangs, it is sometimes possible to insinuate an informant or undercover agent into the ranks of the conspirators and thereby monitor and eventually thwart the conspiracy. Terrorist organizations vet their operatives carefully. Also, we have few operatives, if any, capable of passing as native speakers of Arabic or Pashtu or Urdu, or as convincing members of those cultures. In any event, infiltration entails much time and high risk and yields only spotty results. That leaves questioning of captured terrorists as a necessary and important way to gather reliable human intelligence.

Why gather human intelligence at all? Isn't signals intelligence, captured in real time from the actual malefactors, far more reliable than information from human beings, who may be motivated to lie or may err even in the best of faith? Well … no. One veteran intelligence hand has analogized the process of gathering and weighing intelligence to trying to put together a huge jigsaw puzzle without looking at the picture on the box. Occasionally, he notes, a human being who has actually seen the picture, or a part of it, comes to hand, and it then becomes vital to get as many details of that picture as possible.

Those charged with gathering intelligence in the wake of the Sept. 11 attacks understood that. They relied on Congress's Authorization for Use of Military Force to justify gathering signals intelligence even under circumstances that might violate then existing statutes and standards under the Fourth Amendment clause barring unreasonable searches and seizures. They argued that one of the functions of the military in times of war was to gather intelligence, and any such intelligence gathering was, by definition, reasonable. As memories of the Sept. 11 attacks faded, safety begat complacency, and this reading of the congressional resolution came to be seen by many as overly aggressive. What became known as the Terrorist Surveillance Program was the subject of a bitter tug-of-war between President Bush and Congress, last resolved in 2008, when that program was folded into existing law and portions placed under the scrutiny of the Foreign Intelligence Surveillance Court.

The struggle over the gathering of human intelligence was another matter. In March 2002, an al Qaeda operative named Abu Zubaydah came into the hands of the CIA following his capture by Pakistani agents. He was seriously wounded and was believed to be in possession of essential information about al Qaeda. He was treated for his wounds in the custody of the CIA by the finest medical talent available in the United States. While still recovering from his wounds and dependent on his interrogators for comfort, he gave up some information voluntarily. He inadvertently disclosed the alias ("Mukhtar") of Khalid Sheikh Mohammed (KSM), the mastermind of the Sept. 11 attacks. But having been essentially the travel agent for al Qaeda operatives all over the world and one of only a few people who had direct contact with the top level of al Qaeda, Zubaydah was believed to harbor much more valuable information. His initial questioning was led by the FBI, but as he grew both physically and psychologically stronger and less communicative, he was turned over to the CIA.

That agency devised a regimen of techniques for inducing cooperation during interrogation, later to become known by the Orwellian euphemism "enhanced interrogation techniques." Using the word *enhanced* could not have been more unfortunate. Such an anodyne term, more suggestive of a washday detergent or a suntan lotion than a method of breaking a person's will, looked like a disingenuous verbal flinch, an attempt to fool the listener into excusing the inexcusable. The techniques were rough stuff, including firm but openhanded slaps to the side of the face or the abdomen; banging the subject's shoulders against a specially constructed wall that exaggerated with sound the apparent force involved; sleep deprivation; and ultimately waterboarding – a technique, which will be discussed further, that induced in the subject the panic that accompanies drowning.

The CIA, mindful of the domestic statutory bar on torture, submitted the proposed techniques, which included one or two not mentioned above, to the Justice Department. It included a precise description not only of the techniques themselves but also of the precise manner and the limitations and safeguards, including medical safeguards, with which they were to be administered to a population that would necessarily select itself based on resistance to less coercive measures. Further, such techniques were to be administered only by people specially trained in them, only to people believed to have vital actionable intelligence, and only with the direct approval of senior CIA leadership. In detailed but hurriedly prepared memos, the Justice Department approved as lawful most, but not all, of the proposed techniques. These hurriedly prepared memos eventually were withdrawn, and others were substituted in 2005 as more soundly reasoned. But the conclusions remained the same. The techniques in question did not violate the torture statute.

These memoranda would come to be known collectively in the popular media as the "torture memos," notwithstanding that they were drafted with the intention of avoiding any technique that constituted torture while marking out the limits of what the law allows. For all of the controversy over the memos and the interrogation program pursued by the CIA, of the many thousands of terrorists captured by U.S. forces, fewer than 1,000 were detained in the CIA's so-called black sites; of those, fewer than a third were subject to any of the harsh interrogation techniques discussed in the memos; and of those, three – Abu Zubaydah; Khalid Sheikh Mohammed; and Abd al-Rahim al-Nashiri, the mastermind of the USS *Cole* bombing – were waterboarded. According to those in a position to know, all three provided actionable intelligence following their exposure to these methods.

Notably, Zubaydah, according to both George Tenet and Gen. Michael Hayden, former CIA directors, provided information that led to the capture of Ramzi bin al-Shibh. In addition to having been the principal communications link between the 9/11 hijackers in the United States and al Qaeda leadership abroad, al-Shibh was arrested while he was completing plans to stage another 9/11-style attack on the Canary Wharf business district in London and on Heathrow Airport. Intelligence officials had known nothing of these plans before the arrest. In addition, he provided information that led to the arrest in Chicago of Jose Padilla, an American-born jihadi who, after he served time for manslaughter in this country, undertook a journey of personal discovery that led to an introduction to KSM and other al Qaeda luminaries. Padilla was known principally for what seems to have been a fanciful plot to build and detonate a "dirty bomb" – a device that yields a small explosion but a high level of radiation. Far more serious, and unprosecuted because the necessary evidence could not be presented in a federal court, was his plan with an accomplice to acquire apartments in Florida, seal them, fill them with natural gas, and detonate them simultaneously to cause widespread civilian death and destruction. He was convicted of lesser charges of aiding overseas terrorist activities but nonetheless received a lengthy sentence.

Zubaydah also revealed that he and others in al Qaeda had been trained to resist interrogation but were also taught that they were permitted by Allah to disclose information when they reached the limit of their ability to withstand physical and psychological pressure. This in itself was invaluable intelligence. Moreover, a later claim by FBI agent Ali Soufan, that the information about Padilla had been obtained by his establishing rapport with Zubaydah, was belied by Soufan's own partner and a report by the Justice Department's inspector general into interrogation procedures.

When the lessons learned from the questioning of Zubaydah were applied to KSM, including the lesson about reaching the limits of resistance, the result was an intelligence bonanza. KSM became the tutor to his captors and disclosed both general information on how al Qaeda moved money and people and specific information that led to the interruption of other plots. These included yet another plot involving airplanes, aimed at the Library Tower in Los Angeles, to be carried out by members of a South Asian terrorist affiliate called Jemaah Islamiyah led by a man named Hambali. When further information was received as the result of leads from KSM, he was questioned yet again and disclosed a key telephone number that identified a circle of terrorist plotters. Still further information from KSM identified an al Qaeda program to develop a biological weapons capability in the United States that included the production of anthrax, and the capture of people involved in that program led to yet further intelligence.

Al-Nashiri, the USS *Cole* mastermind, provided out-of-date information when first questioned. But after he was subjected to harsh interrogation techniques, including waterboarding, he provided important information about al Qaeda's current operational planning.

It is important to note both how these techniques and the actual questioning interacted, and how intelligence is used. These techniques were not applied by those who conduct questioning and debriefings but by operators or interrogators specially trained to apply them. Each was applied not alone but in tandem with other techniques in a regimen that had to be approved in advance by senior CIA personnel, and then only after a detainee had been noncompliant. Still further restrictions applied to waterboarding. Once the detainee indicated that he was ready to be compliant, a debriefer resumed questioning. So it is not possible to say with certainty that this or that particular technique yielded this or that particular item of information, only that after these three detainees were subjected to techniques that included waterboarding, they provided actionable intelligence when they had refused to do so before and that others subjected to some subset of other techniques did likewise.

There is no substance to the claim that these techniques are not productive because a detainee would do anything to stop the discomfort, including lie. If the object were to elicit confessions, the claim might be valid. Subject anyone to enough waterboarding, and he might confess to having shot Abraham Lincoln. But the object is not confessions; it is intelligence. Facts disclosed by detainees under interrogation are not taken at face value. They are fit into the matrix of other facts known to intelligence officers in order to test their reliability.

In any event, with both mounting criticism of coercive techniques and increasing knowledge about al Qaeda that could be used to interrogate captured operatives, waterboarding was abandoned as a part of the CIA interrogation program in 2003. It could not, under rules applied during the Bush administration, be restored to the program absent a specific request from the director of the CIA and the approval of both the president and the attorney general. The CIA interrogation program as a whole, however, including waterboarding, remained classified. In the seven-plus years following Sept. 11, 2001 – although several plots aimed at us had been broken up, both within the country and outside it – there had been no successful terrorist attacks within the United States.

In his inaugural address on Jan. 20, 2009, President Obama announced, "As for our common defense, we reject as false the choice between our safety and our ideals." Two days later, at a White House ceremony, he promised to return America to the "moral high ground" in the struggle against terrorism. He signed three executive orders. One directed that the military detention facility at Guantanamo be closed within a year. A second order said that no one being held in the custody of any government department or agency in any armed conflict could be interrogated using any technique other than one authorized in the Army Field Manual. The third halted all military commission proceedings pending further review and also effectively halted a Supreme Court appeal by Ali Saleh Kahlah al-Marri, who, by his own admission, came to the United States on direct order of KSM to help organize a second wave of attacks following the Sept. 11, 2001, atrocity and was the only person then held in the mainland United States as an unlawful enemy combatant.

The closing of Guantanamo, Obama said, would "restore the standards of due process and the core constitutional values that have made this country great even in the midst of war, even in dealing with terrorism." Restricting interrogators to the Army Field Manual "reflects the best judgment of our military that we can abide by a rule that says we don't torture but that we can still effectively obtain the intelligence that we need." All in all, he said, the orders reflected "me following through ... on an understanding that dates back to our founding fathers, that we are willing to observe core standards of conduct not just when it's easy but also when it's hard."

Guantanamo is a military, not CIA, installation. When it was first set up to house unlawful combatants captured abroad, it was primitive and became the focus of invective, most of it ill-informed, about prisoner abuse. This was particularly true in the aftermath of the Abu Ghraib incident in Iraq, in which prisoners were tormented and humiliated simply for the amusement of undisciplined soldiers. Guantanamo was upgraded at great cost when it became clear that we needed a place to house unlawful combatants and try those who could be charged with war crimes.

I visited Guantanamo in February 2008, while serving as attorney general, and had occasion when I was a district judge to visit federal detention facilities in the United States. Guantanamo is a state-of-the-art facility that compares favorably with even medium-security federal prisons in this country. Because it is remote and located on an island, there is less need for the restrictive conditions that prevail at maximum-security facilities here. I saw where the most noted detainees are housed and would have seen KSM himself had he not been meeting that day with representatives of the International Committee of the Red Cross. In his absence, I was able to visit his cell and adjoining exercise area, which featured the same make and model of elliptical machine that I used in the gym at the building where I lived in Washington, D.C., although of course I, unlike KSM, had to share the machine with others. Detainees may choose from a menu of nutritionally balanced halal meals (my lunch came from that menu), and they are provided with a copy of the Koran in a bag to assure them that it was not touched by infidels. The base itself includes new courtrooms in which to try military commission cases, with secure electronic communications and storage equipment that can handle information at any level of classification from anywhere in the world. It has a gallery for press and other observers that can be electronically screened off when classified information is being presented but otherwise has a full view of the proceedings accompanied by simultaneous translation. This trial facility was built at a cost of tens of millions of dollars and is unequaled at any courthouse in the United States.

That is not to say that there isn't violence at Guantanamo. There is plenty of it, but it is directed by the prisoners toward the guards, not the other way. I saw the plastic face shields that guards must wear when they approach or enter cells to protect them from the cocktails of urine, feces, and semen that are regularly hurled at them along with verbal and physical abuse. I saw the collection of weapons fashioned by detainees to attack guards, as well as the rigorous standards imposed on the guards in responding to these provocations. Any lapse of behavior or demeanor by a military guard results in swift discipline or transfer. Prisoners receive better medical care at Guantanamo than their captors. Notwithstanding prisoners' access to a substantial library of Arabic videos, the most frequently viewed were episodes of *Walker, Texas Ranger*. Despite the abuse these guards take and the thankless rigor of their day-to-day existence, I received only one request from any of them: Please tell people what this place is really like.

The Army Field Manual, to which the president confined interrogators in one of his Jan. 22, 2009, orders, was written to set limits for battlefield interrogations that could be carried out by young recruits. The limits of that manual were not set with experienced and closely supervised interrogators in mind. The manual itself has long been available on the Internet and has, in fact, been used to help train al Qaeda operatives, who now know precisely what they face not only from soldiers in the field but from any U.S. captor.

The president's new secretary of the Department of Homeland Security, Janet Napolitano, shuns the terms "terrorism" and "war," as does the president, preferring to describe the former as "man-caused disasters" and the latter as "foreign contingency operations." When Napolitano first assumed office, she was unaware that it was a crime for an alien to enter this country unlawfully and thought the 9/11 plotters came to this country from Canada.

For his attorney general, the president chose Eric Holder, a man who said during the 2008 campaign that the government had "authorized the use of torture, approved of secret electronic surveillance against American citizens, secretly detained American citizens without due process of law, denied the writ of habeas corpus to hundreds of accused enemy combatants, and authorized the use of procedures that violate both international law and the United States Constitution." He added, "We owe the American people a reckoning." During his confirmation hearing, although he had not been briefed on details of classified CIA interrogation practices, he stated flatly that waterboarding is torture, a position with which he found no conflict even when it was pointed out to him at a later hearing that Navy SEALs and other special forces are waterboarded routinely as part of their training. Training was not torture, he said, because the intent was different, although he continued to maintain that waterboarding in other settings, apparently regardless of how it was administered or with what purpose, was torture, notwithstanding that the one and only relevant statute that defines torture states that it is an act committed under color of law and "specifically intended to inflict severe physical or mental pain or suffering." Asked during an appearance in Berlin whether he would cooperate with foreign or international courts trying to prosecute former Bush administration officials for engaging in torture, he responded, "This is an administration that is determined to conduct itself by the rule of law. And to the extent that we receive lawful requests from an appropriately created court, we would obviously respond to it."

In April 2009, what seemed to be the promised "reckoning" would begin with the release of the theretofore classified Department of Justice memoranda analyzing the legality of the CIA's interrogation procedures adopted in the aftermath of 9/11, which included a detailed description of the procedures and limits of each technique. That disclosure, made in the name of openness, was transparently intended to stir a wind of outrage that would drive further "reckoning."

As to waterboarding, the memos disclosed that it involved binding a detainee to a tilted bench, head downward, covering his nose and mouth with a cloth and pouring water on the cloth, with the result that airflow is restricted for 20 to 40 seconds, causing a resulting increase in the carbon dioxide level in the blood and an automatically increased effort to breathe. The presence of the cloth inhibiting breathing and the increased carbon dioxide level created in the detainee a reflexive feeling of "suffocation and incipient panic," even if the detainee was aware he was not going to drown, as he would be after an initial application. If a detainee tried to defeat the technique, for example by holding his breath or turning his head to the side, the operator could wait until the detainee started to breathe before applying water, or cup his hands around the detainee's nose and mouth to dam the runoff and prevent breathing. This procedure was applied only with a physician present and monitoring a detainee's physical condition; it caused virtually no physical pain and caused no lasting psychological damage. In addition, it could be authorized only if the CIA had credible information that a terrorist attack was imminent, that the subject had actionable intelligence with respect to it, and that other techniques had failed or were unlikely to yield timely actionable intelligence.

Disclosure of these memos did not elicit the outrage that was anticipated. Rather, it was obvious that the CIA, with the concurrence of the Justice Department, had taken extraordinary care to avoid inflicting torture. It became obvious as well that the equation drawn by politicians and pundits linking the CIA procedure and the practices of the Japanese during World War II or the Khmer Rouge in Cambodia was absurd. Those practices included forcing water down a prisoner's throat until his innards were painfully swollen, then stepping on his stomach to force the water out, or submerging a prisoner's head in a tank of water while he was handcuffed to the bottom until he either nearly or actually drowned. Although both were called "waterboarding," the CIA procedure bore as little resemblance to the cruelty of the Japanese or the Khmer Rouge as an arduous hike did to the Bataan Death March. What certainly was achieved by these disclosures, however, was broadcasting to our enemies the precise legal limits to which any president could press them, thus permitting them to train for the absolute worst.

Hard on the heels of disclosure of the memoranda came more "reckoning" – the attorney general's appointment of a prosecutor to reconsider whether criminal charges should be brought against CIA interrogators in cases that had already been reviewed by career prosecutors and deemed insufficient to warrant prosecution. Although those prosecutors prepared detailed memoranda describing the facts and the legal reasons for their conclusions, the attorney general conceded, astoundingly, that he had not read those memoranda before directing the reopening of those cases.

In early June, Ahmed Ghailani, confined at Guantanamo for numerous war crimes that could have been tried before a military tribunal, would be brought instead to New York to face already pending civilian charges in connection with the 1998 bombing of U.S. embassies in East Africa. After experiencing confinement in a civilian jail, Ghailani has asked to be returned to Guantanamo to await his trial, a preview of what is to come if Guantanamo detainees are brought here.

November and December 2009 brought additional examples of the current administration's approach to Islamic terrorism. The first came in November, at Fort Hood, Texas. Nidal Malik Hasan was an Army psychiatrist who held the rank of major and had a history of anti-American and pro-jihadi statements even while he treated soldiers returning from combat at Walter Reed Army Medical Center in Washington, D.C. He had been detected to be in communication with a fanatic Muslim cleric named Anwar al-Awlaki, also an American, who had preached to at least two of the 9/11 hijackers while they were in this country. Hasan shouted "*allahu akbar*" – Allah is great – before opening fire on waiting patients in Fort Hood's Soldier Readiness Center, killing 13 and wounding about 30. The president warned the country against jumping to conclusions about the nature and motive of the act.

Also in November, Attorney General Holder announced that he had decided to terminate military commission proceedings against KSM and others charged with planning the 9/11 attacks, as those proceedings were about to start and KSM had already declared his intention to plead guilty. Instead, KSM and the others would be brought to New York to be charged and stand trial in a civilian proceeding in federal court in Manhattan, blocks from where the World Trade Center stood. This, he said, would show the world that we were committed to upholding the rule of law. He did not specify which law, although it certainly could not be the law that permitted unlawful combatants, or unprivileged enemy belligerents, as they are now called, to be tried before military commissions. Nor did he explain how treating those who violate the Geneva Conventions and other laws better than those who obey them would promote the rule of law. A chorus of criticism, arising from the obvious threat and disruption to New York City that would result from such a trial and the cost of protecting against it, has resulted in reconsideration of where that trial will be held. But it is by no means clear that the obvious alternative of continuing the military commission proceeding in Guantanamo even will be considered.

On Christmas Day 2009, in an airplane over Detroit, Umar Farouk Abdulmutallab, a Nigerian terrorist trained by al Qaeda in Yemen, allegedly tried to ignite a bomb secreted in his undershorts that would have killed 289 passengers and crew, plus untold others on the ground. He was seated in the particular seat on the airplane where an explosion would have caused the maximum damage. His apparent lack of manual dexterity, combined with the heroic intervention of passengers and crew after he had gotten as far as starting a fire, prevented the explosion. His father had warned State Department officials that he had become radicalized; electronic intercepts months before had warned of an incipient plot involving a Nigerian; he bought his ticket for cash and carried no luggage. Yet withal, he was allowed to board the airplane. Further, after he landed and was willingly disclosing information of substantial intelligence value to FBI agents, the attorney general directed that civilian rather than military processes be employed and that he be warned of his *Miranda* rights to silence and counsel. Upon the advice of his lawyer, Abdulmutallab provided no further information. A day after the incident, the secretary of the Department of Homeland Security pronounced that the system had worked and a day after that was ready to say that there was no larger terrorist plot. The director of national intelligence, after testifying that if consulted, he would have sent Abdulmutallab to a special interrogation group put in place to question high-value detainees, conceded that that group was devised to deal only with detainees apprehended abroad, and in any event did not yet exist. As of this writing, Abdulmutallab's family, flown here from Nigeria, persuaded him to continue his disclosures some five weeks after he stopped. What sort of arrangement has been offered him in return is not yet clear. Abdulmutallab has been indicted in Detroit and apparently is to be prosecuted in a civilian court. Curiously, that indictment did not initially contain a conspiracy charge, which would tend to show that his initial disclosures, at least, did not contain enough information to charge anyone else.

What was known, for all its shortcomings of nomenclature, as the global war on terrorism appears to have fallen victim to a mindset in which the pure and the lofty trump reality. All we have to do, the president said in his inaugural address, is choose hope over fear, reject as false the choice between our safety and our ideals, and we can have it all – yes we can. If we strike the right pose, the world will applaud. So it is thought to be of no real significance that both the president and his chief law enforcement officer call for a civilian trial that will showcase the fairness of our legal system, even as they guarantee, when righteous indignation seems more to the taste of the gallery, that the outcome of that trial will be conviction and the death penalty. Nor does it matter that in treating unlawful combatants more favorably than lawful ones, we undo more than a century of effort to civilize the rules of warfare, and we undermine our own safety in the process. A world like that, where choices have no consequences, is a world inhabited only by children, and then only in their fantasies. If we try to live in it, we do so at peril to ourselves and our children.

GLENN HARLAN REYNOLDS

THE HIGHER EDUCATION BUBBLE

I. The Problem in a Nutshell

Something that can't go on forever, won't.
Economist Herbert Stein

The buyers think what they're buying will appreciate in value, making them rich in the future. The product grows more and more elaborate – and more and more expensive – but the expense is offset by cheap credit provided by sellers who are eager to encourage buyers to buy.

Buyers see that everyone else is taking on mounds of debt, and they are more comfortable when they do so themselves. Besides, for a generation, the value of what they buy has gone up steadily. What could go wrong? Everything continues smoothly until, at some point, it doesn't anymore.

Yes, this sounds like the housing bubble, but I'm afraid it's also sounding a lot like a still-inflating higher education bubble. And despite (or because of) the fact that my day job involves higher education, I think it's better for us to face up to what's going on *before* the bubble bursts messily. Because that's what's likely to happen.

No one disputes that college has gotten a lot more

expensive. A recent *Money* magazine report notes, "After adjusting for financial aid, the amount families pay for college has skyrocketed 439 percent since 1982.... Normal supply and demand can't begin to explain cost increases of this magnitude." Consumers would balk, except for two things.

First – as with the housing bubble – cheap and readily available credit has let people borrow to finance education. They're willing to do so because of (1) consumer ignorance, as students – and, often, their parents – don't fully grasp just how harsh the impact of student-loan payments will be after graduation; and (2) a belief that whatever the cost, a college education is a necessary ticket to future prosperity.

Bubbles form when too many people expect values to go up forever. Bubbles burst when there are no longer enough excessively optimistic and ignorant folks to fuel them. And there are signs that this is beginning to happen already where education is concerned.

A recent *New York Times* profile featured Courtney Munna, a 26-year-old graduate of New York University with nearly $100,000 in student-loan debt – debt that her degree in religious and women's studies did not equip her to repay. Payments on the debt are about $700 per month, equivalent to a respectable house payment and a major bite on her monthly income of $2,300 as a photographer's assistant earning an hourly wage. And, unlike a bad mortgage on an underwater house, Munna can't simply walk away from her student loans, which cannot be expunged in bankruptcy. She's stuck in a financial trap.

Some might say that she deserves it: Who borrows $100,000 to finance a degree in women's and religious studies that won't make you any money? She should have wised up, and others should learn from her mistake instead of learning too late, as she did: “I don’t want to spend the rest of my life slaving away to pay for an education I got for four years and would happily give back.”

But bubbles burst when people catch on, and there’s some evidence that people are beginning to catch on. Student-loan demand, according to a recent report in *The Washington Post*, is going soft, and students are expressing a willingness to go to a cheaper school rather than run up debt. Things haven’t collapsed yet, but they’re looking shakier – kind of like the housing market looked in 2007.

So what happens if the bubble collapses? Will it be a tragedy, with millions of Americans losing their path to higher-paying jobs?

Maybe not. College is often described as a path to prosperity, but is it? A college education can help people make more money in three ways.

First, it may actually make them more economically productive by teaching them skills valued in the workplace: computer programming, nursing, or engineering, say. (Religious and women’s studies, not so much.)

Second, it may provide a credential that employers want, not because it represents actual skills but because it’s a weeding tool that doesn’t produce civil-rights suits as, say, IQ tests might. A four-year college degree, even if its holder acquired no actual skills, at least indicates some ability to show up on time and perform as instructed.

And third, a college degree – at least an elite one – may hook its holder up with a useful social network that can provide jobs and opportunities in the future. (This is truer if it’s a degree from Yale than one from Eastern Kentucky – unless, maybe, you’re planning to live in eastern Kentucky after graduation – but it’s true everywhere to some degree.)

While an individual might rationally pursue all three

of these, only the first one – actual added skills – produces a net benefit for society. The other two are just distributional: They're about who gets the goodies, not about making more of them.

Yet today's college education system seems to be in the business of selling parts two and three to a much greater degree than part one, along with selling the even harder to quantify "college experience," which often boils down to four (or more) years of partying.

Post-bubble, perhaps students – and employers, not to mention parents and lenders – will focus instead on education that fosters economic value. And that is likely to press colleges to focus more on providing useful majors. (That doesn't necessarily rule out traditional liberal-arts majors, so long as they are rigorous and require a real general education rather than trendy and easy subjects, but the key word here is *rigorous.*)

My question is whether traditional academic institutions will be able to keep up with the times or whether – as Anya Kamenetz suggests in her new book, *DIY U* – the real pioneering will be in online education and the work of "edupunks" who are more interested in finding new ways of teaching and learning than in protecting existing interests.

I'm betting on the latter. Industries seldom reform themselves, and real competition usually comes from the outside.

In this Broadside, we'll look briefly at how the higher education bubble came to be, at the problems it is creating, and about what is likely to happen when, and after, the bursting takes place. We'll also look at a few things you can do for yourself and for the country.

* * *

II. How We Got Here

Higher education has been around for a long time. The University of Bologna was started in 1088, and many other European universities date from the 12th, 13th, and 14th centuries. It has been a presence in the United States from the very earliest days of colonization – long enough ago that Harvard University supposedly once offered Galileo a job. But for most of that time, a college education, to say nothing of graduate study, was a luxury: Colleges and universities catered mostly to the rich and to the clergy, with the occasional deserving scholarship student thrown in.

College was not seen as the primary way for a young man (it was pretty much always a young man back then) to get ahead, at least not unless the young man was planning a career as a man of the cloth. Most lawyers – and even most doctors – learned more through apprenticeship and on-the-job training than through formal education, which is not surprising since that was the way most people, from blacksmiths to generals, learned what they needed to know for their jobs.

Instead, a college education was mostly a way for a young man of distinction to obtain a degree of social polish – and wider social connections – while sowing a few discreet (or sometimes not so discreet) wild oats. College was not sold as an economic investment in the future but rather as a stage in life, and no one was handing out loans to aspiring entrants.

This began to change after the Civil War, and the reason was, naturally enough, federal money. Even before the Civil War, reformer Justin Morrill had talked up the idea of colleges and universities dedicated to training farmers, mechanics, and soldiers rather than clergymen and lawyers. Morrill's original scheme involved colleges

College Tuition vs. Medical Care vs. Home Prices vs. CPI

ALL ITEMS 1978–2011 INDEXES=100 IN 1978

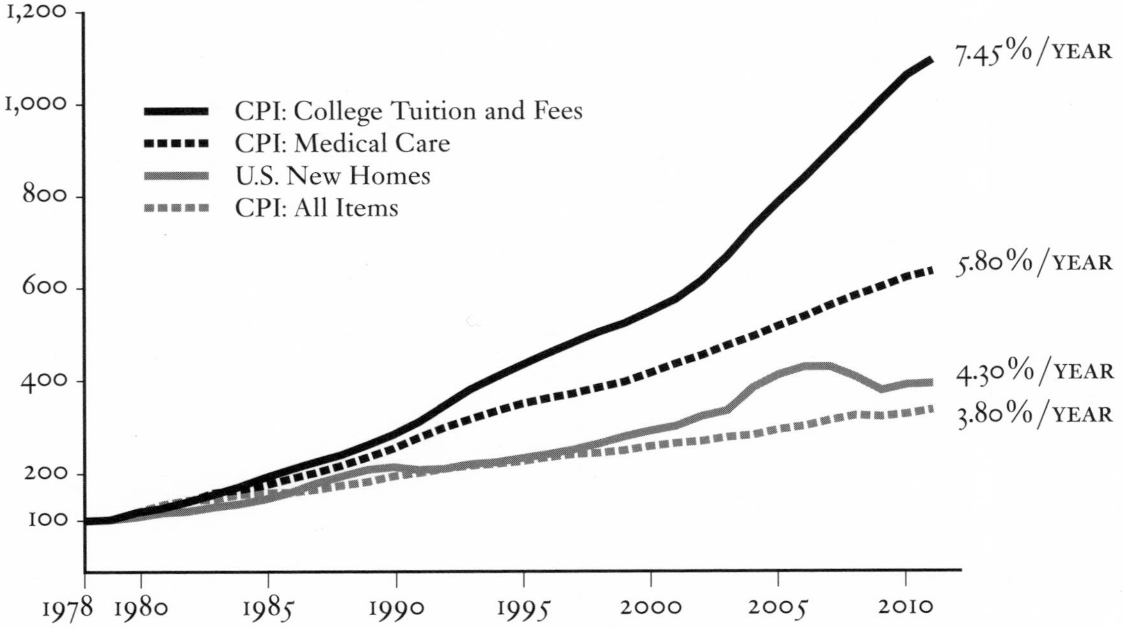

Sources: mjperry.blogspot.com

modeled on West Point, with free tuition and admission via congressional nomination. This proposal went through several different versions, one of which was vetoed by President James Buchanan on the eve of the Civil War, but a later bill was signed into law by Abraham Lincoln.

As it was finally passed, the Morrill Act offered land grants to institutions that would offer education in farming and mechanics, along with a spot of military training. Though the traditional colleges looked down on these upstarts as little better than trade schools, many became elite universities such as Virginia Tech, Texas A&M, the University of Tennessee, the University of Wisconsin, MIT, and Cornell. Historians now regard the Morrill Act as a major step forward in education and a major booster for the U.S. economy, and many believe that the (then required) military training played a major role in America's success in World Wars I and II.

Well, if some is good, more must be better. That was the thinking after World War II, when policymakers – wondering how to receive a flood of returning GIs – hit upon the idea of sending them to college. The GI Bill gave millions of discharged soldiers the option to go to school instead of hitting the job market all at once. Many took advantage of it, and colleges and universities, anxious to accommodate them (and to share in the federal largesse), embarked upon ambitious programs of expansion.

By the time the flood of veterans from World War II and Korea was slowing to a trickle, the Baby Boomers were beginning to show up, and the Vietnam War soon added yet another reason for college: student draft deferments. Enrollments swelled again, and colleges expanded further. By the 1970s, the infrastructure was there for more college students than the population was ready to produce on its own. The solution? Expanded federal aid in the form of Pell Grants, guaranteed student loans, and other support. This really took off in the mid- to late 1970s.

The result was predictable. As with any subsidized product, prices rose to absorb the subsidy. And as colleges saw that increases in tuition didn't hurt enrollment – higher tuition often made a school seem more prestigious, and anyway there were cheap government loans to make up the difference – the rate of increase climbed even further. How much further? Just look at the graphic on page 259, adapted from Professor Mark Perry at the Carpe Diem economics blog.

As you can see, at an annual growth rate of 7.45 percent a year, tuition has vastly outstripped the consumer price index and health care prices, while the growth in house prices under the housing bubble looks like a mere bump in the road by comparison. For a while, parents could look to increased home values to make them feel better about paying Junior's tuition (the so-called wealth effect, in which increases in asset values make people more comfortable about spending) or could at least borrow against the equity in their homes to fund tuition. But that equity is gone now, and tuition is still climbing.

So where does that leave us? Even students who major in programs shown to increase earnings, like engineering, face limits on how much debt they can sanely amass. With costs approaching $60,000 a year for many private schools and out-of-state costs at many state schools exceeding $40,000 (and often closing in on $30,000 for in-state students), some people are graduating with debts of $100,000 or more – sometimes much more.

That's dangerous. And the problem is not a small one. According to Professor Richard Vedder, writing in the *Chronicle of Higher Education*, the number of student-loan debtors actually equals the number of people with college degrees. How is this possible? "First, huge numbers of those borrowing money *never* graduate from college. Second, many who borrow are not in baccalaureate degree programs. Three, people take forever to pay their loans back." Total student-loan debt in America has passed the trillion-dollar mark, more than total credit-card debt and more than total auto-loan debt.

The rule of thumb is that college-debt payments should account for less than 8 percent of gross income. Otherwise, watch out – and remember that loan payments are usually not dischargeable in bankruptcy. The loans can follow you for decades. Students graduating with heavy burdens of student-loan debt must choose (if they can) jobs that pay enough money to cover the payments, often limiting their career choices to an extent they didn't foresee in their student days. And even students who can earn enough to service their debts may find themselves constrained in other ways. It's hard to get a mortgage, for example, when you're already in effect paying one in the form of student loans. (This has implications for the housing bubble too, of course, since the traditional source of new home buyers and move-up home buyers – people a few years out of college or grad school – now suffers from an unprecedented debt burden. But that's a topic for a different book.)

It's even worse, of course, when graduates *can't* find jobs that will let them cover the payments. Regardless of the student's employment circumstances, the debt still comes due. Students can enter forbearance, but that only reduces or stops the payments for a while; the principal continues to grow. Only death or (sometimes) disability will get rid of the debt, and for private student loans, co-signers may remain liable. The whole scheme, as several commentators have noted, seems like the debt-slavery regimes used by coal mines and plantations to keep workers and sharecroppers in debt peonage for life. (Some newer graduates may be eligible for "income-based repayment" schemes, which make things somewhat better, but not much.)

For some of these unfortunates, the debt is enough to quash marriage plans (who wants to marry someone with huge amounts of unpayable debt?), prevent homeownership, and generally wreak havoc on the debtors' lives. These people may wind up living in their parents' basements until they are old enough to collect Social Security, which may wind up being garnisheed – no joke – for unpaid student debts.

It's a big problem, and more and more students and potential students are becoming aware of just how bad student debt can be. That's causing them to change their behavior. Some are eschewing college entirely in favor of military service, skilled trades, or lower-cost alternatives like community college. Others are skipping expensive private colleges (especially those outside the top tier) in favor of less expensive state schools. Some are pursuing their educations online. And even those still going to traditional colleges or universities are looking more closely at their majors and the employment prospects after graduation. Nor are graduate programs immune: The number of students taking the Law School Admissions Test, for example, has fallen by 25 percent over the past two years, leading some to predict that lower-tier law schools may be entering a "death spiral."

These are all rational responses to the fact that the traditional approach to higher education no longer makes as much sense. When education was cheap enough that students could pay their own way through by working part time, "study what interests you" was reasonable advice.

Some criticize today's students for being more concerned about return on investment, but when the investment runs well into six figures, students would be crazy *not* to worry about the return. A six-figure consumption item is well beyond the resources of college students: Nobody would advise an 18-year-old to purchase a Ferrari on borrowed money, but if a college education is a consumption item, not an investment, that's basically what they are doing.

But as the behavior that led to the bubble changes, the bubble itself will burst, and things in the higher education world will never be quite the same. That has significant ramifications for both students and institutions. The next chapter looks at some of those.

III. What Happens When the Bubble Bursts?

For the past several decades, higher education has been living high on the hog. Faculty salaries have grown significantly, administrative salaries have grown dramatically – seven-figure pay for university presidents isn't even news any more, and at most schools, there are scores of lower-level officials who still make more money than anyone else on campus except coaches – and institutions of higher learning have been on a building boom, running up new administration buildings, athletic facilities, dormitories, recreation centers, and classrooms.

All of this is predicated on the money continuing to roll in. But what if it stops? Already, state and local aid to higher education is shrinking as states face pension shortfalls and other budget pressures. State and local spending on higher education hit a 25-year low in 2011, and nothing suggests a significant upturn in years to come. Schools have tried to make up the difference by raising tuition, but for the first time, we're beginning to see significant buyer resistance. Federal money is still there, but it's not growing the way it once was, and with the federal government running massive deficits, the prospects for its filling the gap also seem poor. So what will happen?

At first, of course, the answer will mostly be denial: short-term solutions, efforts to raise quick cash, and a suggestion that what's going on is just temporary. Later there will be more-significant changes, mostly aimed at cost cutting. (If experience is any guide, administration – especially sacred cows like diversity programs – will be cut last; actual teaching will be cut first.) Finally, there will be mergers and even outright closings of schools that can no longer operate. The schools that are left will be those that can survive in the new environment.

This won't be the end of higher education, of course, and the schools at the top of the food chain – the Ivy League and similar schools; top engineering schools like MIT, CalTech, and Georgia Tech; and the better flagship public universities – will survive comparatively unscathed. But the transformation will nonetheless be wrenching. Less-expensive alternative-education and certification schemes will arise, and existing institutions will do their best to marginalize and neutralize them by employing everything from PR offensives to accrediting powers to outright legal assaults, but over time those assaults will largely fail.

We're already seeing some of this. Even as the once-mighty University of California system slashes programs and raises tuition, it has created a new systemwide "vice chancellor for equity, diversity, and inclusion." This is on top of the already enormous University of California diversity machine, which, as Heather Mac Donald notes, "includes the Chancellor's Diversity Office, the associate vice chancellor for faculty equity, the assistant vice chancellor for diversity, the faculty equity advisors, the graduate diversity coordinators, the staff diversity liaison, the undergraduate student diversity liaison, the graduate student diversity liaison, the chief diversity officer, the director of development for diversity initiatives, the Office of Academic Diversity and Equal Opportunity, the Committee on Gender Identity and Sexual Orientation Issues, the Committee on the Status of Women, the Campus Council on Climate, Culture and Inclusion, the Diversity Council, and the directors of the Cross-Cultural Center, the Lesbian Gay Bisexual Transgender Resource Center, and the Women's Center."

While the UC system loses top cancer researchers to Rice University, it is creating new chaired professorships in, you guessed it, diversity studies. Likewise, in North Carolina, UNC-Wilmington is combining the physics and geology departments to save money while diverting more funding to campus diversity offices. This sort of thing illustrates the kind of priorities that emerge in a bubble that is not only financial but also intellectual. It will not survive in the new environment, but administrators will fight a grim rear-guard action as long as they are allowed, even though research suggests that the programs aren't doing much good – as students grow less, not more, committed to racial and gender equality the longer they are in college. (Read more on what to do about that administrative resistance in a later chapter.)

For a time, many schools will try to maintain their enrollments by discounting tuition – usually disguised as increased financial aid – but there are limits to that approach. First of all, to the extent that they need tuition money to survive, schools won't be able to afford these discounts for long. Second, as more schools adopt this strategy, we're likely to see a race to the bottom. And third, once word of heavy discounting gets out, parents who are expected to pay full freight will feel like suckers and either demand discounts for themselves or take their business elsewhere.

For the most vulnerable schools, the problem won't be one of priorities but of survival. Generally speaking, the most-vulnerable schools will be those private schools with modest reputations and limited endowments but with high tuitions. A generation or two in the past, such schools could maintain enrollment via legacies or, in some cases, religious affiliations. But when you're nearly as expensive as (or even more expensive than) Harvard but lack the reputation of Harvard, attracting students won't be as easy. And since schools with modest endowments can't supplement tuition income with endowment income, there will be sharp limits to their ability to cut their prices anyway, at least without engaging in dramatic cost cutting first. In my own world – legal education – some fourth-tier schools that had plenty of applicants a few years ago are already having trouble filling seats. That's just the beginning.

The upshot is that higher education is facing a major structural change over the next decade or so, and the full impact is likely to strike sooner than most people expect. Change is coming, and it is unlikely to be either modest or gradual.

But how should people prepare for this change? Assume that I'm right, and that higher education – both undergraduate and graduate, including professional education like the law schools in which I teach – is heading for a major correction. What will that mean? What should people do?

* * *

IV. What to Do

Piece of advice No. 1 – good for pretty much all bubbles, in fact – is this: Don't go into debt. In bubbles, people borrow heavily because they expect the value of what they're borrowing against to increase. In a booming housing market, for example, it makes sense to buy a house you can't quite afford, because it will increase in value enough to make the debt seem trivial, or at least manageable, so long as the market continues to boom. But there's a catch. Once the boom is over, all that debt is still there, but the return thereon is much diminished. And since the boom is based on expectations, things can go south with amazing speed once those expectations start to shift.

Right now, people are still borrowing heavily to pay the steadily increasing tuitions levied by higher education. But that borrowing is based on the expectation that students will earn enough to pay off their loans with a portion of the extra income their educations generate. Once people doubt that will happen, the bubble will burst. And there's considerable evidence that the doubting is already well under way.

So my advice to students faced with choosing colleges (and graduate schools and law schools) this coming year is simple: Don't go to colleges or schools that will require you to borrow a lot of money to attend. There's a good chance you'll find yourself deep in debt for no purpose. On the other hand, all that tuition discounting may mean that there will be bargains to be had. Just don't expect them to always be obvious bargains; you may have to research, and even dicker a bit, to get the best deal. Don't be afraid to dicker. Schools may act like that's unheard of, but you won't be the only one.

And maybe you should rethink college entirely.

According to a recent report in *The Washington Post*, many people with college educations are already jumping the tracks to become skilled manual laborers: plumbers, electricians, and the like. And the Bureau of Labor Statistics predicts that 7 of the 10 fastest-growing jobs in the next decade will be based on on-the-job training rather than higher education. (And they'll be hands-on jobs that are hard to outsource to foreigners: If you want your toilet fixed, it can't be done by somebody in Bangalore). If the *Post* is right about this trend, a bursting of the bubble is growing likelier.

What about higher education folks? What should they (er, we) do? Well, once again, what can't go on forever, won't.

For the past several decades, colleges and universities have built endowments, played *Moneyball*-style faculty-hiring games, and constructed grand new buildings while jacking up tuitions to pay for all these things (and, in the case of state schools, to make up for gradually diminishing public support). That has been made possible by an ocean of money borrowed by students – often with the encouragement and assistance of the universities. Business plans that are based on the continuation of this borrowing are likely to fare poorly.

Just as I advised students not to go into debt, my advice to universities is similar: Don't go on spending binges now that you expect to pay for with tuition revenues (or government aid) later. Those revenues may not be there as expected. Some colleges have already gotten in trouble by borrowing money in the debt markets to support capital improvements that state funding won't pay for, only to face difficulty paying the money back. Expect more of this down the line unless my advice is followed.

It's also time to think about curriculum reform and changes in instructional methods. Post-bubble, students are likely to be far more concerned about getting actual value for their educational dollars. Faced with straitened circumstances, colleges and universities will have to look at cutting costs while simultaneously increasing quality.

Online education and programs that focus more on things that can help students' earnings than on what the faculty want to teach will help deliver more value for the dollar. In some areas, we may even see a move to apprenticeship models or other approaches that provide more-genuine skills upon graduation.

The first step is to ensure that students are actually learning useful things. This isn't much of a problem in engineering schools and the like, but in many other areas, core subjects have been shortchanged. A recent survey of more than 700 schools by the American Council of Trustees and Alumni found that many have virtually no requirements. Perhaps that's why students are studying 50 percent less than they were a couple of decades ago.

A recent book, *Academically Adrift*, by Richard Arum and Josipa Roksa, surveyed college students and found that there wasn't a lot of learning going on:

> *45 percent of students "did not demonstrate any significant improvement in learning" during the first two years of college.*
>
> *36 percent of students "did not demonstrate any significant improvement in learning" over four years of college.*

Prices have been going up, but learning seems to have been going down. The primary reason, according to the study, is that courses aren't very rigorous. There's not much required of students, and the students aren't doing more than is required. If higher education is going to justify its cost, there needs to be much more return on investment, which means much more actual learning, which means more-rigorous course content and less fluff.

Once this issue is addressed, there's plenty of room for improvement on the technological front. In the old days, professors were few, and it made sense for students to travel hundreds of miles to study with them. But today, once you move onto a campus, much of your learning, especially in the first couple of years, takes place in huge lecture halls where one professor addresses hundreds of students – or gets a teaching assistant to do it.

Some students are saving money by doing their first two years at community college. The quality of instruction is often better, and the classes smaller, than in four-year institutions where professors focus more on research than on teaching.

That's a worthwhile strategy, but innovation at four-year institutions could help too. Now that webcasts are a routine feature of corporate training, perhaps it's time to make better use of the Web for education. Take the top teachers in a field and let students at multiple colleges access their lectures online. (Sure, there's not a lot of one-on-one interaction that way – but how much is there in a 200-student lecture class, really?) Once the basic information is covered, students can apply it in person in smaller advanced classes. Would this save money? Possibly – and it would almost certainly produce better results.

The online approach is used by the popular Khan Academy, where students view lectures at their convenience and perfect their skills via video-game-like software, and the follow-up is done in a classroom with a teacher's oversight. The idea is to take advantage of mass delivery when it works best and allow individualized attention when it helps most.

The Khan Academy has gotten a lot of attention, but it's not the last word in technological progress in education. Many for-profit online schools, like Kaplan or Strayer University, are using their standardized course content and large enrollments to perform deep statistical analysis of how students perform and how changes in course content and course presentation can improve learning. This is a knowledge base that is unavailable to traditional universities.

What's striking is that most of the potentially revolutionary change we're seeing has come from outside the educational establishment. Then again, breakthroughs often come from people working outside the old industries. Kamenetz's book *DIY U* talks about "edupunks" who are exploring unconventional thinking about teaching and learning. In fact, the best way to master many subjects may be for students to find their own path, with the role of the education establishment being more to certify competence than to actually teach. In one way, that's how it works already.

Right now, a college degree is an expensive signifier that its holder has a basic ability to show up on time (mostly), to follow instructions (reasonably well), and to deal with others in close quarters without committing serious felonies. In some fields, it may also indicate important background knowledge and skills, but most students will require further on-the-job training. An institution that could provide similar certification without requiring four (or more) years and a six-figure investment would have a huge advantage, especially if employers found that certification to be a more reliable indicator of competence than a college degree. Couple that with apprenticeship programs or internships, and you might not need college for many careers.

The major problem with this plan is that college now serves largely as a status marker, a sign of membership in the educated "caste," and as a place for people to meet future spouses of commensurate status. However, the sight of college graduates buried in debt may change that. We're already seeing signs of a shift in popular culture, with advice columns and news articles appearing that discuss women and men whose huge student debt makes them unmarriageable. At any rate, American culture at its best values people more for what they do than for their membership in a caste – and now seems like a good time to reassert that preference.

Perhaps online programs from prestigious schools will bridge the gap. MIT has already put many of its courses online. At present, you can learn from them, and even get certification, but there's no degree attached. It wouldn't be hard for MIT to add standard exams and a diploma, though, and if they do it right, an online degree from MIT might be worth a lot – not as much as an old-fashioned MIT degree, perhaps, but quite possibly more than a degree from many existing brick-and-mortar schools. We're beginning to see the beginnings of this with accredited schools like Western Governors University. There's also a new online start-up, Minerva University, that aims to compete with elite brick-and-mortar schools, and it includes such big names as former Harvard president Larry Summers.

Meanwhile, for the states and big donors who fund those portions of higher education that the students don't, a post-bubble world will bring some changes too. Many states have been cutting aid to higher education, content to let higher tuition pick up the slack. Some may choose to change that (if they can afford it), but regardless, I expect more direct oversight of state institutions from those who fund them. Universities' priorities will be brought closer to states' priorities, and we can expect more outside pressure for increased rigor and fewer courses and majors in areas that seem to be more about politics or trendiness than substance. We can also expect resistance from those with investments in those fields, but it is unlikely to prevail as the money runs out.

For private schools, government oversight is less direct – but to an even greater extent than state schools, private institutions have been dependent on a flood of government-guaranteed credit, and they are likely to see more scrutiny as well if that is to continue.

As former British Prime Minister Margaret Thatcher famously remarked, the problem with socialism is that you eventually run out of other people's money, and that's likely to be the problem facing higher education too: not enough of other people's money.

Graduation rates, employment after graduation, loan-default rates, and so on are likely to get a lot more attention. Institutions may even be forced to absorb some of the cost of student-loan defaults as an incentive to encourage students to not take on more debt than they can repay or to major in fields in which employment prospects are dim.

Finally, for the entrepreneurs out there, this bubble's bursting may be an opportunity. One of the underpinnings of higher education, as mentioned above, is its value as a credential to employers. A college degree demonstrates at least moderate intelligence and, more important, the ability to show up and perform on a reasonably reliable basis, something that is of considerable interest when hiring people, a surprisingly large number of whom (as most employers can attest) do neither.

But a college degree is an expensive way to get an entry-level credential. New approaches to credentialing, approaches that inform employers more reliably while costing less than a college degree, are likely to become in-creasingly appealing over the coming decade.

If I were an employer, I'd find a reliable non-college-based credentialing system pretty appealing. First, it wouldn't have to be all that great to be a more-reliable indicator of knowledge and skills than a typical college diploma. Second, all things being equal, I'd much rather hire someone who wasn't burdened by six-figure debt. Such employees are likely to be more cheerful, less financially stressed (which can lead to problems with embezzlement and worse) and, significantly, willing to work for less since they don't have big student-loan payments to cover.

What's more, someone who successfully completes a rigorous program online is likely to be more self-disciplined, more of a self-starter, than someone who completes college in the traditional fashion. For a lot of employers, that's sure to be a significant plus.

So there's a need for an alternative credentialing system. Filling that need will make someone rich. To any entrepreneurs reading this, good luck – and once you hit it big, please remember the impecunious law professor who put this idea in your head.

V. Politics

Wrenching economic change is easy to endure, as long as it's happening to other people. Thus, as blue-collar workers suffered the pangs of economic transitions in the 1980s and 1990s, it was easy for white-collar workers and academics to talk about the benefits of globalization and of technological progress in the workplace. They may have been right about all that, but don't expect academics to be so enthusiastic when their jobs are being eliminated and their pay is being cut.

The bursting of the higher education bubble is pretty much inevitable, a product of economic forces that politics cannot control. But that doesn't mean that there won't be a political firestorm or two along the way. And while politics won't prevent the bubble from bursting, the political response can make a big difference in how well things go. What kinds of responses can we expect?

At one end of the spectrum, we may see the sort of die-hard job protection that we've seen in other shrinking sectors, where the focus is on (1) keeping competition down for as long as possible; and (2) preserving the jobs, perks, and salaries of senior workers at all costs. If that is the main response, we'll see bitterly contested efforts to use accrediting agencies and other gatekeepers to block the rise of new, lower-cost approaches to higher education. At the same time, we'll see existing tenured faculty fighting to retain their positions, while new academic hires become non-tenure-track contract appointments. (Already, many universities have turned many or most introductory courses over to low-paid adjuncts or visiting professors who don't have tenure and in many cases don't get health or retirement benefits.) In the short term, this will reduce the pain for faculty members and administrators, but the end result will be a hollowed-out university.

At the other end, we may see serious efforts to rebuild the higher education model. Instead of looking at what faculty want and then telling students that's what they get, we may instead look at what skills and knowledge students need to possess at graduation – and can afford to pay for – and structure programs accordingly.

In practice, of course, it won't be an either/or thing: Because higher education is decentralized, we'll see all sorts of different responses. Some will succeed and some will fail. Those who learn from the experience of others will be better able to make their own choices. Those who don blinders will learn only from their own experience, which may well turn out to be bitter.

Where state institutions are concerned, there will be an opportunity for the public to take a hand, if people are interested. Ordinarily, running state universities is left to administrators and trustees, with perhaps a bit of attention from the legislature, mostly where budgets are concerned. But as things begin to change, new ideas from outside will get a hearing.

Interested citizens should consider attending trustees meetings, talking to legislators, and in general making noise about the priorities of state institutions and whether or not they are serving the public. Does it make sense to cut science funding while expanding diversity programs? Is a new gym or stadium really a top priority? It is quite possible that we will see a broad-based popular movement for higher education reform. University spokespeople have been telling us for years that higher education is a matter of public interest. It should not be surprising if the public becomes interested as it becomes clear that the existing model has failed. My advice to outside agitators: Master the arcana of the budget process. Even many university administrators don't really understand how it works.

Private institutions do not enjoy (if that is the word) the same degree of outside scrutiny – but here, too, alumni, students, parents, and other interested parties will have more of a chance to weigh in than has been usual. And given that private institutions are actually more dependent on federal student-loan money than state institutions are, they will be particularly subject to pressures for reform that are tied to eligibility to receive federal funds.

Students and prospective students will have an effect – and, indeed, already are doing so – simply by becoming better informed and less willing to pay top dollar for an inferior product. Ultimately, you can't run a college if you can't fill the seats with paying students, and that will be harder and harder to do for schools that don't produce visible value. The schools that get ahead of the curve will prosper, while those that lag behind will not.

There will likely be at least one major effort to secure federal bailout money for the higher education sector, but the prospects for that relief seem poor. The nation is already in sad financial shape, and higher education already received a substantial slug of "stimulus" money in 2009 that was mostly used to conduct business as usual for a bit longer.

The higher education bubble isn't bursting because of a shortage of money. It is bursting because of a shortage of value. The solution is to improve the product, not to increase the subsidy.

Conclusion

There's nothing evil or unnatural about a bubble or about the people who participate in one. Bubbles are an inevitable part of human nature and appear in almost every field of endeavor. When bubbles burst it's painful – but the sources of the pain lie not so much in the bust as in the poor decisions made during the preceding boom. Resources were allocated in ways that didn't make sense, because the bubble made them *seem* to make sense for a while. The consequences of that misallocation account for the pain.

And it's not the end of the world when a bubble bursts, either. When the tech bubble burst, people lost money (some people lost a *lot* of money) and some people lost jobs, but the Internet didn't go away, and neither did Internet businesses. Likewise, the bursting of the higher education bubble won't mean the end of higher education. It'll just mean that there will be less "dumb money" out there to be harvested.

But inevitably, change will come, and that's not so bad. This is the 21st century. It's not shocking to think that higher education will go through major changes over the coming decade or two. What would be shocking would be if things stayed the same, when rapid change has been the norm lately in every other knowledge-based industry.

I don't pretend to know how it will all work out, but I hope the thoughts in this Broadside have been useful to readers, and I encourage you to join in the conversation in the years to come.

RICH TRZUPEK

HOW THE EPA'S GREEN TYRANNY IS STIFLING AMERICA

UNDER THE LEADERSHIP of U.S. EPA Administrator Lisa Jackson and "energy czar" Carol Browner, the Obama administration continues to develop an unprecedented amount of new draconian environmental regulations that will severely damage America's beleaguered industrial sector. The scope of these initiatives is breathtaking, going well beyond anything that has ever been attempted in the name of ecological purity in America. While many of us share a sense of foreboding about what the EPA has been doing, few really understand the issues. After all, cap and trade is dead, is it not? With that job-killing, economically disastrous idea out of the way, most people seem to believe that the EPA's ability to interfere with the free market in general and with industry in particular will remain pretty much the same as ever: an expensive annoyance to be sure, but a manageable annoyance nonetheless.

Unfortunately, the hard reality of the situation today is very different and far from encouraging. Cap and trade may be dead, but that doesn't mean that the EPA and other governmental entities aren't pursuing other ways to sabotage America's ability to use cheap, abundant fossil fuels in order to generate power, which is a vital component of fueling economic recovery. The fact is that the Obama administration and its liberal allies are conducting a full-scale assault on America's energy sector, and on our industrial base, in the guise of environmental protection.

Environmental Protection in America: A Brief History

If we are going to fairly consider where America is today with regard to protecting the environment, we must start with an evaluation of where we have been. Forty years ago, President Richard Nixon signed into law the two landmark statutes that were designed to reverse decades of environmental damage that built up in the industrialized era: the Clean Air Act and the Clean Water Act. Few people, regardless of their ideological bent, could argue against the need for either piece of legislation. People who lived in or near large urban centers could see firsthand how dirty the air was. The evidence ranged from the unnatural color of the sky to the coating of dust that would appear on automobiles parked in the city overnight. Burning rivers and dead lakes testified to the fact that numerous waterways were as dirty as the air.

The Clean Air and Clean Water acts were designed to clean up the mess we had made. At the time they were passed, environmental advocates set reasonable, achievable goals. First, the EPA set up numeric standards for pollutants in the air and water. These were the targets. For example, air would be considered "clean" only if no more than *X* parts per million of particulate matter and *Y* parts per million of carbon monoxide were detected. A similar but more complex scheme was used to define clean water, depending on how the water would be used. Having set these goals, the EPA, along with various state and local regulatory authorities, then started building the regulatory structure that would allow the nation to reach those targets. New standards forced automobile manufacturers to install pollution-control devices on vehicles; oil refineries to introduce new fuel blends; and thousands of factories and power plants to install expensive pollution-control devices.

Business owners grumbled, of course, wondering if the expense was necessary and whether the added costs would put American manufacturers at more of a competitive disadvantage relative to foreign competitors. But ultimately, everyone did what they had to do. Americans paid a little more for their automobiles, power, and a host of products, but the expense wasn't enough to really catch anyone's attention, much less to cause concern. Business owners learned that they had to add a new line item on the expense side of the ledger labeled "Environmental Compliance," and while new expenses are never welcome, this one turned out to be manageable in the broad scheme of things.

The results were astounding. The amount of particulate matter (that's dust, to you and me) and lead in the air quickly decreased almost a hundredfold. Concentration of other air pollutants, such as carbon monoxide and ozone, dropped precipitously. Fish returned to waterways that had been horribly polluted just a few years before. Lake Erie rose from the dead to become a sportsman's paradise.

But there was another side to the amazing, and amazingly rapid, success stories called the Clean Air Act and the Clean Water Act. Meeting the requirements of both pieces of legislation required a new kind of support infrastructure, and what we have come to call "green jobs" were born. This included everything from the Sierra Club lobbyist pushing Congress to pass more legislation, to the company that makes state-of-the-art pollution-control devices, to the armies of federal, state, and local bureaucrats who make sure that everyone follows the rules. Law firms sprouted environmental departments to help companies that ran afoul of the EPA, and consultants (like me) began to earn a living by guiding businesses through the tangle of regulations that grew more confusing each year.

As is always the case, once you build up a multifaceted industry like the environmental industry, it's extremely difficult to tear it down or even shrink it a little. This is particularly true when government alone has the power to reduce the size of an industry that – like any service industry – does nothing to create wealth but instead saps capital generated by wealth creators. Absent government mandates, the environmental industry would be a fraction of the size that it is today, for there are few free-market forces that would support such an industry.

And thus we come to the essential conundrum that dominates the increasingly schizophrenic nature of the EPA and environmental policy in this country. On one hand, every administration is anxious to establish its environmental bona fides and trumpet its green triumphs. The agency, likewise, wants everyone to know that it is using taxpayer dollars wisely and is thoroughly protecting the environment. However, nobody is going to declare victory and go home. Nobody is going to say, "That's clean enough, America – let's cut back the size of the EPA and the environmental industry and just go into a maintenance mode." Admitting that we've finished the job, in any facet of environmental protection, would mean that great swaths of the environmental industry would go out of business, from the big companies that produce pollution-abatement equipment to the environmental advocacy groups that provided those companies with a reason to exist. Thus, we have the Zeno's paradox version of environmental policy in America today: We can approach the target of a green planet by halves, but we're not allowed to actually get there.

Thus, even though the goals of the original Clean Air and Clean Water acts have long been fulfilled just about everywhere, those achievements didn't represent an end but rather a beginning. Congress drew up legislation to address other environmental concerns. Bills were passed that aimed to clean up old, poorly managed hazardous-waste dumps (the Comprehensive Environmental Response, Compensation, and Liability Act, also known as "Superfund"); better manage hazardous-waste generation and disposal (the Resource Conservation and Recovery Act); better manage toxic chemicals (the Toxic Substances Control Act); enhance community safety (the Emergency Planning and Community Right-to-Know Act) and do a host of other good things in the name of environmental protection and to enhance our quality of life. There is little doubt that many of these measures were justified, even if the environmental activists usually employed a healthy dose of hyperbole to make manageable problems sound like we were near the end of the world as we know it.

But as more and more environmental legislation was passed, the environmental industry grew larger and larger. The EPA used the authority that Congress granted it to keep environmental goals moving, raising the bar whenever a particular goal was met. Consider ozone, for example.

While ozone is a good thing when it's high in the atmosphere, protecting us from the harmful portion of the sun's rays, ozone is not so welcome at the ground level, where people can breathe it in. Ground-level ozone is commonly called smog and is the primary component of the orange-hued haze that one sometimes sees when flying into a big city on a hot summer day. The original ozone target in the first Clean Air Act was a concentration of 120 parts per billion (ppb) in the air. In other words, if cities controlled air pollution well enough to reduce ozone in the ambient air to 120 ppb or less, then the EPA would define the air as clean – at least with respect to smog.

Around the mid-1990s, it became obvious that just about every metropolitan area, except those located in Southern California, was going to meet the 120 ppb standard. (Southern California is a special and virtually unsolvable case because of the region's geography and weather.) What to do? The Sierra Club and the American Lung Association, along with other environmental groups, pushed for a new lower ozone standard, 80 ppb, and the EPA under the Clinton administration agreed. (That "averaging period" was also changed during the Clinton administration. Ozone concentrations used to be averaged over a one-hour period, but following this change, they have been averaged over an eight-hour period.) More emissions reductions were made, and it became clear that this standard would be met as well. So in 2008 the EPA under the Bush administration lowered the standard again, this time to 75 ppb.

In other words, it doesn't matter whether a Republican or a Democrat is living in the White House. The EPA is its own beast with its own agenda. A particular administration may influence how aggressive the EPA is in cracking down on violations of EPA rules, but the agency's rule-making and standards-setting machinery continues to chug along, no matter who is in charge. For 39 years, from 1970, when the original Clean Air and Clean Water acts were passed, until the end of the Bush administration in 2009, that machinery generated new standards and rules at a fairly consistent, predictable rate. Then Barack Obama took the oath of office, and virtually everything about environmental regulation in America changed.

A Radical Shift at the EPA

Things changed at the EPA when Barack Obama took office and named Lisa Jackson EPA administrator and Carol Browner energy czar. The agency could never be described as a friend to industry, but before Jackson, there were voices within the bureaucracy who listened to the industry side, who understood that evaluating risks versus rewards should include consideration of economic issues, and who served to check some of the more radical voices within the agency. Under Jackson, the craziest tree-hugging inmates of the EPA are now effectively, if not officially, in charge of the asylum. As a result, the EPA has radically changed course. Rather than increasing the regulatory burden and tightening down on standards at a measured pace (whether or not such actions were actually needed), Lisa Jackson's EPA has shifted the agency into hyperdrive. The EPA has never before used its authority to make and propose anything that comes close to the kinds of sweeping, radical changes in environmental regulation that we have seen in the past two years.

It was, I suppose, inevitable that this would happen. According to popular leftist mythology, George W. Bush was an awful president as far as the environment was concerned. There's not a bit of truth to that statement. Under Bush, the air, water, and soil continued to get cleaner than it was under Clinton, just as the air, water, and soil was cleaner under Clinton than it was under George H. W. Bush, and so on. Environmental activists didn't like Bush because 1) he was a Republican; and 2) he didn't sue as many "evil" corporations for violations of obscure requirements of environmental regulations as did his predecessor. Whenever George W. Bush's EPA proposed a change in a regulation or standard that would reduce pollution, environmental groups would complain that he didn't go far enough. Sure, the EPA under Bush published rules to reduce mercury emissions from power plants, for example, but he should have reduced them even more. That complaint, when translated by the technically challenged mainstream media, then morphed into the claim that Bush supported an "increase" in mercury emissions in order to protect his buddies in the power industry.

It was all hooey – politically motivated propaganda with no basis in actual fact. But because few people have the time to understand the intricate technical details involved in environmental policy and because the mainstream media generally defaults to reporting whatever environmental-advocacy groups believe as truth (since, in the mainstream media's mind, the Sierra Club or the American Lung Association have absolutely no self-interest when it comes to environmental policy), the idea that Republican administrations are "anti-environment" and Democratic administrations are "pro-environment" has become accepted dogma within the halls of the University of Conventional Wisdom. Given the extreme, irrational anger that the left directed at the last Bush administration, it's no surprise that an administration swept into office on an anti-Bush platform would use its EPA to clearly distinguish itself from its hated predecessor and to help establish its progressive credentials.

There is no way that Barack Obama's EPA could adhere

to the same policy of gradual but measured "regulatory creep" in the environmental arena to which George W. Bush, Bill Clinton, George H. W. Bush, Ronald Reagan, Jimmy Carter, Gerald Ford, and Richard Nixon had all subscribed. Barack Obama needed to prove that he was the polar opposite of his predecessor in every way possible. If he couldn't do that by closing Gitmo or by pulling out of Iraq when he said he would, then environmental policy would have to do. That was a place where he could clearly distinguish himself from George W. Bush – and at very little cost. Industry would bitch and moan, but industry always bitched and moaned. Ultimately, they did what they were told to do, and America chugged along. Shoot, if Lisa Jackson played it right, they might even be able to convince Americans that environmental regulations actually *created wealth.* America's economy has expanded by leaps and bounds since 1970, when the Clean Air and Clean Water acts were first passed. Why not link the two together? How about this: "What's good for the environment is good for the economy!" That slogan has a fine ring to it, especially when the unemployment rate is hovering near 10 percent.

And so Barack Obama's EPA has become the darling of the environmental left this side of ecoterrorist groups like Earth First. The policies, regulations, and initiatives that Lisa Jackson's EPA have created guarantee that all facets of the environmental industry will continue to grow for decades to come. And yet there is a caveat that goes with that statement. The only way that all facets of the environmental industry will continue to grow for decades to come is if the wealth-creating portions of America's economy continue to grow and prosper, as well. No service industry like the environmental industry can survive unless the wealth creators who pay them remain profitable. One cannot, for example, continue to enjoy the largesse of energy companies – either in terms of consulting fees or eco-contributions – if those companies disappear as the result of excessive, economically destructive regulations. Have we now crossed that line under the current administration? More and more evidence suggests that we have indeed.

An Unparalleled Record of Extremism

Under the leadership of Lisa Jackson and with the encouragement and support of Obama's ultra-leftist energy czar Carol Browner (a former EPA administrator who in January 2011 resigned her position), the EPA has now tossed aside any pretense of steering a middle course. Remember that, as we have seen, the agency never actually steered anything approaching a middle course when it came to balancing the interests of the environment and the economy, but it was near enough to the middle to avoid catastrophic damage. The economy grew, and America prospered in spite of – not because of, as Lisa Jackson would have us believe – the added burdens that increasingly puritanical environmental regulations place upon the nation's wealth creators.

Rather than balancing the interests of the economic health of the nation against the notion of environmental purity, Lisa Jackson's EPA has gone all in on the latter side of the equation. In justifying the draconian measures proposed by the agency she leads, Jackson has repeatedly said that the EPA cannot legally consider the economic effects of its proposed actions. Under Jackson's leadership, the EPA has abandoned any pretense of considering the advice of the industrial sector in anything but a pro forma way as the agency develops new standards and regulations. Jackson justified the agency's radical change of course because, according to her, the EPA was simply following the "latest scientific advice" available. In turn, the "latest scientific advice" largely consists of studies and opinions authored by committees of the EPA's Science Advisory Board (SAB), an organization established in 1978 that is an artifact of the Carter administration. The SAB and its subordinate committees are – in theory – independent, unbiased scientific working groups that serve as both a check and a balance on the EPA. In fact, the SAB and its committees consist almost entirely of left-wing academic types who, if anything, believe that the EPA isn't nearly aggressive enough when it comes to environmental policy. By deferring to the SAB and its committees, Jackson isn't following the "latest scientific advice" available; rather, she's using the SAB as a convenient excuse to justify an ultra-leftist, neon-green agenda. Let's consider a couple of examples.

Economically Disastrous Revisions of the Ozone Standard

When we briefly reviewed the history of environmental regulation in America, we used the ambient air ozone standard as an example of the way that "regulatory creep" ensures that the EPA, environmental groups, and companies that produce environmental products always have something to do. The first ozone standard was in place for 27 years before it was changed. Then the second ozone standard was superseded by a new one 11 years after that. One of the first actions taken by Lisa Jackson's EPA was to propose reducing the ozone standard yet again, even though the Bush-era standard had not been in place for even a year. And Jackson not only wants to reduce the ozone standard after such a ridiculously short period, but the administrator is also proposing a reduction to ludicrously low levels that will allow the EPA to vastly expand its reach in order to clean up air that has suddenly, by regulatory fiat alone, become "dirty."

Jackson has proposed reducing the current ozone standard of 75 ppb to something between 60 to 70 ppb. (All of these standards are based on eight-hour averages.) In addition, the EPA is proposing a new "secondary standard" that will result in creating more "dirty air" in more areas of the country. Going from 75 ppb to 70 ppb (or less) doesn't seem like much of a change, but even that best-case reduction will have enormous effects on industry and the economy.

See page 292 for a map showing which counties do not currently meet the existing 75 ppb standard.

On page 293 let's take a look at counties that would be out of compliance if the standard is lowered to 60 to 70 ppb.

The difference between the two maps is striking. Depending on the final standard the agency chooses, the number of counties that don't meet the ozone standard will increase by 60 percent (70 ppb standard) to more than 100 percent (60 ppb standard). For the most part, the counties that don't meet the existing Bush-era standards are large metropolitan areas that are used to managing emissions that form ozone. (Ground-level ozone forms when two pollutants, nitrogen oxides and volatile organic compounds, react with the aid of sunlight on warm days, typically when winds are light and calm.) Big cities sell the low-vapor-pressure gasoline that fights ozone formation in the summer, for example. Many have vehicle-inspection programs in place to ensure that catalytic converters and other pollution-control equipment continue to function

Counties with Monitors Violating the March 2008 Ground-Level Ozone Standards

0.075 parts per million

(Based on 2006–2008 Air Quality Data)

322 of 675[1] monitored counties violate the standard

NOTES:

1. Counties with at least one monitor with complete data for 2006–2008
2. To determine compliance with the March 2008 ozone standards, the 3-year average is truncated to three decimal places.

Counties with Monitors Violating Primary 8-Hour Ground-Level Ozone Standards

0.06–0.070 parts per million

(Based on 2006–2008 Air Quality Data)

EPA *will not* designate areas as nonattainment on these data,
but likely on 2008–2010 data, which are expected to show improved air quality.

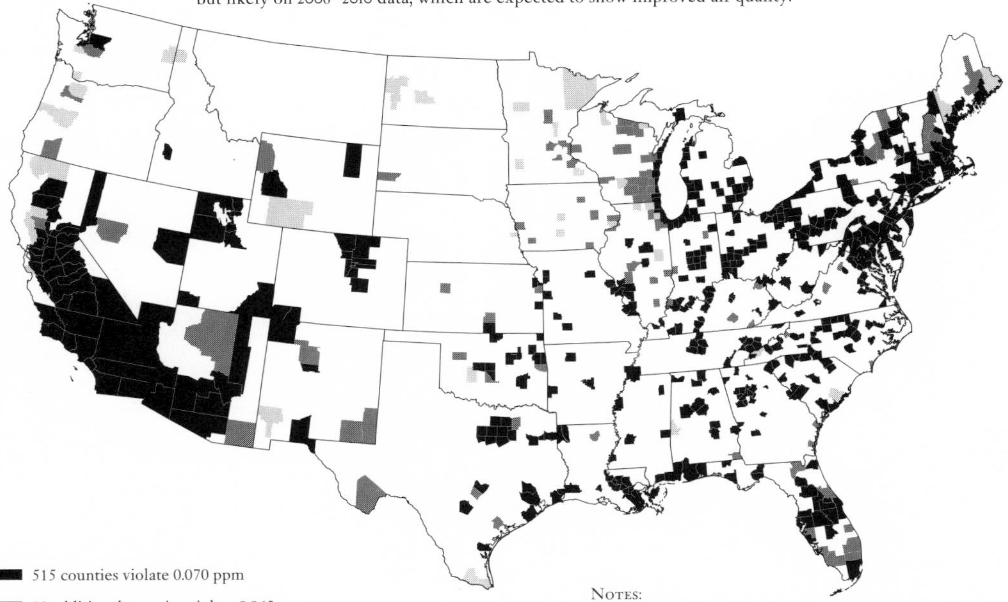

- 515 counties violate 0.070 ppm
- 93 additional counties violate 0.065 ppm for a total of 608
- 42 additional counties violate 0.060 ppm for a total of 650

Notes:

1. No monitored counties outside the continental U.S. violate.
2. EPA is proposing to determine compliance with a revised primary ozone standard by rounding the 3-year average to three decimal places.

Counties with Monitors Violating Secondary Seasonal Ground-Level Ozone Standards

7–15 parts per million-hours

(Based on 2006–2008 Air Quality Data)

EPA *will not* designate areas as nonattainment on these data, but likely on 2008–2010 data which are expected to show improved air quality.

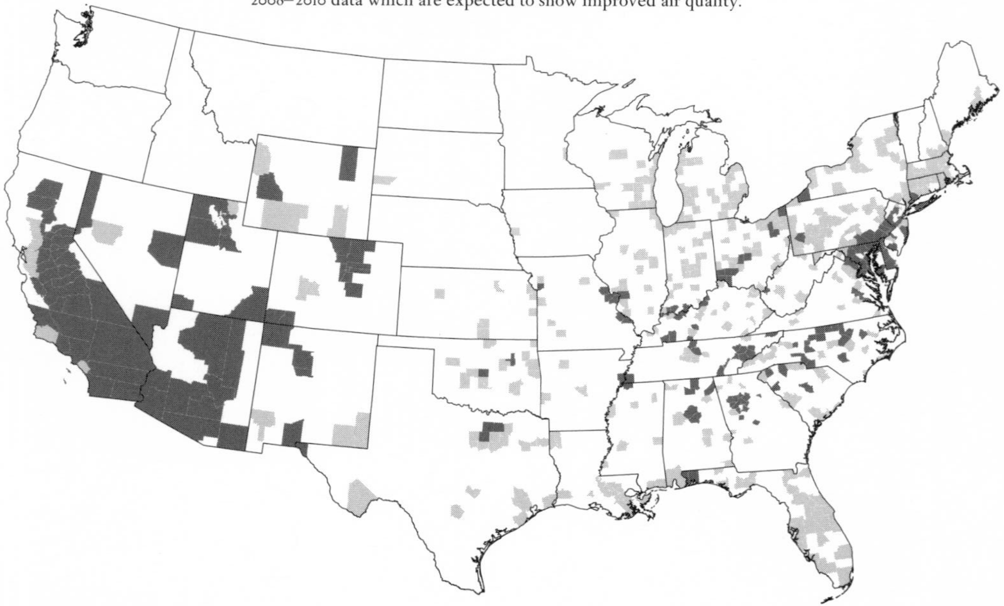

196 counties violate 15 ppm-hours

383 additional counties violate 7 ppm-hours

properly. Industrial sources in and around big cities are subject to stringent control requirements. Few of these structures exist in the many smaller towns and rural areas that would be affected by the imposition of Jackson's draconian standard. The cost of production and the cost of transportation will increase in parts of America that have never felt the heavy hand of the EPA, at a time when the nation can least afford such environmental largesse. As Ted Steichen, policy adviser for the American Petroleum Institute, said during his testimony before Congress regarding the proposed new standard: "To cite a football analogy, EPA is effectively proposing to move the goalposts in the middle of the game. Many local communities will be saddled with new costs that will hurt both large and small businesses and prevent expansion and growth. Fuels that cost more to manufacture would be required in more areas. Jobs will unnecessarily be lost."

On page 294 take a look at the counties that will be affected by the new secondary ozone standard.

This is not, as the Obama administration hopes you will believe, business as usual in the world of environmental regulation. This is something different, something new and radical and untested. This is a demand (and the agency is making a lot of them) for a level of environmental purity that no nation on earth has ever felt the need to attain before. How can the EPA justify this level of regulation? There are three components to the agency's "green marketing" strategy: minimize, rationalize, and marginalize. Here's how it works:

1) Minimize the Effect – Very few people really understand the technical issues that are at the heart of environmental initiatives, so the agency's party line has been that these new rules aren't really a big deal

at all. Without the kind of in-depth analysis that the media just aren't equipped to provide (even if they were of a mind to), the EPA's assurances that nothing has really changed in the world of environmental regulation will satisfy most people. In a speech marking the 40th anniversary of the Clean Air Act, Jackson defended her agenda and sneered away any suggestions that the agency has radically shifted course. "We can take on the remaining challenges of pollution in our air," she said. "I know because the Clean Air Act took on big challenges – and it worked. We can come together in a collaborative effort, ignore the doomsday exaggerations, and build a common-sense plan together. I know because we've done it before – and it worked."

2) Rationalize the Benefits – The longer our economic woes continue, the more you will hear the following slogan: What's good for the environment is good for the economy. In the course of a few sentences that simply boggle the mind for their absurdity, Jackson tried to link the economic growth that America has experienced during the past four decades to the existence of the Clean Air Act. "And as air pollution has dropped over the last 40 years, our national GDP has risen by 207 percent," she said. "The total benefits of the Clean Air Act amount to more than 40 times the costs of regulation. For every one dollar we have spent, we get more than $40 of benefits in return. Say what you want about EPA's business sense, but we know how to get a return on an investment. In short, the Clean Air Act is one of the most cost-effective things the American people have done for themselves in the last half century."

Where do these amazing economic benefits come

from? The rationale that the EPA uses to identify economic savings when it comes to pollution reductions almost always involves one of two areas: fewer worker sick days (and thus increased productivity) and decreased mortality. More about those two issues later on, but as spurious as those overused claims are, they are exceptionally dubious when it comes to Jackson's ozone-standard proposals. The health benefits are linked to a study in which a small number of test subjects showed increased lung capacity when breathing in a few parts per billion less ozone. The increase in lung capacity was small and not really statistically significant, but it was enough for the academics "advising" (read: dictating policy to) the EPA to demand a reduction in the ozone standard. The other common justification for the new ozone standard is the indisputable fact that incidences of asthma are on the rise in the United States. However, no one in the EPA, Sierra Club, or American Lung Association has yet to explain how reducing ozone will help, since we've made drastic reductions in urban ozone concentrations in the past 40 years, while asthma has increased at the same time. If anything, the empirical evidence suggests that we should be pumping more ozone into our breathing air, not less.

3) Marginalize Opposing Voices – In addition to its mandate to protect the environment, the agency's agenda under Jackson includes a new role: guardian of truth. While it is a fact that industry often disagreed with the EPA's actions, industry always had a place at the table when those actions were being considered. The agency generally steered a middle course between the wishes of environmental lobbyists and industry

> lobbyists, even if it leaned toward the former direction. Today all the industry side gets from the EPA is lip service. The industry side still has a seat at the table – sort of – but nobody at the agency is really interested in what they have to say. Jackson's sneering attitude toward industrial concerns was obvious as she dismissed them in two terse sentences during her Clean Air Act anniversary speech: "Today's forecasts of economic doom are nearly identical – almost word for word – to the doomsday predictions of the last 40 years," she said. "This 'broken record' continues despite the fact that history has proven the doomsayers wrong again and again."

Is Jackson right? Has environmental regulation been a profit-making enterprise? Or might the converse be true? Could it be that American economic growth occurred despite, not because of, all of the environmental regulation that has sprouted up in the past 40 years? I am reminded of cereal commercials that were popular 30 or so years ago. They would feature an awful sugary cereal in a bowl, surrounded by eggs, oatmeal, orange juice, toast, and a glass of milk. The announcer would then happily announce that the cereal was "part of a complete breakfast." Not really. The cereal was in fact *adjacent* to a complete breakfast. Such is the case when we look at the relationship between environmental regulation and economic growth.

There are many factors that determine where investors will spend their money to build new factories and create new jobs, but it's beyond naive to believe that the environmental regulatory bureaucracy doesn't play a significant role in those decisions. In my own career as an industrial consultant, I've personally witnessed countless examples of investments not made where the decision was ultimately influenced by concerns about environmental costs.

The real cost of the Clean Air Act and other environmental regulations was paid in jobs. Whether Jackson understands it or not, the increased power of the EPA drives jobs away, because that's a big factor when companies choose not to reinvest in existing American factories and when other companies choose not to build new ones here. Of course it's not the only factor – clearly things like labor costs, health care, and OSHA play big roles – but it's an important one. Consider employment data in four industries that were hit hard by environmental regulation: the iron and steel, motor-vehicle, paper, and printing industries:

INDUSTRY	TOTAL EMPLOYMENT		
SECTOR	1970	1990	2009
Iron and Steel	627,000	276,200	91,200
Motor Vehicles	799,000	812,000	321,900
Paper	700,900	696,700	418,000
Printing	1,104,300	1,569,400	552,200

In addition to losing jobs in industries that once helped form the backbone of our economy, those increases in productivity that the EPA is always talking about cannot be tied to Americans working longer hours because a cleaner environment keeps them healthier. See page 300 for a graph that shows the trend in the length of the workweek for the average American worker.

* * *

Average Hours Worked Per Week: 1947–2009

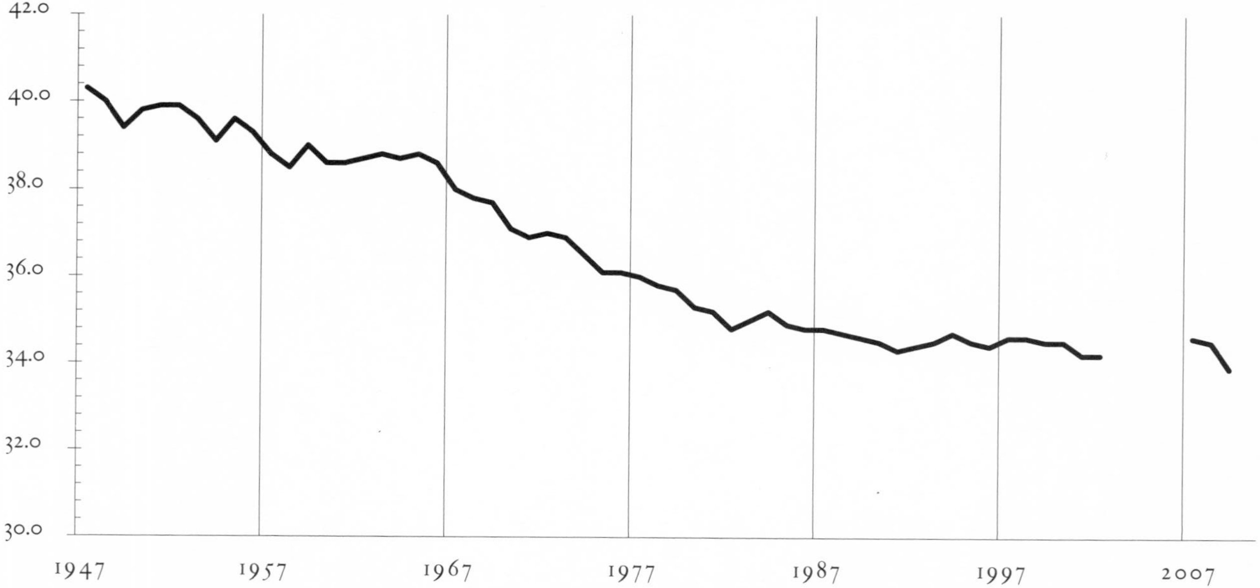

Playing Hardball over Greenhouse Gases

The EPA's claim that it saves billions upon billions of dollars because a cleaner country decreases mortality is equally spurious. The reasons that people live longer today involve advances in medicine and health care, not infinitesimal further reductions in pollution. And as we know very well, thanks to America's intense debate about health care, our increasingly aging population is increasingly more expensive to care for. Thus the EPA's assertion that increased regulation saves money because Americans live longer is ridiculous on two counts: 1) EPA regulations aren't responsible for increased longevity; and 2) if they were, then those rules would cost people more, not less.

Many people who don't buy into the theory that man-made emissions of greenhouse gases are changing the climate of our planet celebrated when cap and trade was officially declared dead in Congress in 2010. Those celebrations were quite premature. The unfortunate fact is that "global warming" disciples have already put a massive, poorly understood infrastructure in place to limit the nation's use of cheap, abundant fossil fuels, and the EPA is aggressively pursuing a regulatory agenda that will further chip away at America's ability to use home-grown energy resources to fuel economic recovery.

Few realize it, but there is no longer any need for the EPA to regulate greenhouse gases in order to reduce greenhouse-gas emissions in the United States. National greenhouse-gas emissions are down to mid-1990s levels. Some of that reduction is due to economic conditions, but a good deal is the result of state and regional initiatives that require continuing decreases in the amount of fossil fuels burned.

Thirty-three states currently have renewable portfolio

standards (RPS) in place. Under these rules, electricity used in the state must be generated using less and less fossil fuel each year. In order to make up the difference, renewable sources that don't emit greenhouse gases must be used in ever increasing percentages. For example, New York's RPS specifies that 24 percent of electricity used in the state has to originate from renewable sources by the year 2013. Illinois's RPS calls for 25 percent renewable generation by 2025. All in all, more than 75 percent of the people in America live in states with RPS programs in place. More are sure to come.

In addition, there are three regional cap-and-trade programs in the United States. East Coast states have banded together under the Regional Greenhouse Gas Initiative, a cap-and-trade program that has been up and running since 2009. West Coast states are developing their own program, called the Western Climate Initiative, while Midwest states are doing the same under the Midwestern Greenhouse Gas Reduction Accord.

The EPA has promulgated new Corporate Average Fuel Economy standards that will reduce greenhouse-gas emissions associated with vehicle emissions. Several EPA initiatives, including drastically reducing ambient air standards for pollutants like ozone, nitrogen dioxide, and sulfur dioxide, are backhanded ways of reducing energy use as well. These standards are so stringent that it would be virtually impossible to get approval to build a large source that burns fossil fuel, because such a source would inevitably violate one or more of the standards. Yet in spite of all that has been done to reduce greenhouse-gas emissions in the United States, the agency is bound and determined to use the "command and control" system set forth in the Clean Air Act to reduce them even more.

Rather than going through a formal rule-making process

to set standards and specify control strategies for greenhouse emissions, the EPA has decided to rely upon the existing permitting provisions of the Clean Air Act to regulate these emissions, at least in the short term. The EPA began greenhouse-gas regulation on Jan. 2, 2011. It will use a two-phased approach. In Phase One, which will run from Jan. 2, 2011, through June 30, 2011, facilities that would trigger permitting requirements based on their emissions of other (non-greenhouse-gas) pollutants must address greenhouse-gas emissions in the permitting process. (The term the EPA uses for these sources is "anyway sources," meaning that they would have been subject to federal permit requirements "anyway.") In Phase Two, starting on July 1, 2011, any source that is a major source of greenhouse gases must address those emissions when going through the federal permitting processes.

To make greenhouse regulation feasible, the EPA had to figure out a work-around to avoid existing permitting thresholds: 250 tons per year for construction permits and 100 tons per year for operating permits. A relatively small commercial establishment – a church or even a large home – could emit 100 tons per year of greenhouse gases. Accordingly, if the EPA stuck to the permitting thresholds specified in the Clean Air Act, the universe of regulated sources would be impossibly large. By the EPA's own admission, sticking to the Clean Air Act in the case of greenhouse gases would inflate the number of operating permits from several thousand to more than 1 million. The regulatory structure could not possibly manage that many permits. Arguably, this is clear evidence that the Clean Air Act was not designed or intended to be used to regulate a "pollutant" such as carbon dioxide and other greenhouse gases. If the nation chooses to limit greenhouse-gas emissions, Congress should pass legislation that defines how that is to be done and delegate authority to the EPA to implement its will. However, the EPA has decided to press forward using its authority under the Clean Air Act, even though a strict interpretation of the act means that the agency will be required to regulate a universe of emissions sources far too large for it to actually regulate.

In order to avoid the problem, the EPA has creatively interpreted the Clean Air Act through the so-called Tailoring Rule. Through the Tailoring Rule, the EPA declared that it can alter the permitting threshold in the case of greenhouse gases. Well, sort of. Clearly anticipating a legal challenge, the EPA retained the 250- and 100-ton-per-year thresholds when it comes to *unmodified* total greenhouse-gas emissions, but it has added another test as part of the formula: the amount of "carbon dioxide equivalent" emissions.

Theoretically, it's not just carbon dioxide that causes global warming. Other chemicals like methane (the primary component of natural gas) can cause global warming too. But the theoretical global warming "power" of each of these chemicals is somewhat different. A pound of methane in the atmosphere, for example, helps retain about 21 times more heat than a pound of carbon dioxide. In order to get every compound that theoretically causes global warming on the same page, the environmental community uses the term "carbon dioxide equivalent." Basically, you multiply the global warming power (called global warming potential, or GWP) of each compound to get to the equivalent amount of carbon dioxide that each compound represents. Carbon dioxide equivalent is commonly abbreviated CO_2e. Thus, one ton of methane emissions (with a multiplier of 21) is calculated as 21 tons of CO_2e. The multiplier for nitrous oxide is 310, and the multipliers to get to CO_2e for certain refrigerants are in the thousands.

When a facility calculates its total greenhouse-gas emissions, it does two calculations. The first, as we have seen, is to calculate the total amount of greenhouse-gas emissions without using any multipliers. This total is compared to the 100- and 250-ton-per-year thresholds, but it really doesn't mean anything, because the facility still has to do the CO_2e test. In this test, you apply the multipliers and then add up all of the emissions as CO_2e. Permit requirements kick in only if that total is over 75,000 tons per year for construction permits or 100,000 tons per year for operating permits. This additional test allows the EPA to drastically narrow the universe of regulated greenhouse sources, because this CO_2e threshold is very high. This is the "tailoring" that the agency is using to avoid the absurdity that naturally comes from trying to regulate greenhouse gases under the Clean Air Act.

Having decided that it can force states to exercise permitting authority over greenhouse-gas emissions through the Clean Air Act, the EPA then told the state agencies that issue the permits what standards to use when considering greenhouse-gas emissions controls. In guidance issued in November 2010, the EPA directed state agencies to focus on energy efficiency when evaluating greenhouse-gas control. In order to determine that a facility is operating at optimum energy efficiency, the EPA tells state agencies that they should delve into the design and operational details of proposed projects and that their decisions on such matters should be codified in permit documents. Examples of ways that state agencies are to impose themselves in design and operational decisions include the choice of the type of a boiler, the way that energy is used, the amount and manner in which waste heat is recovered, and the way that parts of a process are maintained and operated.

It's important to note that very few permit writers working in state agencies have the experience or skills to make these kinds of decisions. With few exceptions, most permit writers are recent college graduates or "old-timers" who do not possess the skill sets to flourish in the private sector. Expecting such individuals to impose their will in a process that has heretofore been guided by free- market principles is a recipe for disaster.

As troubling, the EPA has directed state agencies to ignore the issue of manufacturer guarantees when evaluating greenhouse-gas controls. Traditionally, a proposed control technology need not be considered unless the manufacturer of the technology was willing to guarantee a certain level of performance. This sensible policy protected buyers and kept the number of vendors selling the environmental equivalent of snake oil to a minimum. However, the EPA has abandoned this policy when it comes to greenhouse gases. As part of their guidance, the EPA told state agencies that the lack of a performance guarantee is not sufficient reason to reject a proposed control measure. Doubtless, the EPA hopes this will encourage innovative control measures, but it is more likely to generate a host of unworkable, technically flawed "magic solutions" that always seem to spring up when unscrupulous vendors sense a government-mandated opportunity. Industry will no longer be able to ignore such vendors, and state agencies will be in a position to force such vendors' products onto buyers.

In summer 2010, 13 states pushed back and asked the EPA for the three years that the Clean Air Act allows them to revise their regulatory strategies. Known as State Implementation Plans, or SIPs, these plans are the blueprints that state and local agencies use to achieve clean-air goals. The act formalized the idea that the federal agency should define where the nation wanted to be in terms of air quality, but the individual states should be allowed to figure out the best way to get there. The SIP approval process has been a key feature of the Clean Air Act since that particular piece of legislation was passed. Yet when it comes to greenhouse gases, Lisa Jackson's EPA is demanding that state and local authorities ignore those provisions of the act and submit new SIPs immediately, even though the feds haven't even established definitive emissions targets for greenhouse gases. Essentially, the states have been asked to put their faith in the EPA in the expectation that the feds' decision will ultimately be "the right thing."

Of the 13 states that asked for the time to which they were statutorily entitled before revising their SIPs, only Texas stuck to its guns. In a scathing letter, Texas Attorney General Greg Abbott told Lisa Jackson that the Lone Star State would not "pledge allegiance to the USEPA," thus offering further proof that it's never wise to mess with Texas. In turn, the EPA can be expected to withhold approval of any federal permits that are issued in the state in the future. This is thus a game of chicken on the big stage. Texas is going to press forward with its permit program on the state's own authority, while the feds hope that their refusal to play along will scare away potential developers in one of the nation's few economic bright spots. The outcome of this battle will likely define the future of greenhouse-gas regulation in the United States. If Texas wins, the road to rolling back the enormous and enormously expensive greenhouse-gas-regulation infrastructure that has been put into place will be wide open. If Texas loses, we're in for a very challenging few decades.

Recently, the EPA's all-out attack on coal was expanded to include three especially troubling regulatory proposals:

the Boiler MACT rule, the Utility MACT rule and a New Source Performance Standard for electric utilities that limits the amount of carbon dioxide that power plants can emit. Combined with all of the EPA's other regulatory initiatives, these three rules will ensure that President Obama keeps his campaign promise of making it too expensive to build any more coal-fired power plants in the United States.

The Boiler MACT and the Utility MACT rules are supposed to create standards for the amount of potentially toxic emissions (called Hazardous Air Pollutants in EPA-speak) from industrial boilers and electric utilities. The applicable control standard is called Maximum Achievable Control Technology, from which we get the MACT acronym. The fact that these rules were created could lead one to believe that emissions of potentially toxic compounds from boilers and utilities are a hazard to public health and the environment. They aren't. EPA's extensive monitoring network shows that the concentrations of potentially toxic compounds in the air we breathe are far, far below any levels of concern. The EPA's vast database cataloging the sources of emissions shows that boilers and utilities emit a fraction of the overall total of these pollutants in any case. However, thanks to the misguided Clean Air Act Amendments of 1990 (signed by George H. W. Bush, by the way), the agency is not required to show that MACT requirements are *necessary*: It only needs to demonstrate that they are technically *feasible*, and hang the cost.

Lisa Jackson used these rules to attack coal from yet another direction. Boiler MACT and Utility MACT limits are so ridiculously small that many coal boilers will be forced to shut down because it will be impossible to comply. This is bad enough in the utility sector, which generates the electricity we need, but it's a disaster for many manufacturers who have depended on cheap, plentiful coal to provide the power they need. There is little doubt that many of the plants that are affected will be forced to move operations to other countries.

And then came the death blow. In March 2012, the EPA released Subpart TTTT of New Source Performance Standards, a rule that will limit carbon dioxide emissions from new power plants. No coal-fired power plant can meet the emission limit (1,000 pounds of carbon dioxide per megawatt of power produced), although natural-gas-fired power plants can.

As a result of all this, it is now estimated that about 50,000 to 80,000 megawatts of coal-fired power will be retired from the grid over the next few years. Coal-fired power is base-load power (that is, power that has to be available all of the time), and neither solar nor wind can provide base-load power anywhere but in the president's green fantasies. Biomass (wood, energy crops, etc.) can provide base-load power, but there's not nearly enough of the fuel to replace so much coal. More nuclear power could easily shoulder the load, but there's no way that we can permit and build enough nuclear plants in the time available. That leaves natural gas as the only fuel that can possibly be used to replace all of that coal.

Right now, natural gas is looking pretty good. Thanks to shale gas, we have abundant supplies (over 100 years of proven reserves, even in the worst-case demand scenario) and prices are incredibly low. New, highly effi-cient combined-cycle gas-fired power plants are actually competitive with coal-fired power at today's prices.

Replacing all that coal with natural gas should soothe global warming alarmists as well. (I say "should" because everyone knows that the environmental doom industry cannot and will not ever admit that it is satisfied with any level of reductions until we're living in caves.) Natural gas generates much less carbon dioxide per unit of energy as compared with coal and, as noted above, natural-gas-fired power plants can be much more efficient. The combination of these two effects means that carbon dioxide emissions in the United States, which have been declining for the past five years in any case, will drop even more precipitously in the future.

So one might be tempted to ask: What's the big deal? If natural gas is cheap and if burning natural gas might cause at least a few hysterical enviro-types to lower the volume of their incessant shrieking just a tad, it's all good – right? Well, not quite.

Historically, natural gas prices have been very volatile and, despite the current glut, there is no reason to believe that supply will so greatly outstrip demand in the long run. The big energy players in natural gas – companies like Chesapeake, Cabot, and Chevron – are working hard to create new markets, increase demand, and thus get prices back up. A major South African chemical company recently announced plans to build a plant here that will produce gasoline from natural gas feedstock. Several players in the energy market are in the initial stages of planning Liquefied Natural Gas (LNG) terminals, with exports to Europe and Asia in mind. There are plans in the works to create more natural gas infrastructure so the nation's truck fleet will convert over from diesel to natural gas.

Perhaps most important, using natural gas to generate thousands of megawatts of power will consume huge quantities of the fuel, thus necessarily causing prices to rise as more new power plants come on line. It's no surprise that the two big manufacturers of natural-gas-fired turbines – GE and Siemens – have been flooding the airwaves with commercials extolling the virtues of their wares. Both companies stand to make a whole lot of money in the next few years, thanks to the Obama administration's all-out war on coal.

In contrast to the volatility of natural gas prices, coal prices have always been pretty steady. Thus the coal fleet (along with the nuclear fleet) has helped dampen any fluctuations in natural gas that affect that relatively small portion of energy production in the United States. As we shift away from coal and put more of the energy burden on natural gas, electricity prices are likely to fluctuate more than they ever have and are likely to increase substantially over the long term as well.

It's a shame that we're knowingly abandoning such a cheap, reliable, and plentiful resource like coal in a foolish effort to fulfill a ridiculous crusade led by eco-puritans. It's maddening that such a decision was made not by Congress, nor by the voters, but by a few faceless bureaucrats hiding behind global warming pseudo-science that has become the 21st century's version of alchemy.

The Tip of the Iceberg

We've examined a couple of environmental initiatives in some depth, but we've hardly scratched the surface. Barack Obama's EPA is introducing new regulations at a pace and scope that we have never seen before in virtually every area that the agency touches. The agency is also studying new ways to micromanage America in the name of environmental purity.

There's a working group that's studying new ways to address the pollutants in stormwater runoff, for example. Mind you, new and more stringent stormwater rules were just put in place during the previous administration, but

– by definition – nothing that the EPA did while George Bush was president could possibly be good enough for Lisa Jackson. Accordingly, the stormwater working group is considering, among other things, expanded use of the EPA's licensing authority in order to control the manufacture and use of consumer products that might impact stormwater runoff. If that sounds like a stealthy way to introduce more government control into the economy and raise a little revenue to boot, it's probably because that's what it is.

Another task force is considering ways to improve waterway management, including ocean management. This group's activities were the source of the "Obama wants to ban fishing" story that made the rounds in 2010. While the Interagency Ocean Policy Task Force has not been directed to ban sportfishing or even to explore that issue, looking at fishing regulations and policies is most definitely within the task force's scope of work. Is a fishing ban in our future? Almost certainly not. But are additional rules on the way that will affect commercial fishing and, perhaps, sportfishing in some areas? Almost certainly so.

The Obama administration's breathtakingly shortsighted decision to kill the Keystone XL pipeline after more than three years of study while gas prices approach the $5-per-gallon mark infuriated many Americans. It is yet another example of the way in which the president has abandoned any hint of pursuing a prudent energy policy in favor of satisfying environmental zealots. And recall that the administration was only being asked to approve the border crossing. That's all. The individual states, the EPA, and a host of other regulatory organizations would review and approve the details of the plan. Yet when Congress backed the administration into a corner after it had spent over 36 months wringing it hands, the president claimed that his team didn't have enough information to make a final decision about the border crossing within two more months! It was a ludicrous explanation.

This is the most aggressive EPA that the nation has ever seen. Its tentacles are reaching out into society and the economy in ways that very few members of the public can possibly imagine. We're looking at the tip of a huge iceberg that will affect America for years to come. And, like another famous iceberg, this one has the ability to sink the ship that has been this nation's amazing vessel of prosperity.

KEVIN D. WILLIAMSON

THE DEPENDENCY AGENDA

LBJ AND THE GREAT CONUNDRUM

I'll have them niggers voting Democratic for 200 years.
LYNDON BAINES JOHNSON, 1964
as reported in Ronald Kessler's
Inside the White House

IN THE MID-1960S, the administration of President Lyndon Baines Johnson was in crisis. The Democrats enjoyed a crushing victory in 1964, but December of that year also saw the first march against the war in Vietnam, an unpopular military misadventure that was regarded as being mainly a Kennedy-Johnson project – which, of course, it was, though the sainted JFK has largely been exempted from blame for it. While Johnson's Democratic Party was still largely dominated by fiercely anti-Communist hawks such as Sen. Henry "Scoop" Jackson – who had been a trenchant critic of what he considered the recklessly soft national-defense posture of the Eisenhower administration – it was increasingly the political home of the more radical elements of the left and those who sympathized with them. That the Democrats became the partisan home of the far left in the '60s is illuminating in that it speaks to the political calculations that were made regarding the two thorniest issues of that decade: the confrontation with the Soviet Union abroad and the wrenching debate over African Americans' rights at home.

The left could not make common cause with the Republican Party, even though the party had been – in both its legislative and executive branches – a champion of the political and economic rights of African Americans. Republicans had a tradition of consistent and energetic anti-Communism, which extended back to the pre–New Deal era, and a refreshed postwar commitment to free enterprise over state central planning. But the left found that it could make common cause with the Democratic Party under Johnson, which was curious. On top of prosecuting an unpopular war as president, Johnson – as Senate majority leader only a few years earlier – had rallied such Democratic worthies as Sen. Robert Byrd, a veteran of the Ku Klux Klan, and Sen. William Fulbright, a remorseless segregationist and signer of the Southern Manifesto, in undermining President Dwight D. Eisenhower's Civil Rights Act of 1957. That Johnson did so while successfully posing as a champion of civil rights is testament to his unique political genius, unmatched on the national scene until the presidency of Bill Clinton. Contrary to the popular myth, Democratic opposition to Eisenhower's landmark civil-rights bill was hardly confined to the so-called Dixiecrats: Sen. John F. Kennedy voted against it, while his eventual Republican nemesis, Richard Nixon, had helped shepherd the bill through Congress. Johnson, for his part, not only opposed civil-rights legislation but also Republican-backed antilynching legislation – and had done so consistently.

While President Eisenhower was finally successful in getting the 1957 act through Congress – in spite of an unprecedented marathon 24-hour filibuster by Democratic Sen. Strom Thurmond (who regaled the Senate with, among other things, his grandmother's biscuit recipe) – Sen. Johnson succeeded in watering down the key provisions of what he called in private the "nigger bill," excising its enforcement clauses and thereby rendering the legislation almost entirely toothless.

Some years later, President Johnson, one of the canniest political operators in American history, could draw upon his own deep experience in legislative politics to calculate where this would all end. While racial animus was indeed a ghastly fact of life in American politics, particularly in Southern politics, he knew that there were stronger forces at play. As *The New York Times* put it, "He won his seat in Congress because, in 1937, central Texas was still deep in the Depression and he was able to demonstrate a connection to Franklin D. Roosevelt, who was a god there." Johnson's constituents during his time in the House may have broadly shared his troglodytic racial outlook, but it was the New Deal, not the Lost Cause, that had brought Johnson to Washington. When he became a U.S. senator, the *Times* says, Johnson found himself representing a constituency that "made up for being less intensely segregationist than the rest of the South by being more intensely anti-Communist."

Johnson found himself and his party in a position that would in the long term prove untenable. The elements of the Democratic Party that were strongly anti-Communist and in favor of civil rights – the faction represented by Sen. Jackson and others of that stripe – were sure to be repelled by the influx of leftist radicals that the antiwar movement was bringing into the fold. At the same time, those who were mainly motivated by the paramount domestic issue of fully integrating African Americans into national political and economic life had the recent experience of watching the Democrats, led by Johnson, do red-in-tooth-and-claw battle against the Civil Rights Act of 1957 and again against the Civil Rights Act of 1960. The latter act sought to remedy some of the defects of the earlier legislation and again found Sen. Johnson in the shadows leading Senate Democrats in a record-breaking continuous filibuster, this one lasting some 43 hours. In 1960, as in 1957, the disproportionately Republican congressional civil-rights caucus overcame Democratic parliamentary obstacles and sent landmark legislation to the desk of a Republican president.

All of this puts paid to the utterly dishonest account of the '50s and '60s cultivated by the Democratic Party today: that conservative Southern Democrats exited the party en masse to join up with a Republican Party that shared their primitive racist views. Conservative Southerners did in fact abandon the Democrats during and after the '60s, but they did so to join a Republican Party whose legislators and president had achieved significant civil-rights progress over bitter Democratic opposition. Whatever their motive was, it was not for the sake of racism that they were abandoning the party of the Ku Klux Klan and Byrd (who held the ridiculous title of Exalted Cyclops in that ridiculous organization) for the party of Abraham Lincoln, Eisenhower, and the Civil Rights Acts of 1957 and 1960 – or because of later landmark civil-rights legislation either. Even Johnson's own keystone civil-right legislation, the Civil Rights Act of 1964, was much more strongly supported by congressional Republicans (75 percent voted for it) than by Democrats (just over half voted for it).

The question of what really happened with the political realignment of the '60s and the subsequent decades, which saw great numbers of conservative Democrats leaving their party and joining the Republicans, is complex. The short version is that the left valued the toleration of revolutionary socialism abroad and the piecemeal implementation of the welfare state at home over the civil rights of African Americans, and it therefore made common cause with the segregationist Johnson Democrats over the anti-segregationist Eisenhower Republicans, while many conservative Democrats – dedicated to opposing the welfare state at home and Communism abroad – followed the opposite course. The antiwar movement and the radicalization of the Democratic left certainly played a leading role in that drama, particularly among national security conservatives. But the most critical factor was President Johnson's decision to try to maneuver his way out of the mess he found himself in by revisiting the political agenda that first brought him to Congress: the New Deal. Not to put too fine a point on it, but the Democrats were on the verge of losing both the blacks and the rednecks, and Johnson had a plan to buy their loyalties with a program he called the Great Society.

The New Deal and the Politics of Control

The New Deal differed from the Great Society and most subsequent additions to the welfare state in important ways. It was adopted during a time of national (indeed, global) emergency. The Great Depression had led to an unprecedented decline in U.S. economic output and the sudden impoverishment of millions of Americans. (Many New Deal programs, notably the intentional reduction of U.S. agricultural production, would in fact make this problem worse, contrary to the economic theory under which Roosevelt and his advisers were operating.) In the background, the increasing possibility of another war in Europe informed a great deal of economic thinking at the time. This was true well before Adolf Hitler's formal ascent to power, though it is notable that this happened during the same dark year – 1933 – that saw the first New Deal programs instituted. The European situation was a critical factor for two reasons. First, Roosevelt was far from alone in his belief that a United States in economic disarray was poorly positioned to be a credible military actor in an unstable world. The second and less well-understood fact is that a great many American intellectuals and politicians considered the totalitarian systems of the early 20th century to be successful to varying degrees: Roosevelt famously spoke well of Benito Mussolini ("that admirable Italian gentleman"), while leaders ranging from Henry Ford to David Lloyd George found things to admire about the Third Reich and its charismatic leader. Further, the rapid industrialization of the Soviet Union under Communism had made an impression in the West, much as the rapid industrialization of China under Communism at the turn of the century would make on similarly naive American intellectuals. For a great many U.S. leaders in the 1930s, it seemed apparent that fascism, Nazism, and Communism had all taken steps toward solving what they believed to be the pre-eminent problem of the day: the failure of capitalism and its necessary replacement with rational central-planning regimes. As the influential liberal economist John Kenneth Galbraith noted, "Hitler also anticipated modern economic policy … by recognizing that a rapid approach to full employment was only possible if it was combined with wage and price controls. That a nation oppressed by economic fear would respond to Hitler as Americans did to F.D.R. is not surprising.… In economics, it is a great thing not to understand what causes you to insist on the right course." Galbraith, who became a senior official in Roosevelt's

Office of Price Administration during the war, was typical in his view of the necessity of centralizing government power to ameliorate the vagaries of capitalism.

The New Dealers may be partly exonerated for the subsequent sins of statism inasmuch as the ideas behind their program were largely untested; in the context of the 1930s, a centrally planned economy under the management of teams of highly specialized experts and selfless elites must have seemed a plausible alternative to the economic dislocations of the time. No similar exculpation can be offered to the architects of the Great Society, who were not operating during an international emergency and who had plentiful experience in which to root sensible expectations about the likely effects of their agenda. The social-welfare and wealth-transfer aspects of the Great Society were to play the role for middle-class whites that Johnson's loveless embrace of civil rights played for blacks (and, inevitably, for other groups in subsequent years): a tool for building a permanent Democratic majority under which the interests of the state would be made identical to the interests of the Democratic Party – and state dependents made in effect dependents of the Democratic Party.

The New Deal, for all its failures, was not in the main a project dedicated to the cultivation of economic dependency for the purposes of political gain. Indeed, Roosevelt himself worried about creating long-term dependency. In his 1935 State of the Union speech – in which he proposed the creation of Social Security, federal unemployment benefits, and what would become Aid to Families with Dependent Children, he declared:

> *A large proportion of these unemployed and their dependents have been forced on the relief rolls.... The lessons of*

history, confirmed by the evidence immediately before me, show conclusively that continued dependence upon relief induces a spiritual disintegration fundamentally destructive to the national fiber. To dole our relief in this way is to administer a narcotic, a subtle destroyer of the human spirit. It is inimical to the dictates of a sound policy. It is in violation of the traditions of America. Work must be found for able-bodied but destitute workers.

The federal government must and shall quit this business of relief.

Roosevelt's solution was to have the government become an employer rather than a caregiver:

I am not willing that the vitality of our people be further sapped by the giving of cash, of market baskets, of a few hours of weekly work cutting grass, raking leaves, or picking up papers in the public parks. We must preserve not only the bodies of the unemployed from destitution but also their self-respect, their self-reliance, and courage and determination.

. . . This group was the victim of a nationwide depression caused by conditions which were not local but national. The federal government is the only governmental agency with sufficient power and credit to meet this situation. We have assumed this task, and we shall not shrink from it in the future. It is a duty dictated by every intelligent consideration of national policy to ask you to make it possible for the United States to give employment to all of these 3½ million people now on relief, pending their absorption in a rising tide of private employment.

It is my thought that, with the exception of certain of the normal public building operations of the government, all emergency public works shall be united in a single new and greatly enlarged plan.

> *With the establishment of this new system, we can supersede the Federal Emergency Relief Administration with a coordinated authority which will be charged with the orderly liquidation of our present relief activities and the substitution of a national chart for the giving of work.*

If it occurred to President Roosevelt that an American employed by the government on noneconomic terms is as much of a dependent as one receiving welfare payments, he does not ever seem to have spoken of the fact. But it is clear that – with some important exceptions such as the creation of Social Security – much of the New Deal was intended as a set of temporary emergency measures. The various initiatives of the Works Progress Administration, the Civil Works Administration, and the Rural Electrification Administration were intended to be closed-end projects. (Many inevitably achieved immortality, the Tennessee Valley Authority prominent among them.)

What was intended to be permanent about the New Deal was not the creation of government jobs for unemployed Americans but the extension of federal power over large swaths of the economy through the central-planning authority of the National Recovery Administration (unanimously ruled unconstitutional in 1935), the Federal Deposit Insurance Corporation, the Glass-Steagall Act, the National Labor Relations Act, the Fair Labor Standards Act, and the like. Fortunately, much of President Roosevelt's statist overreach was blocked by the judiciary on solid constitutional grounds or was repealed piecemeal by Congress. Though Roosevelt went to his grave beloved, the imperial, Bismarckian style of his economic program was not destined to sit well with a nation fresh from vanquishing German authoritarianism. The Great Society attempted no such obvious domination of the economy. The New Deal was an iron first; the Great Society is a velvet glove.

Unlike the New Deal, the Great Society's hallmark programs were not enacted in response to an emergency of any kind, much less one so deep and broad as the Great Depression. When Medicare was adopted, the elderly were the single wealthiest group of Americans, as they are today. The first Job Corps office opened when the unemployment rate was under 5 percent. The poverty rate had been declining steeply for years before the War on Poverty was announced. It was nearly halved before the Great Society began to be implemented in earnest, falling from nearly 19 percent in 1959 to less than 10 percent in 1968. After the first skirmishes in the War on Poverty, the rate began to climb: War was declared, and poverty won. Its upward march was not reversed until the Reagan administration.

This was by design. The War on Poverty was not designed to help the poor.

This was apparent from the beginning; indeed, it was the subject of hot controversy during the debate over the creation of Johnson's marquee program, Medicare, as Charlotte Twight discusses in her meticulously documented "Medicare's Origin: The Economics and Politics of Dependency." Rep. Thomas B. Curtis, R-Mo., during the 1963 debate cited a University of Michigan study that found that 87 percent of households headed by people age 65 or older had a net worth at least equal to the average of people ages 45–65 and on average higher than those under 45. He asked the reasonable question of why the nation should offer subsidized medical benefits to 100 percent of those over 65 when only 15 percent of them had below-average levels of personal wealth. Why not "direct our attention to the problems of the 15 percent, rather than this compulsory program that would cover everybody?" Sen. Huey Long, D-La., class-conscious man that he was, demanded, "Why should we pay the medical bill of a man who has an income of $100,000 a year or a million dollars a year of income?" One wonders what Long would have made of the Great Society's ugly grandchild, the 2009 Patient Protection and Affordable Care Act (PPACA), which, if it stands, would offer federal health insurance subsidies to families making nearly $100,000 a year.

Long's question was a fair one. The answer from Secretary of Health, Education, and Welfare Anthony J. Celebrezze will not surprise anybody who followed the 2009 debate over health care reform: We must, he said, treat health care "as a right and in a way which fully safeguards the dignity and independence of our older people." The theme of dependence was hit upon constantly throughout the debate. Celebrezze spoke often and disparagingly of "dependence" and "dependency," as did other Great Society architects. Others saw through that transparently false rhetoric. The proposal was "another step toward destroying the independence and self-reliance in America, which is the last best hope of individual freedom for all mankind," declared the insightful if florid Sen. Karl Mundt, R-S.D., adding that the program would be "exceedingly difficult to discontinue without breaking faith with those who have to pay the tax." For all the talk of protecting the "independence" of the elderly, the program, as Twight notes, had the opposite effect: "Medicare heralded enhancement of political job security by creating new and broad-based dependence on government."

While Celebrezze argued that Medicare would enable elderly Americans to "avoid dependence," it in fact achieved only a *transfer* of dependence: Old people who may have been dependent upon family members, charity, or local institutions would henceforth be dependent upon President Johnson's health care program – and, presumably, "voting Democratic for the next 200 years." Worse still, Americans who had previously been dependent only upon themselves and their own means would gradually be made dependent upon President Johnson's health care program as payroll taxes diminished their ability to save for their own retirement needs and as the federal government used its political muscle to price private health care competitors out of the marketplace in favor of Medicare. It is worth noting that under the status quo ante, the poor were largely dependent upon family members, churches, and other institutions that had nothing to gain from their dependency. Under the Great Society and its later permutations, they became dependent upon a professional class whose highly paid members were themselves dependent upon the dependency of their clients. Dependency became a valuable commodity. At the apex of the dependency food chain are the highest-ranking members of a political machine ultimately dependent upon dependency and highly invested in its spread.

So intent was the Johnson administration on cultivating the dependency of all retirees – rather than the poor elderly alone – that Secretary Celebrezze and his department carried out what Sen. Mundt described as a program of "deliberate sabotage" against legislation passed in 1960 to establish a need-based program of medical assistance for the elderly. As Twight reports, Mundt complained that public meetings were closed to supporters of the 1960 legislation while the Johnson administration was deploying "public servants, paid with public funds, traveling at public expense, charged with administering a federal law, going about the country trying to destroy public confidence in a law enacted by this Congress." For this, they must have had their inspiration in President Roosevelt's strategy in creating Social Security: Once the middle class is paying into a program, it develops a sense of – what shall we call it? – *entitlement* to future benefits. "With those taxes in there," Roosevelt said, "no damn politician can ever scrap my Social Security program." So far, history has proved him correct.

A Program for the Poor Is a Poor Program

Hooking the poor on government benefits is child's play. Hooking the middle class is a little more difficult, though well within the powers of such masterly politicians as Roosevelt and Johnson. But the really neat trick is hooking the rich.

It is a truism among self-styled social reformers that "a program for the poor is a poor program," and there is no paucity of examples to illustrate that fact. Ronald Reagan denounced "welfare queens" in the 1980s, and by the 1990s, Bill Clinton was reluctantly signing legislation to dethrone them. But the main middle-class entitlements – Medicare and Social Security – are untouchable, to say nothing of specialized programs such as the federal Export-Import Bank and virtually the entire Department of Agriculture, which exist for the sole purpose of transferring wealth to the wealthy. The growth of the middle-class entitlement state and the expansion of corporate welfare are well-understood and widely publicized phenomena. Less well understood is the government's intentional co-opting of the private social-services sector of the economy, a process that began in the early 1960s and one upon which we again find the grimy fingerprints of Lyndon Johnson.

In the early 1960s the budding profession of social

work was confronted with a problem. The social-work programs were turning out graduates, but there were few jobs for them and little money in those. Rather than see their members go to work as minor functionaries in the government's welfare bureaucracies, the social workers' professional organizations hit upon a new strategy: Social workers would not go to work for the federal government, but the federal government would nonetheless pay them to be social workers by offering them *contracts* to provide social services. This provided social workers with the main benefits of government employment – security, lack of accountability or meaningful oversight – with few if any of its burdens and a chance at much higher incomes than those typically enjoyed by government workers. As Roger and Nancy Lohmann put it in *Social Administration*, this was "part of an ongoing struggle by the social work profession to legitimize itself and find an institutional and resource base in modern industrial society."

The U.S. government in 1962 and 1967 amended key pieces of social-welfare legislation to allow for the contracting out of welfare services, and it did so, according to Philip Popple and Leslie Leighninger in *Social Services, Social Welfare, and American Society*, guided by "social workers and other experts who contended that providing intensive social services would rehabilitate and bring" – can you guess what? – "financial *independence* to the poor."

The outcome was precisely the opposite, as the Lohmanns document. "Rather than leading to decreases in the welfare rolls as promised, it immediately preceded enormous increases in public welfare eligibility during the following decade." "Moreover, in many cases the rhetoric and actions of social workers were deliberately provoking such increases.... [G]radually expanding the American welfare state became the proximate goal of the social work profession, and public purchases of services became an important means for pursuing that end." Under the Kennedy administration, that was a simple matter of intragovernmental exchanges. The Johnson administration had bigger ideas: "The 1962 amendments made it possible for departments of public welfare to purchase specified social services for eligible clients from other public agencies. The 1967 amendments expanded this to nonprofit and proprietary agencies in cases where state agency staff were not available to provide the needed services." Here, "proprietary" means "for-profit." The effects were once again entirely predictable: an explosion in social-welfare spending and in welfare-dependency rolls. Meanwhile, business was booming in the medical-entitlement racket: "[By 1972] medical payments through Medicare and Medicaid – wherein service contracting had been explicitly rejected as an abridgment of the 'autonomy' of the medical profession – grew in excess of $50 billion, more than twenty-five times the level of social service spending."

By the turn of the century, there were some 66,000 government-supported social-service agencies in the United States, most of them private and many of them for-profit. Private, voluntary, and even religious groups found themselves in whole or in part dependent upon government contracts; as a result, their organizations changed in subtle and not-so-subtle ways, and their missions were distorted as they chose to offer a menu of services that matched the availability of government funds. The final effect was the wholesale displacement of private philanthropy by government contracting, which has the double result of making government dependents of both welfare recipients and the workers at the agencies that provide contracted services to them. This has much deeper and even more worrisome consequences than those of having merely the poor hooked on welfare checks: A wide swath of the professional middle class has been put in the same position as the nation's welfare recipients. It will surprise nobody that the National Association of Social Workers quickly developed a sophisticated political operation (called PACE); that it operates a political-action committee; that it created a lobbying arm; that it endorsed both Barack Obama and his signature health care program; that it lists among its top priorities ensuring high levels of funding for Social Security and Medicare; that social workers as a profession are overwhelmingly Democrats; that their organizations overwhelmingly endorse Democratic candidates and support them financially; and that they consistently push the Democratic Party into an ever more statist direction. They may be expected, as President Johnson might have put it, to be backing Democrats for the next 200 years.

Being a government dependent can pay very well. Planned Parenthood, an organization that enjoys very generous contracts from the government, pays its regional office directors salaries averaging $158,000; its national president is compensated in excess of $400,000 a year. The average salary for a nonprofit executive in the United States runs $200,000 a year, or about four times the average family income, with salaries for executives in larger organizations (budgets of more than $50 million a year) running on average from $240,000 to $300,000. Executives of health care nonprofits routinely see compensation packages well into the millions of dollars per year. If a Cadillac owner on food stamps is a welfare queen, these are welfare emperors.

President Johnson did not concoct these innovations out of thin air. In 1909 another great progressive president, Theodore Roosevelt, held the first major presidential summit on child poverty. You will not be surprised to learn that it was called the White House Conference on the Care of *Dependent* Children, and its result was the creation of the federal Children's Bureau. There was some slow and incremental growth in the welfare state in subsequent years but nothing to match what came after President Johnson launched his program to largely co-opt private charity in the 1960s. Once that particular floodgate was open, there was nothing that could hold the waters back.

Another key innovation of the Johnson years was to broaden the definition of who is eligible for social services that are government funded but privately administered. Previously, standards were applied to the individual – a person of *X* age making *Y* income with *Z* assets – but afterward, eligibility was derived from membership in a group. Relatively affluent people became eligible for social services because they lived in relatively poor neighborhoods. Relatively well-off older people became eligible for assistance because they were members of communities with high rates of poverty among the elderly. Children of middle-class parents became eligible for benefits because they attended schools that were mostly poor. Organizations such as the United Way, which had long had a specific policy against the acceptance of government money, soon changed their minds, and, inevitably, the portfolio of social-services "investments" was widened from providing relief to the poor and the sick to programs that were concentrated on more nebulous goals such as "human development" and enhancing the "general quality of life." Thus government welfare payments became mostly separated from government welfare programs, eligibility for anti-poverty benefits severed from the condition of being poor, and the War on Poverty sundered from efforts to reduce poverty. Unsurprisingly, within a decade, only one-fifth of those being served by these organizations were poor.

By the 1980s the overwhelming majority of funding for most privately administered social services came from government sources. In some fields, such as drug-addiction treatment and services for the elderly, nearly all the money now comes from government sources – and that excludes income from "fees" that are in fact simply yet more government money in the form of Medicare and Medicaid payments. Unsurprisingly, the for-profit sector is the fastest-growing element in social services and by many estimates today is larger than the nonprofit sector. These are not tiny firms: As a Mathematica Policy Research paper, "Privatization of Welfare Services: A Review of the Literature," points out, Lockheed Martin was a major provider of services under the Temporary Assistance for Needy Families (TANF) program until the division that handled such contracting was sold off to American Computer Services (ACS). The depth of the firm's involvement in the welfare state is breathtaking: "ACS now administers the entire TANF program in Palm Beach County, Florida," Mathematica reports. "It also administers Florida's welfare reform program, Work and Gain Economic Self-Sufficiency (WAGES) program in 13 regions and employment services in 12 workforce board regions in Texas. It currently holds 26 TANF contracts worth a possible $108 million."

21st-Century Leviathan

Before the Great Society, the share of household income derived from federal payments was vanishingly small – some modest Social Security payments to the relatively few elderly who lived long enough to receive very many of them and a very small array of welfare payments. By 1998 more than one-third of U.S. households were receiving direct entitlement payments; by 2006 it was 44.5 percent, and by 2009 it was 48.5 percent. If current trends continue, that figure will be well more than half in only a few years. Before the Great Society, less than 8 percent of household income came from federal payments; today it is nearly 18 percent. As late as 1979, the majority of federal transfer payments went to the poor; today 64 percent goes to the middle and upper classes, with the most growth at the higher end of the income spectrum. If the 2009 health care legislation stands, that would change even more rapidly. In a country of more than 300 million, there are fewer than 25,000 households that will *not* be eligible for subsidies under PPACA – and most of the adults in those households are either already eligible for Medicare and Social Security or on the cusp of it. We are all welfare queens now, or at least we soon will be.

Beginning as an emergency program for the poor during the Great Depression, federal welfare programs quickly grew into a tool for building political constituencies. Because the United States experienced an unprecedented economic boom from the end of World War II to the turn of the century, there simply were not enough poor to go around to meet the needs of those who would benefit from the cultivation of government dependency. It became necessary then to use various tools – changing the definition of *poor*, substituting group eligibility requirements for individual eligibility requirements, contracting out social services while expanding the mission of social-services agencies, expanding from poverty into health care, etc. – to deepen the pool of potential government dependents. On top of this large pool of primary dependents is the larger, wealthier, and more politically influential class of secondary dependents: those who make their living by acting as intermediaries between federal tax collectors and welfare-dependent tax consumers. It is this second class that is the real product of and constituency for the dependency agenda.

There is one fact that becomes incandescently apparent when studying the origins of the modern welfare state: It is nearly impossible to overestimate the cynicism of Lyndon Baines Johnson. The universal welfare state was only one-half of what President Johnson called his Great Society. The other half was ameliorating the gross injustice inflicted on African Americans up through the 1960s. The latter aspect of the Great Society was a moral imperative, though there is a great deal of debate about whether the particular legislative and constitutional remedies enacted throughout the 1960s and after were the best expression of that mandate, and men of impeccable intentions opposed the Civil Rights Act of 1964 and similar legislation, largely out of concern (subsequently confirmed) that the government would abuse the vast new powers with which it was invested. Sen. Barry Goldwater was one such critic, Gov. Reagan was another; Sen. Johnson was not. There is no shortage of anecdotal evidence that the civil-rights wing of the Great Society was an exercise in Johnsonian self-aggrandizement, but perhaps the most telling was his answer to an aide who asked him why he appointed Thurgood Marshall to the Supreme Court instead of a less controversial African-American candidate. "Son," Johnson declared, "when I appoint a nigger to the court, I want everyone to know he's a nigger." Robert Caro's magisterial Johnson biography contains another illuminating exchange between Johnson and a colleague, with the president telling his fellow Democrat, "These Negroes, they're getting pretty uppity these days, and that's a problem for us since they've got something now they never had before: the political pull to back up their uppityness. Now we've got to do something about this – we've got to give them a little something, just enough to quiet them down, not enough to make a difference." It is necessary to bear this in mind not in order to conclude that Lyndon Johnson was at best a hypocrite and at worst a moral monster – though he was – but to conclude that the Great Society was built for some other purpose than to help those whom Johnson et al. purported to help. There is no doubt that many of the architects of the Great Society were idealistic progressives, but each and every one of them would have had to have been blind not to have seen what they were building and for whom they were building it – a Faustian bargain at best.

It is characteristic of the progressive project that moral necessities are thoroughly blended with political opportunism and statist arrogation. No American – left, right, or center – proposes to let elderly people starve in the streets, to let the poor die of easily preventable ailments, to let poor children go uneducated, to let the disabled founder in misery. The choice before us, now as always, is not between socialism and social Darwinism, between Charles Dickens and Ayn Rand. Rather, we face difficult and sometimes painful questions about how to provide for those who cannot provide for themselves – how, how much, for whom, when, where, and on what grounds. There is abundant evidence that these decisions are best made by applying the principle of subsidiarity, meaning that families first, then neighborhood organizations, and then municipalities, counties, states, etc., attempt to address problems on their own, applying local knowledge close to home rather than relying first and reflexively on the federal

Leviathan. There are many reasons to do this, a main one being that such wealth transfers automatically create their own political constituencies, both among recipients and among administrators. Those constituencies are more easily counteracted, contained, and policed at the local level. At the federal level, they become nearly insurmountable obstacles to reform and sources of financial improbity – which is precisely why today's Democrats prefer Washington-based programs.

We have a great deal of evidence that massive federal entitlement programs do not work. Health outcomes for Medicaid patients are in fact worse than for those who have no health insurance at all. Medicare and Social Security have not reduced poverty among seniors; Head Start, TANF, AFDC, and the like have not reduced poverty among children. These programs are fiscal nightmares, to be sure: Our current unfunded liabilities under Social Security and Medicare amount to more than all the money in the world, literally – more than every bill and coin in every currency around the world, along with all bank-account deposits, CDs, and money-market funds. But the fiscal nightmare, while terrifying, is not as terrifying as the moral nightmare behind it. Millions of Americans are being exploited for the benefit of the permanent political class. In the name of a War on Poverty, we have needlessly impoverished many millions of Americans. We have needlessly ruined many millions of lives. The dependency agenda must be reversed and the federal welfare state dissolved not only because we cannot afford it but because failing to do so ensures that our politics will remain warped by perverse incentives, by unconstitutional seizures of power, and by what amounts to the looting of the fisc by the parasitic political class. That is what is at stake – not merely the national ledger sheet.

And these many decades later, what lesson have we learned? I can only imagine how Barack Obama could possibly have explained to his aides that his party intended to create a new health insurance entitlement program that would provide subsidies not only to the poor but to more than 80 percent of all U.S. households: "I'm going to have those middle-class suburbanites voting Democratic for the next 200 years."

ABOUT THE AUTHORS

JOHN R. BOLTON served as the U.S. permanent representative to the United Nations from August 2005 to December 2006. From 2001 to 2005, he served as undersecretary of state for arms control and international security. He is currently a senior fellow at the American Enterprise Institute.

DANIEL DISALVO is an assistant professor of political science at the City College of New York – CUNY and a Senior Fellow at the Manhattan Institute. He is also the author of *Engines of Change: Party Factions in American Politics, 1868–2010* (Oxford).

RICHARD A. EPSTEIN is the Laurence A. Tisch Professor of Law at New York University, a senior fellow at the Hoover Institution, and the James Parker Hall Distinguished Service Professor of Law Emeritus and senior lecturer at the University of Chicago Law School. His most recent book, *Design for Liberty: Private Property, Public Administration, and the Rule of Law*, was published in October 2011 by Harvard University Press.

PETER FERRARA is a senior fellow at The Heartland Institute and general counsel of the American Civil Rights Union. He served in the White House Office of Policy Development under President Reagan and as associate deputy attorney general of the United States under President George H. W. Bush. He is a graduate of Harvard Law School and Harvard College.

John Fund is National Affairs columnist for *National Review* magazine and a senior editor of *The American Spectator*. He also is a commentator who regularly appears on Fox News and other television programs.

Victor Davis Hanson is a senior fellow in Classics and Military History at the Hoover Institution, Stanford University, and the author of 17 books on ancient, military, and social history.

Andrew C. McCarthy, a former top federal prosecutor, is the best-selling author of *The Grand Jihad* (Encounter 2010) and *Willful Blindness* (Encounter 2008), a contributing editor at *National Review*, and a widely read commentator on national security matters.

Betsy McCaughey, Ph.D., is a patient advocate and the founder of the Committee to Reduce Infection Deaths. She is a constitutional scholar, the author of two histories of the U.S. Constitution, and New York's former lieutenant governor.

Stephen Moore joined *The Wall Street Journal* as a member of the editorial board and senior economics writer on May 31, 2005. He is a regular economic commentator on Fox News Channel and CNBC.

Michael B. Mukasey served as attorney general of the United States from November 2007 to January 2009 and as a U.S. district judge for the Southern District of New

York from 1988 to 2006, where he presided over, among other cases, those involving Sheik Omar Abdel Rahman and Jose Padilla. He is now a lawyer in private practice in New York.

GLENN HARLAN REYNOLDS is the Beauchamp Brogan Distinguished Professor of Law at the University of Tennessee. He writes for such publications as *The Atlantic*, *Forbes*, *Popular Mechanics*, *The Wall Street Journal*, and the *Washington Examiner*. He blogs at InstaPundit.com.

RICH TRZUPEK is a chemist and principal consultant at the environmental engineering and consulting firm Mostardi Platt Environmental. Trzupek is a contributing editor at FrontPageMag.com and the author of McGraw-Hill's *Air Quality Compliance and Permitting Guide* and *Regulators Gone Wild: How the EPA Is Ruining American Industry* (Encounter Books).

KEVIN D. WILLIAMSON is an editor at *National Review*, the author of the forthcoming *The End of Politics (And What Comes Next)*, and a columnist for *The New Criterion*. He began his journalism career at the Bombay-based Indian Express Newspaper Group and has worked as a reporter, columnist, and editor at a variety of newspapers. He directed the journalism program at the Institute for Humane Studies at George Mason University.

INDEX

A NOTE ON THE TYPE

THE NEW LEVIATHAN *has been set in Janson, a type first cut in the seventeenth century. Long attributed to the Dutch punchcutter Anton Janson, the types are now ascribed to Nicholas Kis, a Hungarian punchcutter who studied his art under Dirk Voskens in 1680. Educated in theology and known as a scholar of Greek and Latin, Kis intended to turn his typographic skills to the production of beautiful bibles. His ambitions were thwarted by religious and political strife in his native country, and his name and types fell into obscurity until their revival in the early twentieth century. Used most notably by Daniel Berkeley Updike for his Book of Common Prayer in 1930, the types have enjoyed wide popularity among book designers and have since been recut and digitized. Heavier in color and denser in fit than its Dutch old-style cousin, Caslon, Janson is particularly successful in pages where a rich texture and a distinct personality is desired.*

DESIGN & COMPOSITION BY CARL W. SCARBROUGH